FIRST YEARS OF REVOLUTION
1918–21

By the same author

*

THE EXTRAORDINARY ADVENTURES OF
JULIO JURENITO
THE LOVE OF JEANNE NEY
A STREET IN MOSCOW
THE FALL OF PARIS
RUSSIA AT WAR
EUROPEAN CROSS-ROAD
THE STORM
THE NINTH WAVE
THE THAW
THE SPRING
PEOPLE AND LIFE
CHEKHOV, STENDHAL AND OTHER ESSAYS

Ilya Ehrenburg's portrait by Diego Rivera

ILYA EHRENBURG

+->><<->>><<->>><<->>><<->>><<->>><<->>><<->>><<->>><<->>+

First Years of Revolution
1918-21

—

Volume II of
MEN, YEARS-LIFE

*

Translated by
ANNA BOSTOCK

in collaboration with
YVONNE KAPP

LONDON
MACGIBBON & KEE
1962

FIRST PUBLISHED 1962 BY MACGIBBON & KEE LTD
ENGLISH TRANSLATION © MACGIBBON & KEE LTD 1962
PRINTED IN GREAT BRITAIN BY
COX AND WYMAN LTD
LONDON, READING AND FAKENHAM

TRANSLATORS' NOTE

All quotations from Russian poets are our own translation, with the exception of the passage from Mayakovsky: 'But I mastered myself . . .' on page 40, which is taken from *Mayakovsky*, translated and edited by Herbert Marshall, Dennis Dobson, 1962; and two passages from the Pasternak poem: 'Oh, had I known . . .' on page 54, taken from *Selected Poems by Boris Pasternak*, translated by J. M. Cohen, Benn, 1958.

The footnotes are ours.

ILLUSTRATIONS

Ilya Ehrenburg's portrait by Diego Rivera *Frontispiece*

The following pictures are to be found between pages 96-97

Boris Pasternak

Portrait of Lenin by N. Altman, 1920

Lenin: drawing by N. Altman, 1920

Pasternak, André Malraux, Meyerhold and Malraux's brother

Vladimir Mayakovsky, 1924

Sergei Yesenin and Isadora Duncan

Portrait of Valery Bryusov by Vrubel

Portrait of Meyerhold by Konchalovsky

1

I WAS like du Bellay's lamb that has strayed from the fold: remember that when I first left Russia I was less than eighteen years old. Like a child going to school for the first time, I was eager to learn the ABC; I asked everyone to explain what was happening, but the answer was always the same: 'No one knows'. I tried to start long conversations about Russia's mission, the rottenness of the West, and Dostoyevsky, but people had other things to think about: instead of talking, they only swore and cursed. Some cursed the Bolsheviks, some Kerensky, some the Revolution.

A middle-aged Menshevik lady wearing a pince-nez met us at the Finland Station and invited me to follow her. I replied that I was under guard. She started cursing the guard, and the guard cursed back. She said he was a black marketeer (it is true that he was carrying a large paper bag), and he retorted that she very probably 'stuffed herself with sweetmeats'[1]. I stood amazed. The Menshevik lady took us to a hostel which was dark and crowded. An unidentified young man was screaming at his neighbour: 'Call yourself a revolutionary? You're a Galliffet, you ought to be put against a wall and shot'.

Like all political émigrés, I was granted military deferment; a lieutenant at the police station told me there were enough windbags in the army without me.

I received the fees due to me from the *Birzhevka* (*Stock Exchange Gazette*) and moved into furnished rooms on the Moyka. Each morning I went out into the streets and just looked. The city's architecture, its straight avenues seemed to me extraordinarily lucid, but it was impossible to understand anything at all.

I went to a meeting at Chinizelli's circus. There was a big audience, but I felt at once that everyone was tired of speeches: the enthusiasm of the early months had obviously ebbed and even the windbags had talked themselves to a full stop. The speakers were all people on the fringe of things. A grey-haired lady argued that Esperanto would

---

[1] At the time a popular expression of contempt for the rich.

9

save the Revolution. Nobody listened. The next speaker was an anarchist who said that the State must be abolished immediately; everyone shouted at him; then he started whistling furiously and was pulled off the rostrum. An elegantly dressed young man pleaded that Russia should not be surrendered to the Kaiser. Two soldiers heckled him: 'Ever been in the trenches, you bastard?'

I tried to find the poets with whom I had corresponded. None of them was in town; 'at his *dacha*' or 'in the Crimea', I was told. One day Tikhon Sorokin sent for me: 'Come quickly, Blok is here'. I rushed to the Winter Palace but I arrived too late: Blok had already left. And so I never saw the poet whose verse I loved above everything else.

At the *Birzhevka* I was advised to go to the 'Vienna' restaurant, where poets and artists met in the evenings. I concluded that the Vienna must be something like the Rotonde. But the people who sat at the tables were officers, black marketeers and ordinary bourgeois. One man was shouting: 'What are you signing chits for, you know perfectly well they're worth nothing now! You might as well sign yourself Nicholas II'. A lady screeched: 'Why ever have they let Lenin slip through their fingers?'

Deserters were being hunted in the streets; the patrols checking documents looked like deserters themselves. Once I saw two officers take a bag of granulated sugar from a woman. She howled: 'Bandits!' As she walked away, one of the officers shouted after her that she would soon be shot: Kerensky was on the side of the black marketeers, but Kerensky wouldn't last much longer. Then, paying no attention to the passers-by, the officers shared the loot between them.

In the shops you could buy Havana cigars, Sèvres vases and the poems of the Comtesse de Noailles. In the teashops you were served coffee with honey (sugar had already run out) and, instead of pastries, thin slices of white bread with plum jam. The cabbies no longer talked about oats but only swore in a sinister fashion. A poet whom I met at the *Birzhevka* office said: 'Our only hope is General Kornilov. His first name is Lavr[1]: that's symbolic.'

Soldiers talked about winding up the war. Deserters did not talk about anything at all but just gave people black looks. Girls in military uniform walked up and down the Nevsky; they saluted smartly, and had very large breasts. They held meetings at the corner of Sadovaya

[1] Laurel.

and shouted that Lenin must be found; meanwhile, it would be a good idea to arrest Chernov.

I heard Chernov speak. As in Paris, his tone was very elevated. But in March I had somehow found him moving, whereas in August he struck me as ridiculous. He was a good speaker and altogether reminded me of a French Radical Socialist who promises the voters that if they elect him he will build a bridge across the local stream. Chernov promised that he would give land to the peasants and save Russia from the Germans. He had cunning eyes; I do not think that any of his listeners believed him. I also heard Kerensky. This was like being at the theatre: one had the feeling that at any moment the head of the Provisional Government would burst into tears or run off the stage. By this time Kerensky's glory had entered its decline; all the same, fifty or so women screamed hysterically when he appeared. One of them threw him a bunch of fading asters; he picked it up and, for some reason, sniffed it.

I ran into two or three émigrés whom I had known in Paris. One of them, a Bolshevik called Sashunya, said that Antonov-Ovseyenko was being held at Kresty, that the Mensheviks were traitors and that the time for arguments was past. I asked him whether he was not afraid that the Germans might take advantage of a civil war to seize Petrograd. He shouted that I was talking like a Menshevik, that I was an intellectual 'from top to toe', that the intellectuals were 'in the way', and that the thing to be afraid of now was not the Germans but the *oborontsy*[1].

I spent an hour or two chatting with Savinkov. He was now Deputy War Minister, and I no longer recognized the Savinkov of the Rotonde who used to smile so wryly. He talked about harsh measures, dictatorship and restoring order. He called Kerensky a phrasemonger drunk with the sound of his own voice and spoke contemptuously of the Provisional Government: 'They've lost their nerve, they hold their meetings standing up, not sitting down'.

At the Winter Palace I saw the trappings of the Tsar's life. They were not interesting. The rooms were crammed with tasteless furniture and *petit-bourgeois* knick-knacks. (Later I was to see similar objects at the Peking palace, in the apartments of the last Chinese Emperor.)

[1] 'Defenders' – moderate Socialists who favoured the continuation of the war.

Camp-beds stood among the pouffes, and rifles lay scattered about: the Revolution, which Savinkov wanted to lay prematurely into its grave, stalked the rooms of the Winter Palace. On the stairs, some lady or other buttonholed Savinkov: 'Why is my George still in prison, I'd like to know? Even at school he used to read Herzen'.

Savinkov introduced me to Fedor Stepun. I knew Stepun as a philosopher, the author of an interesting book called *Letters of a Second Lieutenant*, where war was shown without its obligatory glamour. I was not at all prepared to find him functioning as chief of the political department of the Ministry of War. His face was rather that of a dreamer or a Protestant parson. I began telling him, as incoherently and passionately as I had tried to tell Sashunya, that the Germans might occupy Russia and crush the Revolution. He asked me whether I wanted to become a war commissar. I smiled: a commissar must understand, must explain to others, while I could do only one thing: ask questions.

I also went to Smolny. There, people hurled themselves at Chkheidze, shouting that Savinkov was plotting with the generals while workers were being put in prison. Soldiers slept in the passages.

One of the Paris émigrés said to me severely: 'This isn't your Rotonde, you know. Get yourself to the front'. I explained that they wouldn't have me in the army. He gave a vicious laugh: 'So you're a Bolshevik, are you? Wait till I expose you'. An old woman cornered me, weeping: 'Tell them Andryusha's daughter is at the Conservatoire, tell them it was Mishukin who bought the cloth. . . .'

Tikhon Sorokin and Katya, with my daughter Irina, were in Petrograd at this time. They were living with Katya's father, who refused even to hear my name: on top of all my other crimes, I was a Jew. Katya brought Irina to see me without her grandfather's knowledge. The little girl was six years old. I took her to the Café Empire and treated her to some white bread with plum jam. Then we went for a walk along the Nevsky. Irina had once had an Italian nurse who had taught her to pray. The child asked to go to the Kazan Cathedral; once inside, she immediately knelt down and ordered me to follow her example. I disobeyed. Irina began to cry and scream; women praying in the cathedral turned on me: you should be ashamed of yourself, making a child cry in a holy place. Luckily Irina had had enough of prayer and asked me if we might go back to the café.

Tikhon said that Stepun was sending him to the Caucasian front and wanted me to become his – Tikhon's – assistant. I had a good long laugh. Tikhon was even less able to make sense of things than I. He knew a lot about the works of Vladimir Solovyev and early Gothic architecture. What, I wondered, would he discuss with the troops: the 'eternal feminine' or the stained glass windows of Chartres Cathedral?

(In the archives I found a paper signed by the Minister of War, dated September 1917, saying that 'by agreement with the Front sub-committee of the Central Executive Committee of the All-Russian Congress of Soviets of Soldiers' and Workers' Deputies' I was appointed assistant military commissar of the Caucasian military area. By that time I was in Yalta and did not hear of this appointment until both the Minister of War and the Caucasian front had disappeared.)

Everyone was saying that somebody was about to 'take action'. Some thought the 'action' was to be taken by General Kornilov, others by the Bolsheviks. I realized that I wasn't going to understand anything – and left for Moscow.

Back in Ostozhenka, I recognized every shop sign and every alley. At first Moscow struck me as a calmer place, but this was only so in appearance: people here could not understand anything either. I tried to find a few old friends. Eight years had passed, and eight years is a long time. One schoolboy who had attended our meetings in 1907 had meanwhile become a fashionable lawyer; when I said who I was, he shouted at me: 'See what your fooling about has led to! You should have stayed in Paris, at least there's no firing in the streets there'. A schoolgirl called Lusya, who had once had a passion for Lermontov, turned out to be a stout lady with a faint moustache. She gave me tea, but maddened me with her grumbling: there wasn't any sugar, the servants were insolent and it was risky to leave the house at night.

In Tverskaya there was the Café Bom, with red velvet seats, where they served coffee and pastries. Writers used to go there. I met Lidin, a very pink, very neat man who talked about horses, stables and Bunin's masterly style. Boris Zaitsev spoke warmly about the beauty of the Russian Orthodox ritual and the short story. Khodasevich talked maliciously about everyone and wrote tender poems saying that death beckoned to him as sleep beckons to young girls at nightfall. His face was like a skull. Alexey Tolstoy puffed gloomily at his pipe and kept saying: 'It's all muck. Can't understand a thing. They're all off their heads'.

Tolstoy said that I looked like a Mexican gaolbird. Once I dropped into a café in the Arbat and began writing. The waitress came, took away my empty glass and said crossly: 'Where do you think you are? The university?' I had forgotten the Russian way of life and often behaved ridiculously. I thought this was the reason why I could not make head or tail of things. But Alexey Tolstoy did not see any more clearly than I. I have recently re-read Blok's diaries, Korolenko's letters and the articles of Gorky. At that time, everyone accepted and rejected, agreed and protested. A closer look, it seems, revealed that the 'Mexican gaolbird' was just an ordinary member of the Russian intelligentsia. I do not say this by way of justification or excuse. I am merely trying to explain my state of mind in the years 1917 and 1918. Of course I see things much more clearly today, but that is nothing to be proud of: anyone can be wise after the event.

2

THEY say 'one can't see the wood for the trees'; that is as true as that one can't see the trees for the wood. When we read about France in 1793, we see the Convention, the incorruptible Robespierre, the guillotine in the Place de la Révolution, the clubs full of eloquent *Sans-culottes*, political pamphlets, conspiracies and battles. But in the same year Philippe Lebon was sitting in a small laboratory, thinking about gas; Talma was rehearsing a pseudo-classical tragedy; ladies of fashion tried on new hats with ribbons; and housewives scoured the town in search of vanishing foodstuffs.

This is how Alexey Tolstoy described the conversations that went on in the summer of 1917: ' "Are we lost or have we still got a chance? Will there be a Russia or won't there? Shall we intellectuals have our throats cut or shall we stay alive?" Another man says: "Nonsense, my dear fellow, why should they cut our throats? I don't believe it, it's all rubbish. What they *will* do, though, is loot the food shops." A third reports from a reliable source that "by the first of the month the city will start dying of famine".'

It so happens that my notebook for 1917–18 has been preserved by some Moscow friends. The entries are so laconic that I cannot make out many of them, but a few lines have helped me to reconstruct a good deal from memory. Some of the notes concern my first meeting with Valery Bryusov.

It was the summer which Alexey Tolstoy described. I spent several hours with Bryusov. He read me a recent poem of his about Ariadne and we argued about it.

A summary of that part of our talk seems rather surprising for August 1917:

1. Is it true that Theseus suffered pangs of conscience when he deserted Ariadne on an uninhabited island?

2. Is it more correct to render the first letter of Theseus' name in Russian by a T or an F? (Bryusov insisted on the latter.)

3. Should a modern poet write about Theseus? (I said he should not.)

One might deduce that Bryusov was a Formalist, an eternal Decadent, who wanted to oppose his private world to reality. That is untrue. Soon after the October Revolution, when men of his own age as well as poets of a younger generation (including myself) were puzzled and distraught, lamenting many things and outraged by others, Bryusov was already working in the first Soviet institutions. The reason why he talked to me about Theseus was that he believed in the vitality of poetry and respected his own work. His whole life was in books, his own and other people's. As a young man he once confessed that he had 'a silly sensitivity to novels' which he 'lacked entirely to events in real life'.

I went to see him with mixed feelings: I remembered his letters – after all, he had often encouraged me – and I respected him, but I had long ceased to like his poems and was afraid that I would be unable to hide this and would involuntarily offend a man to whom I owed a great deal.

Bryusov lived in Pervaya Meshchanskaya; to get there I had to cross the famous Sukharevka. The Vatican is an independent state in the middle of Rome; Sukharevka was such a state in the Moscow of 1917, not subject to the Provisional Government, or to the Soviet of Workers' Deputies, or to the militia. The splendid tower soared above the enormous market place; it was as though Ancient Russia still went on living here, with its blind men singing their mournful songs, its beggars and its holy fools. Obscenities mingled with lamentations, ancient curses with talk about *kerenkas*[1], bourgeois and Bolsheviks. The variety of people here was limitless: deserters, fat peasant women from nearby villages, governesses, housekeepers and retainers who suddenly found themselves unemployed, stolid wives of government officials, habitual thieves, snotty-nosed boys selling loose cigarettes, priests with cackling chickens. They haggled and swore, shouted and stamped their feet – a human sea.

'And Adam wept: paradise, my paradise!' a blind man chanted. The chant was still ringing in my ears as I approached Bryusov's house. Sukharevka was the indispensable foreword, the key to the complex riddle called Valery Bryusov. One may argue about the value of poems on Theseus, but no one will deny the importance of Bryusov in the development of Russian culture. (He once wrote: 'I wish I were not Valery Bryusov'. But it is a good thing he was.)

[1] Paper currency of the Provisional Government.

It is not Sukharevka alone, of course, that has a right to appear in the foreword: I mention it because Bryusov lived nearby; one might equally well speak of the Zaryadye district with its ancient shops, the 'Society for Free Aesthetics', Kitay-Gorod, the merchant Shchukin who bought the pictures of an unknown painter called Picasso, or the 'Literary and Artistic Circle' in Bolshaya Dmitrovka where Bryusov preached 'scientific poetry' while members of the circle, who managed very well without either poetry or science, played whist. Bryusov dressed in the European style, knew several foreign languages, interspersed his letters with French words and hung pictures by Rops rather than Makovsky on his walls, but he was a product of staid and brazen, reckless and shrewd old Moscow.

His industry and his energy astonished everyone. At that first meeting of ours he criticized me harshly for what he called my 'irresponsible' attitude to a poet's work: 'What has inspiration got to do with it? I write poetry every morning. Whether I feel like it or not, I sit down at my desk and write. Even if I fail to bring off a poem, I can still find a new rhyme or practise a difficult rhythm. Here, look at my drafts', and he started pulling out the drawers of his large desk, filled to the top with manuscripts. He reproached me with frivolousness and dilettantism. He said that there should be a school for poets: poetry was a craft, albeit a 'sacred' one, and it had to be taught.

He was a magnificent organizer. His father had been a dealer in cork, and I am convinced that if Bryusov had not, in his youth, happened to come across the poems of Verlaine and Mallarmé, he would have ended up owning whole forests of cork oaks like those in Estremadura. In his character capacity for work was coupled with ambition. At the age of twenty he wrote in his diary: 'Talent, even genius, can honestly yield but slow success, if they yield it at all. That is not enough! Not enough for me. Another way must be sought. In the darkness a guiding star must be found. I see it: it is Decadent art. Yes! Say what you will, it may be false, it may be ridiculous, but yet it advances, it develops, and the future belongs to it, especially when it has found a worthy leader. I will be that leader! Yes, I!'

He started publishing firms, founded journals, wrote books on the art of poetry, translated Latin authors, argued with recognized authorities, taught the young. He was afraid of one thing only: being left behind by the times.

He often wrote about chaos – this was derived from Tyutchev –

but what he really wanted was to grasp the chaos of which he sang and to organize it. I remember how at the end of 1920 I went to see him in the small building which housed LITO, as the literary department of the People's Commissariat of Education was called. Bryusov talked to me as a departmental chief; offered me a job; pointed at the wall, where hung an extraordinary chart – squares, rhomboids, pyramids – representing literature. It was naïve and at the same time majestic: a silver-haired magician transforming poetry into an office, an office into poetry.

He has often been called a rationalist, a man of dry reason; many have said that he was never a poet. I think that is untrue: for Bryusov, reason was not common sense but a cult; he carried his belief in reason to excess. He was a poet even in the most commonplace, philistine sense of the word: he lived in a schematic world of frenzied constructions. Vrubel painted a marvellous portrait of him: dry, scorching eyes, and a head as though sliced off at the back.

I remember the 'Poets' Café' in Moscow in 1918. People came there who had little to do with poetry: black marketeers, frivolous ladies, young men who called themselves 'Futurists'. Bryusov announced that he would improvise tercets on subjects set by other customers. People would send him idiotic suggestions. He did not seem to notice the waiters with their shouts of 'Two coffees, two!' nor the laughter of tipsy sailors. Solemn and stern, he recited poetry. His voice when he was reciting was strangely harsh and abrupt; his head was thrown back. He looked like an animal tamer, but before him were words, not lions. He composed tercets about Cleopatra, about a girl sitting at another table, about the transparent cities of the future.

He treated everything seriously; his erotic poems are a bit like a guide through the kingdom of Aphrodite. Surrounded by poets under the sway of mysticism, he began studying the 'occult sciences', knew all about incubuses and succubuses, spells and medieval magic.

When the Futurists appeared, Balmont naïvely begged them not to hasten his overthrow; Bryusov tried to do some overthrowing himself. He wrote a poem called 'Futurist Evening'. Mayakovsky wrote: 'Beyond the suns of the streets hobbled a flaccid moon, wanted by nobody'. And Bryusov: 'The moon, a badly-minted coin, is hung above the chimneys'. However, the Futurists did not recognize him as one of themselves, and: 'rip the paper armour off Bryusov's black frock coat' was one of their slogans.

Bryusov discovered in France the little-known poet René Ghil, the founder of 'scientific poetry'. Ghil's ideas appealed to Bryusov: he had always wanted to be a wizard with a university degree, a magician of the academies.

He studied Pushkin, wrote about anagogy, zeugma, procatalepsis and syllepsis, and discovered that in Chapter III of *Eugene Onegin* the pre-accentual sounds agree in seventy-three per cent of the rhymes, whereas in Chapter IV they do so in only fifty-four per cent. He tried to complete Pushkin's *Egyptian Nights* and to write a new version of *The Bronze Horseman*, but those are not works which one is anxious to re-read.

Some people unjustly accused Bryusov of tastelessness. This is a feature common to all Symbolists, and that, evidently, was their taste. Is it not extraordinary that they all admired the poems of Igor Severyanin, which we now regard as models of vulgarity? Shortly before his death, Bryusov was capable of writing: 'I live between worlds. Equal to the foremost, I am a peer where noblemen gather, and my every sigh, my every nerve echoes the higher spirits of the spheres.' I am now thinking of the poetry of the Symbolists. It was an astonishing phenomenon. A great poet, Alexander Blok, was born; it was as though Russian poetry had been freed from bondage. Yet how much more humanly understandable I find the letters, not only of Chekhov, but of his dimmest satellites, than the diaries of Bryusov, the travel notes of Balmont or the correspondence of Blok and Bely!

It was his reason that made Bryusov accept the Revolution: he could see the world of tomorrow. He was then approaching fifty. He worked on the preservation of libraries and the dissemination of poetry, performing many useful and important services. There is a rather ugly German word, *Kulturtraeger*: it precisely defines Bryusov's activities both before and after the Revolution. I prefer a more old-fashioned definition: Bryusov was an enlightener.

He believed that the Revolution would radically change everything; he used to say to me that Socialist culture would differ from capitalist culture as fundamentally as Christian Rome from the Rome of Augustus. He wanted to come to terms with the new world as a poet also, but he was too closely bound up with the old. His poems about the Revolution are full of mythological images; they make use of the Symbolists' familiar vocabulary. During the October days in Moscow he saw the Three Fates of Greek mythology. When Chicherin signed the agreement with the German Republic, Bryusov wrote: 'From the council of the Lemures to the council of Rapallo . . .' This is how he attacked the supporters of capitalism: 'So it was, so it persisted under different flags, from Semiramis to Poincaré . . . Someone, entrenched as the lord of worldly goods, always tightened the fatal ring'. (I well remember that dapper average Frenchman, Monsieur Poincaré; doubtless he would have been flattered to know that someone had mentioned him in the same breath as Semiramis.) From time to time Bryusov would feel depressed, and then he complained as in his youth: 'All men today, formerly and in the future, staring at a fence, the same arpeggios repeated, always the old chords . . .'

He died in the autumn of 1924, aged fifty-one. I was then in Paris. We organized a memorial meeting. When a man dies you suddenly see him in a new way: at full stature. Bryusov wrote some beautiful poetry which remains alive to this day. It may be that the traditional fairy was absent from his cradle, but even if he was not born a poet, he became one. He helped dozens of young poets who later condemned, rejected and deposed him. But this impassioned builder, this tireless sower was of far more use to young Soviet Russia than many a sweet-voiced singer.

I must recall once more my early years in Paris when Bryusov gave me vital support; even his reproaches helped me to live.

At our very first meeting Bryusov brought the conversation round to Nadya Lvova: the wound, it appeared, had not yet healed. Perhaps it was then that I remembered the poem Nadya wrote before her death, where she speaks of Bryusov's 'grey temples'; to me, he seemed a very old man indeed, and I wrote in my notebook: 'Grey-haired, very old' (he was then aged forty-four). I also wrote: 'Life for him is secondary'. Perhaps I was thinking of Nadya when I said this, perhaps of the Revolution; certainly I had in mind his line that 'everything in life is only a means to brilliant, singing verse'.

He gave me a small volume in which he wrote: 'A token of our affinity in some things, our differences in others'. This referred to our argument about poetry. We did not talk of the events of that storm-laden summer. But as I was leaving I could hold back no longer and asked: what's going to happen? Bryusov answered in verse: 'The deluge is gathering strength. But from the firmament, lighting up the dust, like the arc of a rainbow, freedom proclaims days of brightness'.

I was out in Sukharevka once more. The blind man with his 'Adam' had disappeared. A crowd was gathered at the corner of Sretenka: someone had been stabbed with a knife. I stood for a while and then walked on. But I did not think about Theseus. I thought about the deluge.

3

WHEN I met Marina Ivanovna Tsvetayeva she was twenty-five years old. The striking thing about her expression was its combination of arrogance and bewilderment. Her bearing was proud – her head thrown back, with a very high forehead – but the bewilderment was betrayed by her eyes, large and helpless, as though unseeing: Marina suffered from short-sightedness. Her hair was cut short, with a straight fringe. She looked like something between a prim young lady and a peasant boy.

In one of her poems Tsvetayeva speaks of her two grandmothers: one was a simple Russian woman, a village priest's wife, the other a Polish aristocrat. In Marina's nature, old-fashioned courtesy mingled with rebelliousness, arrogance with shyness, bookish romanticism with simplicity of soul.

When I first went to see Tsvetayeva I already knew her poems. Some of them I liked, especially one written a year before the Revolution, where Marina spoke about her own funeral: 'Down the streets of deserted Moscow I shall drive, and you will walk, and many will drop behind, and the first handful will ring against the coffin's lid, and the selfish, lonely dream will be resolved at last. Forgive, O Lord, the noblewoman Marina newly dead of pride'.

Entering the small flat I felt utterly confused: it would be difficult to imagine greater chaos. Everyone in those days lived in a state of emergency, but the outward forms of life were still preserved. Marina, however, seemed to have ravaged her hiding-place on purpose. Everything was flung about, covered with tobacco ash and dust. A small girl, very thin and pale, came up and, clinging to me trustingly, started whispering: 'What pale dresses! What a strange silence! Embraces full of lilies, eyes empty of thought'. Horror chilled me: Tsvetayeva's daughter Alya was then five years old, and she was reciting Blok. Everything was unnatural, contrived: the flat, Alya, Marina's own conversation. She professed a great interest in politics and said she was agitating for the Kadets.

In her early poems Tsvetayeva sang of Stepan Razin's 'freemen'.

She herself was by nature a rebel rather than a supporter of that law and order for which the terrified bourgeoisie longed in the summer of 1917. She had nothing in common with those people, but she drew back from the Revolution and created a romantic *Vendée* in her imagination. She pitied the Tsar (although she condemned him, too: 'Many times our children will remember the Byzantine perfidy of your limpid eyes'). And she repeated again and again: 'O my boyar longing, sorrow of the Tsars . . .'

Why had her husband, Seryozha Efron, gone off to join the White Army? I knew his elder brother, the actor Pyotr Yakovlevich Efron, in Paris; he died young of tuberculosis. Seryozha was like him: a very gentle, modest, thoughtful person. I cannot imagine that he should have wanted suddenly to become a *chouan*.

He left, and Marina wrote raving poems: 'For Sofia against Peter!' and 'André Chenier mounted the scaffold; I am alive, and that is a terrible sin'. She read all these poems at various literary gatherings and no one persecuted her for them. It was all a bookish invention, an absurd romanticism for which Marina paid with her crippled, impossibly hard life.

When, in the autumn of 1920, I got back to Moscow from Koktebel, I found Marina still in her frantic solitude. She had written a book of verse glorifying the Whites, called *The Swans' Encampment*. By that time I had seen many things, including the Russian *Vendée*, and had arrived at many conclusions. I tried to describe to her the true face of the White Guards, but she did not believe me. I tried arguing, but she grew angry. She had a difficult character from which she herself suffered more than anyone else. I have still got her book *Parting*, on the flyleaf of which she wrote: 'For you whose friendship cost me more dearly than an enmity and whose enmity is dearer to me than any friendship, for Ehrenburg from Marina Tsvetayeva. Berlin 29 May 1922'. (Written in the old spelling, although by this time little remained of the firm positions she had once held.)

When, in the spring of 1921, I became one of the first Soviet citizens to go abroad, she asked me to try and find her husband. I was able to discover that Seryozha Efron was alive and in Prague, and I wrote and told Marina. Her spirits rose and she applied for a passport entitling her to go abroad. She said they gave her the passport straight away; Mirkin at the Narkomindel (People's Commissariat for Foreign Affairs) said: 'One day you'll be sorry you're leaving'.

With her, Tsvetayeva carried the manuscript of *The Swans'*
Encampment.

Her meeting with her husband was dramatic. He told her of the
White Guards' atrocities, the pogroms, the spiritual emptiness. In his
accounts the swans were like crows. Marina was badly shaken. In
Berlin I once talked to her throughout a whole night, and at the end
she said that she would not publish her book.

(*The Swans' Encampment* was published in Munich in 1958. Before
returning to the Soviet Union on the eve of the Second World War,
Tsvetayeva left her literary papers at the library in Basle—'a neutral
country'. I do not know how the manuscript got into the hands of
the publishers; their aims were certainly political and contrary to
her wishes. After all, she had spent seventeen years in emigration and
received many offers to publish *The Swans' Encampment,* but she had
always refused.)

I should like to deepen and expand the subject of the *Vendée*
poetically visualized by Marina Tsvetayeva. I want to speak of the
way in which art sometimes turns into a pose, a masquerade, fancy
dress. (I have already mentioned this when writing of my own early
verse.) This applies not only to *The Swans' Encampment* but also to
many works by many other poets, and a few words on this subject
may help, if only partially, towards an understanding of later chapters in this book.

As I have already said, I have kept no old letters. Tsvetayeva brought
a small part of her private papers to Moscow, including the drafts of
some letters addressed to me. In one of these, Marina wrote: 'At that
time, in 1918, you rejected my Don Juans (a "cloak" which neither
covers nor reveals). Now, in 1922, you reject my Tsar-Maidens and
Yegorushkas (Russia in me – that is, a secondary thing). Both then
and now you wanted only one thing from me: myself, i.e. a skeleton,
without cloak or peasant tunic, if possible in rags. Poetic conceits,
figures, expression through something, you saw all this as more or less
a masquerade. You wanted from me the chief thing, without which I
am not myself. I was never able to refute you (myself I have refuted,
continually, and shall again); you turned out to be more far-seeing
than I. Both then, in 1918, and now in 1922, you were cruel: not a
single self-indulgence! You are right. Loose writing in poetry is no
better than loose living (self-indulgence, wilfulness) in life. All the
rest of them fall into two categories: the keepers of law and order –

"Do what you like in poetry, so long as you behave properly in life" – and the aesthetes – "Anything you like in life, so long as you write good poetry". Only you: "No looseness either in poetry or in life. You do not need it". You are right, because that is the thing towards which I am silently advancing.'

She advanced and she arrived at the goal she had set herself, she arrived at it by the road of suffering, loneliness and rejection.

Her relationship to poetry was complex and painful. She wrote many unjust things about Bryusov: she saw the externals and did not try to look or think more deeply. Of course she was bound to be outraged by lines such as: 'Perhaps everything in life is only a means to brilliant, singing verse, and from your carefree childhood onwards you must seek combinations of words'. Tsvetayeva answered: 'Words instead of meanings, rhymes instead of feelings? As if words were born out of words, rhymes out of rhymes, poems out of poems!' Yet she was herself a prisoner of poetry all her life. Remembering the words of Karolina Pavlova, Tsvetayeva called one of her books *Craftsmanship*. In it she writes: 'Find yourself trusting life companions who have not sorted out the miracle by numbers. I know that Venus is the work of hands; a craftsman, I know my craft.'

Marina called many people her friends in the course of her life; suddenly the friendship would break down and she would bid farewell to yet another illusion. But there was one friend to whom she remained faithful to the end: 'There was a being that I loved, and that being was a desk' – her writing desk – poetry.

I have met poets and I know the high price an artist pays for his passion for art, but I do not think there is a figure in all my memories more tragic than Marina. Everything in her history is unstable and illusory – political ideas, critical opinions, personal relationships – everything except poetry. Few people are left alive who knew Tsvetayeva, but her poetry is only just beginning to enter the world of a great many.

From adolescence until death she was lonely, and this was bound up with her own rejection of her environment. 'All things in my life I have come to love and have loved to the end by farewells not by meetings, by parting not by union.' In emigration, Tsvetayeva found herself lonely once again; émigré journals published her unwillingly, and when she wrote enthusiastically about Mayakovsky she was suspected of 'treason'. Tsvetayeva wrote in one of her letters:

'In emigration they publish me at first (in the heat of the moment!) then, when they've recovered their balance, they withdraw me from circulation, sensing something not their own: something from "over there". The content looks like "ours", "but the voice is theirs".'

In what is normally known as politics, Tsvetayeva was guileless, obstinate, and sincere. In 1922, together with the painter Lisitzky, I was publishing a journal called *Veshch* (*Object*); it appeared in Russian, French and German. At her own wish, Marina translated into French Mayakovsky's fighting poem '*Listen, you swine!*' In the thirties, when her passion for the Russian *Vendée* had cooled long ago, she still could not reconcile herself to the New Style – I do not mean in art, but in the calendar. (I remember tales about the first year of Soviet power: at a meeting in Petrograd Blok made an impassioned speech in defence of the old spelling; he accepted everything, but *lyes* – forest – spelt in the new way was no longer a forest to him.)

During the years of the First World War, Tsvetayeva wrote: 'Germany, my madness! Germany, my love!' (She was not alone in that love; Blok, too, spoke of his allegiance to German culture.) A quarter of a century later German divisions marched into betrayed Prague, and Marina cursed them: 'Megalomania! O hollow greatness! You shall burn, Germania! Madness, madness is this you do.'

Our encounters in the thirties were rare, accidental and empty. I did not know how or for what she was living nor did I know her new poems. For Tsvetayeva those were years of great trials and great effort: today I realize how she grew in stature as a poet, how she divested herself of the last 'cloaks', how she found simple, penetrating words.

Her life was extremely hard: 'My husband is ill and cannot work. Our daughter earns five francs a day by knitting little hats and on this four of us live (I have a son aged eight, Georgi), that is to say we slowly die of hunger.'

Efron became a member of the Eurasian movement and, later, one of the organizers of the 'League for the Return to the Motherland'. Addressing her son and all the young people born in emigration, Marina wrote: 'Stop mourning an Eden where you've never been'. Alya went to Moscow; Efron followed her soon afterwards.

But Tsvetayeva herself had never been in the illusory Eden either. The old world seemed to her a lost paradise. 'I, too, liked laughing when laughter was out of place.' She liked many things just because they were 'out of place', applauded at those moments when those sitting next to her did not, sat alone staring at the lowered curtain, walked out of the auditorium and wept in dark, empty corridors.

As a girl Marina had admired *L'Aiglon* and the whole conventional romanticism of Rostand. With the years her enthusiasms went deeper: Goethe, *Hamlet*, *Phèdre* She sometimes wrote poetry in French and in German. Yet she felt a foreigner everywhere but in Russia. Her whole being was bound up with her native landscape, from the 'hot rowan' of her youth to the ultimate elder trees stained with blood. The fundamental themes of her poetry were love, death and art, and she resolved these themes in a Russian way. Love was for her the 'fatal duel' that Tyutchev wrote about. She said of Pushkin's Tatiana: 'What other nation has such a love heroine: bold and dignified, enamoured and unrelenting, clear-sighted and loving?' Worse than anything, Marina hated the substitutes for love: 'How many of them, how many, white and dove-coloured, eat out of my hands! Whole kingdoms coo around your lips, O Baseness!', She herself was 'enamoured and unrelenting'.

In 1939 Tsvetayeva returned home with her fourteen-year-old son. One of her last poems, I believe, was written after the fascists had finished off Spain and invaded Czechoslovakia: 'I refuse to be in the Bedlam of non-humans, I refuse to live. I refuse to howl with the wolves of the public squares'. Efron lost his life. Alya was far away. In Moscow, too, Marina found herself alone.

She came to see me in August 1941. We met after many years' separation, and the meeting was a failure – through my fault. It was in the morning and the radio had already announced 'Our troops have withdrawn from . . .' My thoughts were far away. Marina sensed it at once and gave our conversation the flavour of a business interview: she had come, she said, to seek my advice about translating work. When she was leaving, I said: 'Marina, we must meet and talk'. But we never met again: Tsvetayeva committed suicide in Yelabuga, where the hazards of evacuation had taken her.

Her son was killed at the front. I sometimes see Alya; she has collected Marina's unpublished poems.

I cannot get certain lines of Tsvetayeva's out of my mind: they have taken root in my memory for the whole of my life. It is not only a matter of an intense poetic gift. Our paths were different, and I do not think we ever met at one of those crossroads where people choose, or think they are choosing, their way. But in Tsvetayeva's life as a poet there is something which is very near to me: perpetual doubts about the rightful claims of art, and at the same time an inability to abandon art. She often asked herself what was more important – poetry or the building of real life – and answered: 'With the exception of parasites of all kinds, everyone is more important than we (the poets)'. She wrote after Mayakovsky's death: 'He lived like a man and died like a poet'. She never tried to shelter from life; on the contrary, she wanted to live with human beings. Loneliness, for her, was not a programme but a curse; it had a great deal to do with that only friend of whom Marina wrote: 'that being was a desk'. She had never been to the Rotonde, had never known Modigliani, yet she wrote: 'Ghetto of the elect. A wall, a ditch. Expect no mercy. In this most Christian of worlds, poets are Jews'. The word 'elect' may confuse, but Tsvetayeva looked upon the 'ghetto' not as a proud retreat but as a doom: 'What poet, of those who ever were and are, is not a Negro?'

When I re-read Tsvetayeva's poems, I suddenly stop thinking about poetry and turn to memories, to the fates of many of my friends, to my own fate: men, years—life.

4

BEFORE me is a scrap of faded yellow newspaper, the *Birzhevka* for 24th September, 1917. There is some theatrical news: the Mikhailovsky Theatre is rehearsing *The Death of Ivan the Terrible*, but the play will probably be taken out of the repertoire owing to the smallness of the company and the incompatibility of the play's political tendencies with the events and feelings of the day. The Committee of the Soviet of Workers' and Soldiers' Deputies is arranging a series of symphony concerts for October. Soloists and the orchestra of the 171st Infantry Reserve Regiment will take part. The conductors will be A. Glazunov, A. Ziloti and A. Coates. Next comes a sketch I had sent from Moscow.

'In flat No. 6 where the Symbolist writer lives there is a select gathering: Madame Eleonora the theosophist, an officer with decorations, another rather younger writer and several who are just intellectuals.

' "They all refuse to listen," moans one of these. "Our people are unworthy of freedom. Brutes, rapers, thieves. I had two keys stolen on the tram. They need the big stick. We made a mistake when we gave them their freedom too soon. People say educate them. Educate those *muzhiks*? No thank you! Let someone else try. They'll soon show themselves in their true colours. They'll cut each other's throats, then a general will come on a white horse and tame them and everything will be much better."

' "What are you saying," ' the theosophist lady sighs sadly, "you say a general on a white horse, I thought it would be Milyukov."

"That's quite right, the big stick is what's needed," the officer explains courteously. "Just consider this: before this 'freedom' of theirs, our soldiers had great respect, one might even say affection for an officer who, if you'll excuse me, might on occasion swipe them across the face. And now it's soldiers' committees and all the rest of that nonsense. What, let those 'lads from back home' pass resolutions? No, for the life of me I can't! They wanted to award me the St. George for valour. I turned it down: just one of their tricks! Believe me, they need the big stick, discipline. . . ."

'The Symbolist writer glances vaguely at his guests, rolls his eyes and intones:

' "Withdraw! Hide yourselves! Save our culture, our wisdom, our faith from those barbarians! All our wealth is in our libraries, in our museums, in your souls. Preserve the museums! Shut your ears to the voice of the streets! I never open one of those accursed newspapers, I hardly leave the house. Paeans ring in my ears."

' "As for me, *maître*," declares the younger writer, "I have adopted a slightly different attitude. Remaining impassive in my soul, I watch the play of passions. I am above it, but how much material it provides for my future novel!"

'A general conversation on paeans and iambics, Symbolists and Futurists ensues. A whole quarter of an hour passes before the company returns to earth: someone has mentioned fruit jelly, which now costs seven roubles a pound and has to replace sugar. And again the intellectual moans:

' "Brutes! Big stick! A general!" '

Mocking others, I mocked myself too. Though I did not dream of generals, the big stick or cheap fruit jelly, I was incapable of understanding what was going on.

Moscow lived as if on a railway platform, waiting for the guard's whistle. The town was combed for deserters. There was cursing everywhere, particularly in the trams which crawled along, hung with clusters of human beings. At the Metropole, despairing intellectuals drank French champagne for which they paid with large sheets of uncut *kerenkas*. Out of sheer habit, they muttered about the necessity of saving Russia; I daresay they genuinely wanted to save themselves, but they no longer believed in anything and went on living purely by the force of inertia. Brand-new publishers at the Café Bom swore that they would publish Pushkin's *Gavriliada*, Rasputin's memoirs and the complete works of any one of us; some of them quickly lost their interest in publishing and switched to the garment trade or sugar. In the Shabolovka cafés, people gloomily awaited a dénouement.

My mother was in Yalta; I wanted to see her after my long absence. I managed with difficulty to buy a railway ticket and fought my way into a carriage. I found my mother greatly aged; she coughed, wrapped herself in a knitted shawl and was terrified of street firing (which occurred frequently, for no apparent reason).

I visited Voloshin at Koktebel. He talked about the elements, the

Archpriest Avvakum and the three Furies with their serpents. His eyes reminded me of shuttered windows.

In the train, my fellow-passengers caught a petty thief, a boy of about twelve; they all flung themselves on him and beat him up. To this day I still see the bloodied childish face. At one of the stations the train stopped for about three hours; we all went to the market and bought a lot of apples and bread, after which a meeting was held. A young miss clutching a loaf to her breast yelled hysterically that now even cripples ought to go to the front. A soldier heaped obscenities on her but she still went on shouting. The black marketeers kept an eye on their sacks of food and smiled enigmatically.

When I returned to Moscow there was fighting in the streets. At Krasnaya Vorota I saw an old man lying in the road: he had been killed by a stray bullet.

This is how, in 1921, the author of *Julio Jurenito* described the experiences of the character appearing in the novel under the name of Ilya Ehrenburg: 'I cursed my ill-conceived nature. It had to be one of two things: either I must have different eyes or I must get rid of my useless hands. At that moment outside the window men were making history, not with their brains, their imaginations, their miserable poetry, but with their hands . . . What could be easier, it seemed – just run down the stairs and make history, make it; hurry whilst the substance under your fingers is clay and not granite, whilst history can be written with bullets, not read in a learned German's six-volume edition. Yet there I was, sitting in a closet, munching a cold rissole and quoting Tyutchev. Accursed eyes, eyes squinting, blind or long-sighted, but rotten eyes in any case. What is the use of seeing thirty-three truths if, as a result, you cannot grasp and clutch your very own truth, a bit skimpy perhaps, but blood of your blood and strong, strong? All around they were at least breathing "oh's" and "ah's", rejoicing and praising the All-Powerful for one reason or another. "Thank God Alexeyev's coming, the bandits have been driven away," cried Lelya, a charming girl. "Thank God," said Matryosha, Lelya's maid, with deep feeling, "the Bolsheviks are getting the upper hand." But I am incapable even of that . . . Mark well, O members of so-called posterity, what Ilya Ehrenburg, the Russian poet, was doing during those never-to-be-repeated days!'

I also wrote, in the same *Julio Jurenito*: 'A sort of dirge broke out everywhere. A curious feature was that many people bewailed things

31

they had not even noticed in the past, or had not approved of when they had noticed them: Lelya lamented the autocracy, Seryozha (the one who was for Mikhailovsky) the Church, Fedya, the schoolboy, their younger brother, lamented industry and finance. At least it was something to do, and in the absence of anything better I turned to lamentation . . . I looked back, lamented, wrote poems and read them aloud in numerous "poets' cafés" with moderate success.'

Here the author of *Julio Jurenito* is not speaking of an imaginary hero but of himself, frankly and without any attempt at self-justification or touching up. However, I mocked myself not only three years later but also during the actual days when, bewildered, I searched for a hundred different truths and bewailed a world which had never been mine. I was writing very bad poems at that time: art does not tolerate falsehood, but I was trying to deceive myself; I prayed to a god in whom I did not believe, and dressed myself up in other men's clothing.

Blok's journals contain an entry for 31st January, 1918, where a young man whose name is given as 'Steng' describes to Blok the young people's attitude to poetry: 'First there were the three B's – Balmont, Bryusov, Blok. Then they began to seem tame, and there was Mayakovsky. Now he seems tame as well, and there's Ehrenburg (he makes the most pungent fun of himself, and that is why, very soon, we shall all like no one but Ehrenburg)'.

'Steng' was V. O. Stenich, a young poet whom I met later. He recited Blok's, Mayakovsky's, Khlebnikov's and his own poems pell-mell, and cracked mournful jokes. He lost his life during the thirties. Had Stenich told me at the time that someone was capable of admiring my poems, I would have been very much surprised. I did not like them myself; I debated with myself in my notebook: 'The thing to do is to stop writing, take up market gardening or wait for things to calm down and then buy a camera with a tripod and take portrait photographs at fairgrounds.'

'Happy is he who has visited this world during its fateful moments': thus wrote a twenty-seven-year-old poet who was then second secretary at the Russian embassy in Munich. Reading newspaper accounts of the Paris revolution of 1830 while he lived on in peaceful, sleepy Bavaria, young Tyutchev envied every eye-witness of the storm: 'Spectator of their lofty spectacles . . .' But in reality there is nothing sillier or more humiliating then the spectator's role when history moves out of the textbooks and into the streets and squares of one's own neighbourhood. Someone involved in events understands far more than a cold observer; blindness does not strike the man who loves and hates, but the man who sits in the stalls trying to decipher the flickering pictures of a film.

Once I ran into Alexey Ivanovich Okulov. In Paris I had known him as a gloomy man who drank a great deal and had no clear idea of what to do. He would make notes in a loose-leaf notebook, then he would spread the bits of paper out on his bed and rearrange them to make a short story; once he actually got a prize for one of these. He was classified as a writer, but when he had had a little to drink he would shout: 'What kind of a writer am I? If I'm any good for anything, it's only to use a gun'. His history was tempestuous: membership of militant units, imprisonment, emigration, underground work, more prisons and more emigration. In revolutionary Moscow he felt confident; he told me he was going to the front in a few days' time. His kind of inner gaiety is the privilege of an active participant. The observer's lot is far less happy. Gorky wrote: 'My relations with Lenin in '17–'18 were far from what I should have liked them to be, but they could not be any different. He is a politician. He possessed, in its perfect form, that clearly developed directness of vision which is essential for the helmsman of so vast and ponderous a ship as our leaden, peasant Russia. I, on the other hand, have an organic distaste for politics, and I have not much faith in the good sense of the masses in general and in the good sense of the peasant masses in particular'. Gorky found himself in the role of an observer, and thirteen years later he wrote: 'Let the reader, then, know of this error of mine. It would be good if it served as a lesson to those who are inclined to draw hasty conclusions from their observations'.

(I think that Gorky is wrong on one point: people learn from their own mistakes, not from those of other people. The same mistakes occur too often in history for this not to be true.)

I cannot say that I have always steered clear of politics, or rather of action: I began with underground work and, later, in my maturity, I have often been a participant in events; in future volumes of my reminiscences, political events will often drive books and paintings into the background. But in 1917 I found myself an observer, and it took me two years to realize the significance of the October Revolution. In terms of history two years is a negligible period, but in a human life they represent many troubled days, complicated thoughts and simple human pain.

Forty-three years have passed since then. I should like to remind my readers what France looked like forty-three years after the Revolution of 1789. A kaleidoscope of events lay behind: Thermidor, Madame Tallien, the young Corsican, the Napoleonic wars, the Cossacks in Paris, again the Bourbons, the White terror, the 'little revolution' – and, at the end of it all, Louis-Philippe whose brand of democracy consisted in walking about with an umbrella and acknowledging the bows of his faithful subjects. For the Parisian of 1832 the Revolution of 1789 was an event in an age long past and difficult to understand. I doubt if even one of the hundred people whom I spoke to yesterday can remember pre-revolutionary Russia; for the fifty-year-olds, not to mention those still younger, the Soviet system is not an idea to argue about, not the programme of a particular party, but a natural form of society.

In the West, of course, people do argue, question and deny; but in 1960 it is possible to make comparisons, to use the complex life of a great State as an argument. The Russian intelligentsia in 1917–18 had a far more difficult time.

I mourned for no estates, factories or shares: I was poor and had despised wealth since my childhood. What troubled me was something else. I had grown up with a concept of freedom inherited from the nineteenth century; from my schooldays I had respected disrespect and listened to the voices of the disobedient. I failed to understand that not only regimes change, but also concepts. The new age both brought and took away many things, whilst I tried to measure tomorrow with the yardstick of yesterday.

But there was something that mattered even more. To be honest, I did not yet know the meaning of life, although I was now twenty-six. Slips of the pen, misprints and mistakes hindered me from understanding the true meaning of the text. I noticed much that was ugly, I saw anger and ignorance, but I failed to see the most important thing: what I had dreamt of as an adolescent, what I had glimpsed as a vision in prison cells was coming true. Life is never like dreams. Fortune-tellers speak of the 'line of life': such a line really does exist, not in the palm of the hand but in the fates of men, and the sooner you can see and read it, the easier it will be for you to overcome your doubts. This line is traced not only by lofty ideas but also by real events, not only by

34

attractions but also by repulsions, not only by passionate feelings but also by sober thoughts. I do not in the least want to imply that the end justifies the means: I know too well that the means may alter any end. I am thinking only of the truth of the 'line of life': a man's, a nation's, a century's.

Later, like all my contemporaries, I was to live through many ordeals. I found myself prepared to face them: at forty-six I saw my 'line of life' much more clearly than at twenty-six. I recognized that it is necessary to know how to live with clenched teeth; that one cannot treat events like an exercise in grammar in which all one has to do is to underline the mistakes; that the road into the future is not a macadamised highway. As the poet Tvardovsky has said: 'here you can neither take away nor add'. History, like the life of an individual human being, has many bitter pages, and not everything happens as you would like. Everyone today realizes the act of heroism our people performed when, in a poverty-stricken, dark and hungry country, in the autumn of 1917, they set out on a new, uncharted path. Whereas at the time, not only I but also many writers of an older generation, as well as many of my contemporaries, did not yet recognize the scale of events. But it was precisely then that a young Petrograd poet who was considered a drawing-room artist, pseudo-classical and remote from life, the frail and hypochondriacal Osip Mandelstam, wrote the marvellous lines: 'Well, then let us try: a tremendous, clumsy, creaking swing of the helm. The earth is in full sail. Be manful, men, cleaving the ocean as with a plough: even in the chill of Lethe we shall remember that the earth was worth ten heavens to us'.

However, I shall have occasion later to speak of all these things: of Mandelstam, of the great swing of the helm, and, above all, of that earth which was worth ten heavens to us.

5

I CANNOT remember who introduced me to Mayakovsky. At first we sat in some café or other and talked about the cinema. Then he took me 'home', to a small room at the San Remo lodging house in Saltykovskaya Lane near Petrovka. I had just read his book *Simple as Mooing*, and he was exactly as I had imagined him: large, heavy-jowled, with eyes that were now sad, now stern, a loud and clumsy man ready at any moment to join in a brawl, a combination of athlete and dreamer, of medieval *jongleur* who stands on his head to pray and irreconcilable iconoclast.

As we walked towards the San Remo he droned the epitaph of François Villon written in the expectation of the gallows:

> *Je suis Françoys, dont il me poise*
> *Né de Paris emprès Pontoise,*
> *Et de la corde d'une toise*
> *Sçaura mon col que mon cul poise.*

As soon as we were in his room, he said: 'Now let me read you something'. I sat down on a chair, he remained standing. He read me *Man*, the long poem he had recently finished. The room was small and there was no one in it besides myself, but he read as though addressing a crowd in Teatralny Square. I gazed at the horrid wallpaper and smiled: boot legs were really turning into harps.

Mayakovsky amazed me: poetry and the Revolution, the turbulent streets of Moscow and the new art dreamed of by the habitués of the Rotonde existed side by side within him. I even thought that he might help me to find my way. It did not turn out like that: Mayakovsky has remained, for me, a tremendous phenomenon, both in poetry and in the life of the age; but he had no direct influence on me at all; I always felt him to be near and yet infinitely remote.

It may be a peculiarity of genius, or it may be a peculiarity of Mayakovsky's character: he used to say that poets ought to be 'different', he was the initiator of LEF, New LEF, and REF[1], he wanted to attract and unite many artists, yet round him were only his admirers, sometimes his imitators. He has written how, at a *dacha* near Moscow, he had a conversation with the Sun: he himself was a sun circled by satellites.

I met him in Moscow in 1918 and 1920, in Berlin in 1922, in Paris, again in Moscow and again in Paris (we met for the last time in the spring of 1929, a year before his death). Sometimes our meetings were casual, sometimes significant. I should like to speak of my own interpretation of Mayakovsky. I know what I have to say will be one-sided and subjective, but can a contemporary's evidence be anything else? A multitude of differing accounts, sometimes contradictory, helps to create the image of a man. The trouble is that Mayakovsky, a passionate destroyer of all myths, was translated into a mythical hero with extraordinary speed. It is as though he were fated to appear not as he really was. There are the memoirs of eye-witnesses who can remember a few ferocious jokes. There are the pages of school text-books. Finally, there is the statue. The schoolboy learns extracts from *Good!* by heart. The housewife in the trolley-bus asks anxiously: 'Will you tell me when we get to Mayakovsky?' It is not easy to speak about the man.

Until the mid-thirties Mayakovsky provoked passionate arguments. At the First Congress of Soviet Writers, whenever his name was mentioned, some would applaud enthusiastically, others would remain silent. At that time I wrote in *Izvestia*: 'We did not applaud because somebody had conceived a wish to canonize Mayakovsky: we applauded because Mayakovsky's name means to us the overthrow of all literary canons'. I could not imagine that a year later the canonization of Mayakovsky would really have begun. I did not attend his funeral. Friends told me that the coffin was too short. I have the feeling that Mayakovsky's posthumous fame is also too short, and, above all, too narrow for him.

First of all I should like to speak of him as a human being. He was by no means a 'monolith': he was a great, complicated man with tremendous will power and a tangle of sometimes contradictory feelings. *The Dead Stay Young* is the title of one of Anna Seghers' novels.

---

[1] LEF: The organization and journal 'Left Front' 1923–5. New LEF 1927. REF: Revolutionary Front of the Arts, 1929.

Later impressions nearly always obscure earlier ones. I have already tried to describe the young Alexey Tolstoy; he was one of the first writers I ever met. But often, when I think of him, I see him corpulent and famous, with a loud laugh and tired eyes: I see the man I knew during the last years of his life. Here is a photograph with Alexander Fadeyev – young, dreamy, gentle-eyed – standing next to Mayakovsky. It is very difficult for me to remember Fadeyev thus: the eyes I see are strong-willed, sometimes cold. But Mayakovsky stays young in my memory.

To the end of his life he retained certain features, or rather, perhaps, certain habits of his early youth. The critics do not like to dwell on Mayakovsky's so-called 'Futurist period', although it is impossible, without his early poems, to understand the later works. But I am now speaking not of poetry but of the man. Of course Mayakovsky soon abandoned the slogans, as well as the yellow shirt, of the early Futurist manifestos. Yet the spirit which dictated *A Slap in the Face for Public Taste* remained with him, in his bearing, his jokes, his answers to questions sent up to him at meetings.

I remember the Poets' Café in the winter of 1917–18. It was in Nastasyinsky Lane, and it was a very odd place indeed. The walls were covered with strange paintings and no less strange inscriptions. 'I love to watch children dying': this line from an early, pre-revolutionary poem of Mayakovsky's was displayed in order to stun newcomers. The Poets' Café was quite unlike the Rotonde. No one here talked about art, no one argued, no one suffered; there were actors and there was an audience. The clientèle of the café were people of the sort then known as 'bourgeois who hadn't had their throats cut yet': speculators, literary men and ordinary middle-class people in search of entertainment. Mayakovsky was hardly capable of providing this: although much in his poetry was incomprehensible to them, they sensed the existence of a close link between his words and the sailors strolling along Tverskaya. As for Mayakovsky's little song about the bourgeois stuffing himself with pineapple against the wrath to come, that was understood by everybody: though there were no pineapples in Nastasyinsky Lane, a lump of vulgar pork stuck in the throats of many. Entertainment was derived from other sources. For example, David Burlyuk would mount the rostrum, heavily powdered and holding a lorgnette, to read 'I am fond of pregnant men . . .' Holzschmidt also had a galvanizing effect on the audience; he was billed as a 'Futurist of

Life', and he wrote no poetry but dyed two locks of his hair golden, was exceptionally strong, broke wooden planks and acted as chucker-out. Once this 'Futurist of Life' decided to erect a monument to himself in Teatralnaya Square; the statue was not very large, made of plaster and not in the least Futuristic: all you saw was a naked Holzschmidt. The passers-by were shocked but left the enigmatic monument alone. Eventually someone did smash it.

All that belongs to the distant past. A couple of years ago, David Burlyuk and his wife came to Moscow, a couple of American tourists. In America Burlyuk draws pictures, makes his bit of money and has become respectable in behaviour and looks; there is no trace of the lorgnette or of the 'pregnant men'. Today, Futurism seems to me far more ancient than ancient Greece. But for Mayakovsky, who died young, it remained, if not alive, at least near.

I used to visit the Poets' Café fairly often; once I actually gave a reading and received the appropriate fee from Holzschmidt.

I remember an evening when Lunacharsky came. He sat down unobtrusively at a table at the back and listened. Mayakovsky asked him to speak; he refused. Mayakovsky insisted: 'Repeat what you told me about my poems'. Lunacharsky had to give in. He spoke of Maya-kovsky's talent, but criticized Futurism and commented that self-advertisement was unnecessary. Then Mayakovsky said that he would have a monument raised to him quite soon on the site of the Poets' Café. He was only a few hundred yards out: his monument is not very far from Nastasyinsky Lane.

Lack of modesty? Self-confidence? Many of Mayakovsky's con-temporaries often asked such questions. For example, he celebrated the twelfth anniversary of his poetic activity. He often described him-self as the greatest poet. He demanded recognition during his lifetime; and this was part and parcel of the period, of that overthrowing of idols that Balmont deplored, of the desire to draw attention to the arts at all costs.

'I love to watch children dying . . .' Mayakovsky could not bear to see a horse being whipped. Once a friend of mine cut his finger in a café. Mayakovsky hastily looked away. Self-confident? Yes, of course; he answered criticisms sharply and insulted his literary opponents. I remember the following exchange. Comment: 'Your poems do not warm, do not surge, do not infect.' Reply: 'I am not a stove, not the sea, not the plague.' He used to write in his books when he gave them

39

away: 'For internal use only'. All that is well known. Other things are less well known.

I remember a Mayakovsky reading at the Café Voltaire in Paris. Lydia Seyfullina was among the audience. It was in the spring of 1927. Someone in the hall shouted: 'Now let's have one of your old poems!' As usual, Mayakovsky parried with a joke. Afterwards several of us – Mayakovsky, Lydia Seyfullina, Elsa Triolet and some others – went to a night club near the boulevard St Germain. There was music; a few couples danced. Mayakovsky joked, imitated the poet Georgi Ivanov who had attended the reading, then fell into a gloomy silence looking about him uneasily like a caged lion. We arranged that I should come to see him the next morning, the earlier the better. In the tiny room at the Hôtel Istria where he always stopped, the bed was unused: he had stayed up all night. He was sombre and preoccupied and asked me as soon as I came in: 'Well, do you also think I wrote better poetry before?' He was never self-confident; the pose adopted once and for all was deceptive. I think it was a pose dictated by reason rather than natural inclination. He had a leaning towards romanticism, but was ashamed of it and often cut himself short: 'Who has not spouted philosophy by the sea?' (this after some bitter reflections on his own life), followed immediately by the ironic 'water'. In the article *How to Make Verse* everything seems simple and logical. In reality, Mayakovsky knew all about the sufferings inseparable from creative work. He spoke at length about 'storing up' rhymes. But he also had other stores laid up which he did not like to speak about: stores of emotional suffering. In a poem written just before his death he wrote 'Love's boat has foundered on everyday life'. This was a sop to that romanticism at which he had laughed so often. In reality, his life had foundered on poetry. Addressing posterity, he said what he did not want to say to his contemporaries. 'But I mastered myself and crushed underfoot the throat of my very own song'.

He seemed extremely strong, healthy, full of *joie de vivre*. Yet he was sometimes insufferably glum. He was extremely cranky about his health. He always carried a piece of soap in his pocket, and when he was obliged to shake hands with someone who was for some reason physically repugnant to him, he immediately went and washed his hands very thoroughly. In Paris cafés he drank coffee through a straw, like an iced drink, to avoid touching the glass with his lips. He laughed at superstition yet he was always trying his luck and adored simple gambling games such as heads or tails, odds or evens. In Paris cafés there used to be automatic roulette machines: you put five sous on red, green or yellow, and if you won you got a counter which would pay for a cup of coffee or a glass of beer. Mayakovsky spent hours in front of these machines, and when he left Paris he bequeathed hundreds of counters to Elsa Triolet: he did not want them, all he wanted was to know what colour would come up. He left one bullet in the magazine of his revolver, too: odds and evens.

When Mayakovsky spoke to a woman, his voice changed: normally rough and urgent, it became gentle. I read in Victor Shklovsky's book: 'Mayakovsky went abroad. There was a woman, and there might be love. I have heard that they were so alike, they made such a fine couple, that people in cafés would smile gratefully just to see them'. A poem by Mayakovsky addressed to Tatiana Yakovleva ('Tata') – to whom Shklovsky is referring – was published recently. But I have got a manuscript copy of *The Bedbug*, which Mayakovsky gave to Tata who threw it away when she no longer wanted it. No, she did not resemble Mayakovsky, though, like him, she was tall and good-looking. I do not want to indulge in what Mayakovsky himself rightly called 'gossip', and I mention this episode – by no means the most important in Mayakovsky's life – only to point out once more how unlike the bronze statue of himself and Vladimir the Red Sun, the legendary hero, he really was.

At eighteen he went to art school because he wanted to become a painter. In his poetry he always retained a visual approach to the world: his images are not invented but seen. He loved and understood painting and enjoyed being among painters. He saw the world rather than heard it. (He used to say, as a joke, that an elephant had trodden on his ear.)

I have already mentioned the evening at the Zetlins when Mayakovsky read his poem *Man*. Vyacheslav Ivanov nodded approvingly from time to time. Balmont was obviously on tenterhooks. Baltrushaitis was as inscrutable as ever. Marina Tsvetayeva smiled; Pasternak gazed at Mayakovsky like a man in love. Andrey Bely listened – not just listened but drank it in – and when Mayakovsky had finished reading he leapt to his feet in such a state of excitement that he could hardly speak. Almost everyone present shared his enthusiasm. But Mayakovsky fastened upon somebody's cold polite remark and was angered by it. That was always the way: he appeared not to notice the bouquets but to look only for the thorns. His poems are full of ceaseless battles with real and imaginary opponents of the new poetry. What was behind those recriminations? Was it perhaps an argument with himself?

I have read articles on Mayakovsky, written abroad, whose authors try to prove that the Revolution destroyed the poet. A greater absurdity is difficult to imagine: without the Revolution, there would have been no Mayakovsky. In 1918 he rightly called me a 'frightened intellectual': it took me two years to understand what was going on. Mayakovsky, on the other hand, understood and accepted the Revolution at once. He was not merely inspired by the thought of building a Socialist society, he was absorbed by it. He never trimmed his sails, and when certain people tried to tame him, he snapped: ' "Back to the village" is the slogan: up with the bagpipes, poet friends! But understand: I've only got one face, and it is a face, not a weather vane. An idea isn't cooked in water. Water will damp any idea. Poets have never lived without ideas. What do you think I am – a parrot? A turkey?' He was never in conflict with the Revolution; that is an invention of people who jib at nothing in their struggle against Communism. Mayakovsky's tragedy lay not in the conflict between the Revolution and poetry, but in the attitude of LEF towards the arts. 'Let poets moan, pour out their spittle, their lips snaking contempt. I, who have scrapped the soul, shout about things necessary under Socialism.' (At the time, the newspaper where this poem was published altered a few words, putting: 'I, who have not abased my soul' instead of: 'I who have scrapped the soul.' Mayakovsky restored the original text: it holds the key to his heroism as a poet and a man.)

Mayakovsky admired Léger; their conception of the role of the arts in modern society had something in common. Léger was interested in machines, in town planning; he wanted art to be part of everyday life; he kept away from museums. He painted his canvases and created fine works, works which, in my opinion, are decorative and which in no way undermine our love for Van Gogh or Picasso, but which are undeniably bound up with the new age. Mayakovsky fought poetry for a number of years, not only in articles and manifestos: he wanted to destroy poetry by poems. LEF published a death sentence on the arts: on 'so-called poets', 'so-called painters', 'so-called producers'. Instead of working on easel paintings, artists were advised to turn their attention to the aesthetics of machinery, textiles and household articles;

theatrical producers were enjoined to organize popular festivals and demonstrations and to bid farewell to the footlights; poets to abandon the lyric and write for the newspapers, invent captions for posters and copy for advertisements.

To abandon poetry did not prove easy. Mayakovsky was a man of fortitude and strength. But sometimes even he deviated from his programme. In 1923, when the LEF was still decrying lyric poetry, Mayakovsky wrote *About This*. Not even people close to him understood the poem; his allies and his literary opponents alike abused it; yet with it he enriched Russian poetry.

His rejection of the art of the past grew less harsh with the years. At the end of 1928 New LEF stated that Mayakovsky had publicly proclaimed: 'I am granting an amnesty to Rembrandt'. Let me repeat once more: he died young. He did not live, nor think, nor feel, nor write according to a plan: he was a poet above all else. I remember the rapture with which he spoke of the new industrial beauty of America in those far-off years when the electrification of our own country was only a project, when dim lamps spelt the words 'Children Are the Flowers of Life' in dark, snow-swept Teatralnaya Square. I saw him when he returned from America. Yes, certainly, Brooklyn Bridge was very fine, yes, there were many cars. But how much savagery and inhumanity there was too! He swore, and said how happy it had made him to see the tiny gardens of Normandy again. The LEF programme called for the rejection of Paris, where every house is a relic of a bygone age, and for the glorification of brand-new, industrialized America. Yet Mayakovsky cursed America, and without fear of appearing sentimental, made declarations of love to Paris. What was the reason for this contradiction? LEF was a magazine that lasted a few years, and Mayakovsky was a great poet. In his declarative verse he jeered at Pushkin's admirers and visitors to the Louvre, yet he himself was moved by lines from *Onegin* and by old paintings.

He realized at once that the October Revolution had changed the course of history. But he saw the details of the future in a schematic way, not on canvas but on a poster. It is difficult for us today to be seduced by the antiseptic idyll in the last act of *The Bedbug*. The art of the past seemed to Mayakovsky not so much alien as doomed. His iconoclasm was the fulfilment of a vow, a heroic act. He fought not only critics, not only the authors of sentimental ballads, but himself. He wrote: 'I want my country to understand me, but if it does not, why then I shall pass over it to one side, like slanting rain'. Then he crossed out these lines because he thought them too sentimental. But his country understood him, as it also understands the beautiful lines he deleted.

I remember him in the autumn of 1928, when he spent more than a month in Paris. We met often. I see him glowering in the small bar of the Coupole. He would order White Horse whisky: he did not drink much, but made up a little song in which the English words 'White Horse' rhyme with the Russian *hvost* (tail). One day he said: 'Do you think it's easy? I could write better poetry than any of them'. He remained dedicated to his idea until the end.

Much has been said about the reason for his suicide: difficulties over an exhibition of his literary works, attacks by RAPP[1], affairs of the heart. I do not like speculating; I cannot approach the life of a man I once knew as I would approach a plan for a novel. But there is one thing I should like to say: people often forget that a poet has especially acute sensibilities; that is why he is a poet. Mayakovsky called himself an 'ox', even a 'huge ox'; he said of his poems that they were 'rhinoceroses'; he once said at a meeting that he had an 'elephant's hide' which no bullet could pierce. In actual fact he lived without so much as the ordinary human skin.

According to Christian legend, the heathen Saul having become the Apostle Paul took to smashing statues of gods and goddesses. The statues were perfect, but Paul was able to vanquish his own aesthetic sense. Mayakovsky smashed not only the beauty of the past, but himself. Therein lies the greatness of his heroism. Therein also lies the key to his tragedy.

There was a literary gentleman in Petersburg called Andrey Levinson, considered an expert in choreography. In 1917 he published a squib on Mayakovsky in the journal *Life of the Arts*. Many painters, and also Lunacharsky, replied to him at the time. Levinson emigrated to Paris. When the news of Mayakovsky's tragic death came, he published a disgusting, slanderous piece in the paper *Les Nouvelles Littéraires*. Together with several French writers I drafted a letter to the editor of this paper, expressing our indignation. All decent writers in France, whatever their views, signed this letter: I cannot remember a single refusal. I took the letter to the paper's editor, Maurice

[1] Russian Association of Proletarian Writers.

Martin du Gard. (This was an unremarkable person, not to be confused with the important writer Roger Martin du Gard.) He calmly read the letter, which was extremely sharply worded, and said: 'I would ask you to make one small change'. I answered that the wording could not be toned down. 'I'm not asking that. But perhaps you would agree to insert just one word in the sentence beginning: "We are shocked that a literary journal", to read: "We are shocked that the leading literary journal" . . .' He was willing to receive a slap in the face provided it was duly recorded that the face was a large one. I am sure Mayakovsky would have written up this story beautifully.

The world has dealt strangely with Mayakovsky. Only a short time ago some writers from Equatorial Africa spoke to me about him: that shows how far he has penetrated. He is travelling round the globe. Poetry is, of course, difficult to translate, and the forms which Mayakovsky proclaimed as the forms of the future have in many ways become forms of the past by now. But as man and poet he is as young as ever. Aragon, Pablo Neruda, Eluard, Tuwim, Nezval – none of them ever wrote 'in the style of Mayakovsky', yet all of them owe him a great deal. It was not a new form of versification that he taught them, but the courage of choice.

It is important to distinguish the modern from the merely topical, the spirit of innovation from novelties which will seem out of date a quarter of a century later. A certain poet said to me a few months ago that since Mayakovsky's complex rhymes it is impossible to use rhymes derived from verb forms. That, of course, is too simple. It is perfectly possible to write using such rhymes, and equally possible to write without any rhymes at all. Nine-tenths of the poets starting their career in 1940 wrote 'ladder' poems. Now they imitate other models. Fashions change. Mayakovsky was beaten over the head with volumes of Pushkin, Nekrasov and Blok. Is it sensible to lambast our young poets with volumes of Mayakovsky?

I have already said that at one time I felt Mayakovsky could have helped me to see my way ahead. I remember a conversation late one night in February or March 1918. We had left the Poets' Café together. Mayakovsky asked me about Paris, Picasso, Apollinaire. Then he said that he had liked my poem on Pugachev's execution. 'You ought to be pleased, and here you are whining. That's bad.' I readily agreed: 'Of course it's bad'. Politically he was right, as I soon realized; but we always thought and felt differently. In 1922 he told me that he had liked

Julio Jurenito. 'You've understood many things better than others have.' I could not help laughing: 'I don't believe I've understood anything yet'. We met many times, and yet we never really met.

I have often thought about Mayakovsky and I still think about him. Sometimes I argue with him, but always I admire his heroism as a poet. I do not look at the statue: the statue stands still. But Mayakovsky strides. He strides through the new districts of Moscow, through old Paris, over the whole of our planet. He strides carrying 'stores', not of new rhymes, but of new thoughts and feelings.

6

SOON after my return to Moscow I met Boris Pasternak, who took me off to his place (he was then living near Prechistensky Boulevard). In my notebook there is a brief entry: 'Pasternak. Poems. Strangeness. Staircase'.

Another notebook. 5th July, 1941. Between the words 'The Germans say they have crossed the Berezina' and 'Lozovsky, 5 p.m.' there is an entry: 'Pasternak. Madness'.

1917–41. Over a period of twenty-four years I met Pasternak, sometimes at long intervals, sometimes almost every day. One might suppose that this was enough time to get to know even a highly complex person, but Pasternak often seemed as enigmatic to me as when I had first met him. This explains the 1941 notebook entry. I was fond of him, and I loved and still love his poetry; of all the poets I have met, he was the most tongue-tied, the nearest to the element of music, the most attractive – and the most insufferable. I shall try to describe him as I saw him. The Pasternak I speak of is in the main the Pasternak of 1917–24, when we had many talks and exchanged many letters. We also met fairly frequently in 1926, 1932 and 1934 in Moscow, in 1935 in Paris, then again in Moscow just before the war and during its early weeks. We did not quarrel but drew apart by a kind of tacit agreement; meeting by chance in later years, we shook each other by the hand, said that we really must see each other, and parted again till the next chance meeting. Of course I cannot hope to present the whole of Pasternak, even the young Pasternak: there was much in him that I did not understand and much that I did not even know; but the picture I will give will not be an icon or a caricature but an attempt at a portrait.

Let me start at the beginning. When we met, Boris Pasternak was twenty-seven; it was the summer of that year when, in his words: 'all suffered drought and famine, all were embittered in battle, and no one cared that the miracle of life should be one hour long'. I was depressed and distraught, Pasternak gay and elated. It was a particularly memorable year for him: 'Unforgettable, too, because it swelled with dust, because the wind cracked sunflower seeds, littering the burdocks with the husks, because it led me like a blind man through the unfamiliar mallows to beg for you at every wattle fence'. That year Pasternak experienced a very great emotion. The book, *My Sister, Life* was being born. Here is how I described our first meeting: 'He read me his poetry. I do not know what struck me most: his poems, his face, his voice, or what he said. I went away, filled with sounds, my head aching. The entrance downstairs was locked: I had stayed till 2 a.m. I looked for the porter, but could not find him. I went back, but could not find the flat where Pasternak lived. It was a house with corridors, side passages and blind alleys leading off half-landings. I realized I should not get out till morning and resigned myself to sitting on the stairs. The staircase was an iron one, and the night stirred beneath my feet. Suddenly a door opened. I saw Pasternak. He could not sleep and was going out for a walk. I had sat for a good hour in front of the very flat where he lived. He was not in the least surprised to see me; I was not surprised either.'

Pasternak spoke in interjections. There is a poem of his called *The Urals for the First Time*; it is like a fervent lowing. The strength of his early poetry is that it is 'life for the first time'. In those days his reputation was anything but that of a recluse; he liked being amongst people, was joyous, and the poems of those years are joyous too. To me he seemed lucky not only because he had been granted a great poetic gift but also because he knew how to make high poetry out of everyday details. All of us at that time were slightly sickened by the excessively loud vocabulary which the Symbolists abused: 'eternity', 'the infinite', 'boundlessness', 'decaying', 'transient', 'verge', 'casting of the die', 'doom'. Pasternak wrote: 'Great god of love, great god of detail'. This is how he described the woman he loved: 'It would be very wrong to think you were a vestal; you came in with a chair, took my life as from a shelf, and blew away the dust'.

It was not for nothing that he called his book *My Sister, Life*: unlike not only the older Symbolist poets but also the majority of his contemporaries, he was on good terms with life. The realism of his poems was not associated with a literary programme (Pasternak said many times that he could not understand the various trends and schools) but dictated by the poet's nature. He wrote in 1922: 'The real, living world is a unique concept of the imagination which has succeeded once and is still endlessly successful. Here it is, going on, succeeding at every moment. It is still real, deep, irresistibly absorbing. You are not disappointed in it the morning after. It serves the poet as example to an even greater extent than as prototype and model'.

A young man said to me recently that Pasternak must surely have been a gloomy, unsociable, profoundly unhappy man. Yet I wrote of Pasternak in 1921: 'He is alive, healthy and modern. There is nothing about him of autumn, sunset or any other delightful but unrewarding thing of the kind'. A year later V. B. Shklovsky, who had seen Pasternak in Berlin, wrote: 'Lucky man! He will never be embittered. He is sure to be loved, spoiled and great all his life'.

Here is how Mayakovsky and Osip Brik formulated (to use the jargon of the period) the intentions of different artists: 'Mayakovsky. Experiment using polyphonic rhythm in poems of wide everyday and social range'. 'Pasternak. Application of a dynamic syntax to a revolutionary task'.

All this may come as a surprise to those foreign readers who first learned of Pasternak's existence in 1958. They visualize an unhappy man engaged in a duel with the State. In reality, Pasternak was a happy man, and the reason why he lived outside society was not that the society in question did not suit him but because, being sociable and even gay in the company of others, he was nevertheless able to speak to one man only: himself.

At the end of 1918 he expressed admiration for the Kremlin, that is to say, the Soviet State, in these words: 'It sweeps forward, terrible, crushing everything in its path, through the year not yet ended into Nineteen. Beyond the sea of these squalls I foresee how that year which has not yet begun will set about my upbringing anew, ship-wrecked as I am'. (He did not understand then that no one in the world would seriously undertake 'his upbringing anew'.) Later, in 1930, after Mayakovsky's suicide, he wrote: 'Our State, our State breaking into the ages and accepted into them for ever, our unexampled, impossible State'. He spoke of the blood ties between that State and Mayakovsky. In 1944, he wrote enthusiastic lines about the same State 'breaking into the ages'. He admired as an onlooker: every poet, even the very greatest, has not only a ceiling but also walls; society was outside the walls of the world in which Pasternak lived.

Shklovsky was mistaken in one thing when he wrote: 'This great and happy man sensed the pull of history among the people dressed in their overcoats who munched sandwiches at the counter of the Press

Club'. Pasternak was sensitive to nature, love, Goethe, Shakespeare, music, old German philosophy, the beauty of Venice, he was very sensitive to himself, and sometimes to certain other people who were close to him, but never to history; he heard sounds inaudible to others, he heard hearts beat and the grass grow, but he never heard the footsteps of the age.

The word 'egocentricity' has been used so often that it has become hackneyed; besides, it has a derogatory ring; yet I cannot find another. Boris Pasternak did not live for himself – he was never a selfish man – but he lived in himself and through himself. I remember our meetings long ago: two trains rushing forward, each on its own track. I knew that Pasternak listened to me and yet could not hear me: he could not tear himself away from his thoughts, his feelings, his associations. A talk with him, even an intimate one, was like two monologues.

I recall an amusing incident. In the summer of 1935 Pasternak attended a cultural congress in Paris. The main group of Soviet writers arrived first and was later joined by Pasternak and Babel. Pasternak was cross, saying that he had not wanted to come and did not know how to speak in public. In a short speech he said that it was wrong to look for poetry in the skies: it was a matter of bending down and looking; poetry was in the grass. Perhaps it was these words or, more likely, Pasternak's appearance and personality that impressed the audience; he was given an ovation. A few days later he said to me that he would like to meet some French writers. We decided to arrange a lunch. My wife telephoned Pasternak telling him to come to such and such a restaurant at 1 p.m. He was shocked: why so early? Let's make it three o'clock. My wife explained that in Paris people lunched between twelve and two and dined between seven and nine; at 3 p.m. all the restaurants would be closed. Thereupon Pasternak announced: 'No, I don't feel hungry at one o'clock'.

His concentration on himself (which increased with the years) did not prevent and could not have prevented Pasternak from becoming a great poet. We often say, as much out of habit as anything else, that a writer must be observant. In the recently published diaries of A. N. Afinogenov there is an interesting passage: 'If the writer's skill consisted in the ability to observe, the best writers would be doctors and examining magistrates, teachers and train guards, Party Committee secretaries and military leaders. Yet that is not so, for the writer's skill consists in the ability to observe himself'. Afinogenov is right to reject the old concept of 'observancy'; what the author has experienced and absorbed plays an immense part in the creation of characters in a novel or drama; after all, the inner world of other people is understood by the writer only in so far as he knows, and therefore understands, a particular feeling or passion.

Art, however, is multiform. In a lyrical poem, the author reveals himself; however original he may be, his feelings – elation on a spring day, or a sense of the inevitability of death, the joy of love, or disillusionment – can be understood by thousands or millions of other people. In order to write: 'Oh, how in the decline of our years we love more tenderly, more anxiously', Tyutchev did not have to observe ageing men in the grip of passion: he had only to meet the young Denisyeva at the threshold of his own old age. The young Chekhov, in order to describe the friendship between the old professor and his young ward in *A Boring Story*, had to have a very good knowledge of people, their feelings, habits, characters, their manner of speaking and even of dressing. Boris Pasternak, one of the finest lyric poets of our times was, like every artist, limited by his own nature; when he attempted to represent, in a novel, dozens of other people, an epoch, the climate of the Civil War, to reproduce conversations on trains, he suffered failure: he could see and hear only himself.

He was fascinated, especially towards the end of his life, by the riddle of other men's destinies. In one of his autobiographies he tried to understand what it was that Mayakovsky, Marina Tsvetayeva, Fadeyev felt in their last moments. Reading these conjectures I was somehow embarrassed: Pasternak had a very rich heart, but he did not hold the key to the hearts of others.

I would not attempt to guess what he himself felt in the last years of his life; I did not see him during that time and, even if I had, I might not have known: another man's soul is darkness. I do not know why, in the autobiography I have mentioned, he repudiated his old friendship with Mayakovsky. I should like to speak of that friendship, which I witnessed.

We used to say as a joke that Mayakovsky had a 'spare voice' for women. It was this spare voice, extraordinarily gentle and affectionate, which in my hearing he used to only one man. That man was Pasternak. I remember a Pasternak evening at the Press Club in March 1921. Pasternak read some poems, and then a young actress, Alexeyeva-Meskhieva, read a few others. During the discussion that followed someone ventured to 'point out some shortcomings', as the phrase goes. Then Mayakovsky rose to his full height and began to extol Pasternak's poetry at the top of his voice: he defended it with all the passion of love.

In *Safe Conduct* (1930) Pasternak speaks of his attitude towards Mayakovsky before and during the war and in the first years of the Revolution: 'I was crazy about Mayakovsky', 'I deified him', 'Mayakovsky was the epitome of a poet's fate', 'I was almost glad of the occasion when, for the first time, I spoke to my idol as to a stranger' (this was after one of their minor quarrels), '. . . I felt Mayakovsky's presence with double force. His nature was revealed to me in all the freshness of a first meeting'.

Their quarrels were frequent and tempestuous. Sometimes Pasternak used to tell me about them. I have kept a copy of the *Sovremennik* anthology for 1922 bearing the following inscription by Pasternak: 'To my friend and fellow-fighter in joy and gratitude for *Jurenito*, admiration for which united Mayakovsky, Aseyev and other friends and fellow-fighters who rarely agreed on anything but, more often than not, wandered off in different directions'.

After one of their differences Mayakovsky and Pasternak met again in Berlin; their reconciliation was as tempestuous and passionate as the break had been. I spent the whole of one day with them; we went to a café, then we dined and later sat in a café again. Pasternak read his poems. In the evening Mayakovsky gave a reading of *The Backbone Flute* at the Arts Club; he recited with his face turned towards Pasternak.

Later their ways parted. Yet even in 1926, quoting Pasternak's quatrain 'That day, from your combs to your feet', Mayakovsky called it a 'poem of genius'. Pasternak wrote of Mayakovsky's death: 'I burst into tears, as I had yearned to do for a long time'.

Why did Pasternak, looking back on his past, try to delete so much? Did this perhaps reflect a dissatisfaction with himself? I do not know. For me, his last poems are very close to *My Sister, Life*, whereas he evidently felt a break between the two. Recently I read a letter from Pasternak to one of his French translators, published in the journal *Esprit*. He was trying to persuade the translator not to publish some of his old works. They say that when people tried to get him to talk about his earlier books he would put them off, assuring them that everything he had written before had been only schooling, a preparation for the one really worthwhile thing he had written recently, the novel *Doctor Zhivago*. (In this, as in many other things, Pasternak repeated the mistakes of a number of other artists. I am thinking of Gogol, who regarded *The Inspector-General* and Part One of *Dead Souls* as trifles, and thought he had found the right path when he started Part Two.)

Reading the manuscript of *Doctor Zhivago* saddened me. Pasternak once wrote: 'The inability to find and tell the truth is a fault which cannot be disguised by any amount of skill in telling the untruth'. It was its artistic untruth that struck me about the novel. I am convinced that Pasternak wrote it sincerely; it contains some marvellous pages on nature and on love; but too many pages are devoted to things the author never saw or heard. Some wonderful poems are attached to the novel; they underline, as it were, the spiritual inaccuracy of the prose.

I had never previously succeeded in convincing poetry-lovers abroad that Pasternak was a great poet. (This does not, of course, apply to some great poets, who knew Russian: Rilke spoke enthusiastically of Pasternak's poetry as long ago as 1926.) Fame came to him by another door. He had once written: 'But it was not for nothing that you whispered to me, messenger, in some suburb where not a single two-legged creature . . . I too am some such . . . I have lost my way: this is the wrong city and the wrong midnight'.

I was in Stockholm when the storm broke round the Nobel Prize. I went out into the streets and saw newspaper posters: they bore one name. Trying to understand what was happening, I turned on the radio, and there was only one word I could distinguish: Pasternak. All this was blatant anti-Soviet politics, just another episode in the cold war. The wrong city, the wrong midnight. And the wrong kind of fame: not the fame Pasternak deserved.

I am convinced that it was not part of Pasternak's intention to harm our country. His guilt consisted only in the fact that he was Pasternak; that is to say, while marvellously understanding one thing, he was unable to understand another. He did not suspect that his book would create a vile political sensation and that the blow would inevitably be followed by a counterblow.

Let me return to poetry. Once upon a time anthologists were fond of arranging poems according to subject. If we approached Pasternak with such a criterion, we should find that most of his poems are devoted to nature and love. I believe, however, that his fundamental and constant theme was art, that is to say the theme that inspired Gogol's *Portrait*, Balzac's *Chef d'Oeuvre*, Chekhov's *Seagull*. 'Oh had I known that's how it happens, when I made my stage début, that lines when mixed with blood do murder, will rush into your throat and kill you'. And this poem about poems ends with a confession: 'And there's an end of art and there's a breath of earth and destiny'. He neither shot himself, nor died young, but he came to know the price that is paid for art; he came to know it fully: the power of lines which kill slowly and persistently.

Paul Eluard once said: 'A poet must be a child even if he has grey hair and arterial sclerosis'. There was in Pasternak something childlike. His definitions, which seemed naïve and childish, were a poet's definitions. He said of a certain author: 'How can he be a good poet when he's not a good man?' Seeing Paris for the first time, he exclaimed: 'Why, this isn't like a city, it's more like a landscape'. He used to say: 'It's easy to describe a spring morning; besides, nobody wants that. But to be simple, clear and sudden like a spring morning, that's devilishly hard'.

During the period of which I am writing in this volume, while I went about confused and lost, Boris Pasternak was to me both a guarantee of the vitality of art and a gangway to real life. Young, gay and handsome, looking like an inspired Arab, that is how he remains forever in my mind, although I also knew him aged and grey.

For half a century now I suddenly find myself muttering some poem by Pasternak. You cannot abolish those poems from the world: they are alive.

7

EVERY morning the townspeople carefully studied the decrees still wet and crinkled, pasted on the walls, trying to find out what was allowed, what forbidden. Once I saw a crowd round a sheet entitled 'Decree No. 1 on the Democratization of the Arts'. Someone read aloud: 'Henceforth, together with the destruction of the Tsarist regime, the keeping of art in those lumber rooms and store sheds of human genius – viz. palaces, galleries, salons, libraries and theatres – is hereby abolished.' An old woman squawked: 'Dear O Lord, they're taking away our store sheds now!' The bespectacled man reading the 'decree' explained: 'It doesn't say anything about sheds, but they'll close down the libraries all right, and the theatres too, of course'. The text was composed by Futurists, and the signatures of Maya-kovsky, Kamensky and Burlyuk appeared at the bottom. The names meant nothing to the man in the street, but everyone knew the magic word 'decree'.

I remember the First of May, 1918. Moscow was decorated all over with Futurist and Suprematist paintings. Demented squares battled with rhomboids on the peeling façades of colonnaded Empire villas. Faces with triangles for eyes popped up everywhere. (The art now called 'abstract', which today arouses so much argument both in Russia and in the West, was in those days issued unrationed to all Soviet citizens.) That year, the First of May coincided with Good Friday. Worshippers thronged outside Iverskaya Chapel. Lorries (formerly belonging to Stupin's) drove past draped with non-objective paintings; actors on the lorries presented *tableaux vivants*: 'Stepan Halturin's Heroic Deed', or 'The Paris Commune'. An old woman wailed, staring at a Cubist picture with a huge fish eye in it: 'They want us to worship the devil'.

I laughed, but my laughter was not happy.

I have just re-read an article of mine published in the newspaper *Monday* in the summer of 1918, called 'Among the Cubists'. In it I spoke of Picasso, Léger and Rivera. I said that the works of those artists could be regarded as 'mad ornaments on a house about to collapse, or as the foundations of another kind of structure, never yet seen even in creative dreams'.

It is, of course, no accident that Picasso, Léger and Rivera became Communists. The Futurists, the Cubists and the Suprematists – not the academic painters – were the ones who gathered in Red Square in 1918. What was it, then, that disturbed me about the triumph of artists and poets who resembled – at least outwardly – the best friends of my early youth?

First of all, it was their attitude to the art of the past. Everyone knows that Mayakovsky changed and grew; but in those days he was a passionate iconoclast. 'You find a White Guard: against the wall with him! But have you forgotten Raphael? And what about Rastrelli? It is time for bullets to ping on museum walls. Shoot the past down out of one-hundred-inch throats! Guns are lined up at the edge of the forest, deaf to White blandishments. Why, then, is Pushkin not yet under fire?' This was an attitude I could not understand. Often, as I roamed the alleys of Moscow, I repeated Pushkin's poems to myself, and I cherished my memories of the old Italian masters. Arriving in Moscow, I rushed to the Kremlin almost at once. The fifteenth-century art there moved me deeply: until then I had had no idea of the Russian Renaissance.

Arguments about the values of the past soon died down. Mayakovsky wrote his poem about Pushkin, but today the results of research on Mayakovsky himself are printed in *Literary Inheritance*, an Academy publication. (I have already mentioned the journal *Veshch*; its contributors included many representatives of our 'Left art', such as Mayakovsky, Malevich, Meyerhold, Tatlin and Rodchenko. In an article on the journal's aims, I wrote: 'It is naïve and ridiculous today to "throw Pushkin overboard". There is continuity in the flow of forms, and the masters of today need not fear classical examples. We can learn from Pushkin and Poussin. *Veshch* does not deny the past in the past: it calls for the modern in modern times'.)

It is not difficult to understand Mayakovsky's attitude. His own poems were received with contemptuous laughter. The works of painters who joined the Futurists (Malevich, Tatlin, Rodchenko, Pougny, Udaltsova, Popova, Altman) were objects of ridicule before the Revolution. After October, the imitators of classical poetry began packing their bags. Both Bunin and Repin went abroad. The Futurists, the Cubists and the Suprematists stayed. Like their opposite numbers in the West – the pre-war habitués of the Rotonde – they loathed bourgeois society and saw revolution as the way out.

The Futurists believed that people's tastes could be changed as quickly as the economic structure of society. The journal *Art of the Commune* said: 'We have our claims, and if we were allowed to use State power to carry out our artistic ideas we should not refuse it'. This, of course, was a dream rather than a threat. The main reason why the streets of Moscow were decorated by the Suprematists and Cubists was that the academic painters were in opposition (political, not artistic). And yet the results were regrettable. What matters is not the old woman who mistook a Cubist picture for the devil, but the artistic reaction which followed the brief appearance of 'Left art' in the streets.

Discoveries in the sphere of the exact sciences are subject to proof and the question whether Einstein was right or wrong was decided by mathematicians, not by millions of people who can only remember their multiplication tables. New art forms have always entered the consciousness of people slowly and by devious ways; at the beginning, only a few understand and accept them. Anyway it is impossible to lay down, propagate or enforce tastes. The deities of ancient Greece drank nectar, called by the poets the 'drink of the gods'; but if anyone had tried to pump nectar through a tube into the stomachs of Athenian citizens it would certainly have led to a tremendous amount of vomiting.

However, all that is now ancient history (this goes not only for arguments as to who should decorate the Moscow squares, but for 'Left art' as a whole). Once more I propose to infringe the rule that a writer of memoirs must follow a chronological sequence. I want to understand what happened to me and many other poets and artists of my generation. I do not know who tangled the skein – our artistic opponents or we ourselves – but I want to try and unravel it.

First let me speak about myself. I soon became an adherent of what was then known as Constructivism; but I must confess that the idea of art being dissolved in life both inspired and repelled me. In 1921 I wrote a book called *And Yet it Moves*, a boisterous, naïve book not unlike the declarations of LEF (the LEF journal remarked that 'the conclusions of I. Ehrenburg's group largely coincide with our own'). I declared that 'the new art ceases to be art'. At the same time I mocked my ideas: my *Julio Jurenito* was written in the same year, 1921, and my hero reduces the principles of *And Yet it Moves* to absurdity. Jurenito says: 'The arts are the focal points of anarchy. Artists are heretics, sectarians, dangerous rebels. And so we must unhesitatingly ban the arts as we have banned the manufacture of intoxicating spirits and the import of opium . . . The pictures of the Cubists or Suprematists can be used for a variety of purposes – as plans for kiosks on the boulevards, as wallpaper designs, as models for new shoes, and so on . . . Poetry is adopting the language of the newspapers and business'. I was not being two-faced: duplicity is always bound up with caution or calculation. The simple truth is that I was not entirely convinced of the death of the arts which was being proclaimed by many people, including myself.

Futurism was born at the beginning of our century in provincial, technically-backward Italy, where glorious monuments of the past were to be seen at every step, while the shops sold German knives, French saucepans and English textiles: factory chimneys were not yet trying to butt in on the elegant company of ancient towers. (Northern Italy today rivals the most highly industrialized countries, but in to-day's Italy you will not find a single Futurist calling for the burning down of all museums, and the former Futurists Carra and Severini find inspiration in Giotto and the Ravenna mosaics.) The enthusiasm of Mayakovsky, Tatlin and other representatives of Russian 'Left art' for industrial aesthetics during the first years of the Revolution is entirely understandable: in those years, not only lumps of sugar but even matches were sold by the piece in Sukharevka. This is Maya-kovsky's dream of the future in *Mystery Bouffe:* 'Great hulks of transparent factories and blocks of flats, flung wide open, soar into the sky. Trains, trams and cars stand wreathed in rainbows'. (When an artist presents nature or human feelings, his works do not age. No one can say that women in the twentieth century are more beautiful or more perfect than the Acropolis Nike, created twenty-five centuries ago; no one laughs at the sufferings of Hamlet, or the love of Romeo and Juliet. But as soon as an artist is carried away by technology, his utopias are outstripped or disproved by time. H. G. Wells was a highly cultivated man who believed that he could see into the future; yet the discoveries of modern physics have made his utopian novels comical. How could Mayakovsky have foreseen that the electric tram would soon share the fate of the horse tram, or that trains would seem an archaic method of transport?)

Picasso's Cubist paintings were not the product of a yearning for machines but of the artist's desire to present man, nature and the world by a method freed from accidental detail. Few people today are interested in the books of Metzinger, Gleizes and the other Cubist theoreticians; but the pictures of Picasso, Braque and Léger are alive and able to please, trouble and excite us. Picasso regards himself as the heir of Velasquez, Poussin, Delacroix and Cézanne. He has never regarded electric trains or jet aircraft as the heirs of visual art.

Of course, art has always gradually penetrated into daily life, making changes in building, clothes, vocabularies, gestures and objects of daily use. Medieval poetry, with its cult of the beloved, helped men to find forms of expression for their feelings. Watteau's and Fragonard's pictures were translated into everyday life, influencing the layout of parks, the design of costumes and dances, the shape of sofas and snuff-boxes. Cubism has helped contemporary town planners to eliminate houses disfigured by unnecessary decorations; it finds a reflection in furniture, even in cigarette packets. The use of art for utilitarian purposes, its decorative application, cannot be the artist's aim but only a natural by-product of his creative effort. The reverse process is a sign of creative impoverishment. A non-objective design on a fabric or a pot is perfectly apt, but when it claims the status of an easel painting it does not represent progress but regression.

Recently I visited a retrospective exhibition of Malevich's works in Brussels. His early works (of the 'Jack of Diamonds' period) are very striking. In 1913 he painted a black square on a white ground. That was the birth of abstract art which was to enthral thousands of Western painters forty years later. To me, it seems primarily decorative. Picasso's pictures are a world fraught with so much thought and feeling that they produce delight or genuine abhorrence. Abstract paintings belong to textiles and wallpaper. A woman may wear a scarf decorated with a non-objective design; the scarf may be beautiful or ugly, it may suit the woman or it may not, but it will make no one think about nature, man or life.

The rapid development of technology demands from the artist a deeper understanding of the inner world of man than ever before. The supporters of 'Left art', who had preached industrial aesthetics, realized this very quickly. After seeing America, Mayakovsky declared that techonology must be kept in check. In saying this he was, of course, thinking of the artist's role and not denying the need for technical progress (there was remarkably little technology about Moscow in those days, i.e. in 1925). Mayakovsky understood that, without the muzzle of humanism, technology would turn on man and savage him. Meyerhold, forgetting bio-mechanics, gave his attention to *The Forest* and *The Inspector-General*, and dreamed of putting on *Hamlet*. Tatlin turned to easel painting, Altman did portraits, Pougny became a master of small landscapes. As for the nectar feeding-tube, it passed into other hands, far better suited for operations of that kind.

Our museums have splendid collections of the 'Left art' of early post-Revolutionary years. It is a pity that these collections are not on view. You cannot abolish a link in a chain. I know young Soviet artists who are 'discovering America' in the year 1960 by doing – or rather, trying to do – what Malevich, Tatlin, Popova and Rozanova did long ago. If they could see for themselves the development of those painters, would they not, perhaps, instead of seeking to return to the year 1920, try to produce something new and in keeping with our own times? Our young poets know the works of Khlebnikov and admire his skill, but they do not try to imitate him blindly. Why is Tatlin more 'dangerous' than Khlebnikov? Is it because the idea of a monopoly held by one trend has become particularly firmly entrenched in the sphere of the visual arts?

Of course, the representatives of our 'Left art' during the first years after the Revolution were mistaken in many ways. People are always ready to talk about the mistakes of painters, writers and composers; I rather doubt whether the reason for this is that painters, writers and composers are the only people who make mistakes. Looking back today, I think with gratitude of even that picture which frightened the old woman near Iverskaya Chapel. A great deal was done. An essence always gets diluted. Beneficent traces of 'Left art' can be seen in the works of many writers, painters, producers, film directors and composers of the decades that followed.

I have never in my life been a passionate adherent of any artistic school. I have compared the early Mayakovsky with the Apostle Paul who smashed the statues of false gods. Before his conversion, Paul had the name of Saul. In 1922, when I was defending Constructivism and editing the journal *Veshch*, V. B. Shklovsky in his book *Zoo* called me 'Paul, son of Saul'. This was unkind but just. All my life I have kept my love for certain works of the past: Stendhal's novels, Chekhov's stories, the poetry of Tyutchev, Baudelaire and Blok. This did not prevent me from hating imitations of the old or from loving Picasso and Meyerhold. Paul had to have a father, and it is better to model a new statue than to smash an old one, however high one's motives. For the sculptor who carved at Ellora the images of Indian deities, Brahma, Vishnu and Shiva were gods; for us they are people created by human genius, with passions we can understand and a harmony we can appreciate.

The age of idols is past, not only in religion but also in art. Iconoclasm died with the worship of icons. But does this mean that the desire to say new things in a new way has disappeared? Recently I read in a certain journal the words 'modest pioneering'. At first they made me laugh, then they made me very sad. An artist must be modest in his behaviour, but never moderate, luke-warm, limited in his creative ambitions. I am sure that it is more worth while to scrawl something that is one's own, in one's own way, than to write out old adages in a copperplate hand. I do not believe that collective farmers painted in the manner of the academic (Bolognese) school can give many people pleasure, nor that it is possible to convey the rhythm of the second half of the twentieth century by that profusion of subsidiary clauses which Leo Tolstoy used so brilliantly.

8

AT PRECHISTENKA police commissariat I was asked to fill in my first questionnaire. This was something new, and I stopped to think over every question. What, for example, was my profession? Journalist? Translator? Poet? I put down 'poet' – it sounded nobler than the others – and burst out laughing. I did not in the least feel like a professional writer.

Apart from bad verse, I also wrote pieces for the newspapers. Together with Alexey Tolstoy I wrote a play for the *Chauve-Souris* theatre; it was called *Blanche's Chemise* and was based on a thirteenth-century French *fabliau* that I had translated while still in Paris. I wrote the verse text, whilst Tolstoy tried to liven it up with amusing repartee.

Outwardly, I had more or less settled down; I rented a room for a hundred roubles in a professor's house in Levshinsky Lane; sometimes I ate at a vegetarian restaurant called, if I remember rightly, 'Make the Best of It', but I was quite unable to make the best of anything.

Sometimes I remembered the Rotonde – Picasso, Modigliani, our arguments about art. Dear God, how long ago it all seemed! I tried to write to Chantal, but immediately tore up the letter: you cannot write to another world. Even if the letter reached her, she would never understand what was happening to me.

Many new words appeared in the language: 'mandat', 'cheka', 'domkom', 'psha', 'proletkult'. I still pestered everyone with naïve questions. No one gave me answers.

To my own surprise, I found myself part of a circle of writers; I even became one of its most typical representatives: the others had families, friends, a more or less regular life, whereas I had arrived in revolutionary Moscow with three changes of underwear, no profession, and no contact with the friends of my boyhood.

I have already mentioned the Café Bom in Tverskaya, frequented by writers, where we drank coffee and swapped news. There were other cafés where we worked, that is to say, read our works for thirty or fifty roubles a time to a noisy audience which listened inattentively but stared at us with curiosity, like visitors looking at monkeys in the zoo. These cafés were ephemeral and their names kept changing: 'Poets' Café', 'Three-Leaved Clover', 'Music Box', 'Domino', 'Pittoresque', 'The Tenth Muse', 'Pegasus's Loosebox', 'Red Cockerel'.

The Zetlins fed us on the grand scale, as befitted the last representatives of a tea dynasty. Often we met at Kara-Murza's, where we also got something to eat and where the atmosphere was much simpler and friendlier. Sometimes we went to Alexey Tolstoy's; at other times we gathered at the actress Ludmila Dzhalalova's in Afanasyevsky Lane.

Apart from this, there were the rather boring meetings of the 'circle', where *genre* writers read out their short stories and men of letters demanded various 'freedoms'. At the head of all the 'circles' was Bunin's brother, the delightful Yuli Alexeyevich.

The chairman of the All-Russian Union of Writers was Jurgis Kazimirovich Baltrushaitis, a man of great kindness and great gloom. He had a face like a desert, pale eyes and a mouth clenched in sadness. While Mayakovsky demolished Balmont or Alexey Tolstoy told funny stories, Baltrushaitis, dressed in a tightly buttoned black coat, maintained a stubborn silence. His room was in keeping with his person: bare walls and a crucifix. His poems were equally mournful, bitter and abstract: 'All are made equal by the sign of kinship, by the mark of God's finger, all part of a great orphanhood, of a great vanity'. I remember once going to Kimry for a literary gathering. Baltrushaitis read his poems; then Lidin reads a story about racing and life in the stables. The hall was noisy; someone had to be turned out. A young fellow climbed up on the platform and began singing: 'A deserter I was born, a deserter I shall die; shoot me if you like, I'll never join the Communists'. We all drank vodka. Then they took us to an empty room – our train did not leave till morning – and we slept on the floor. Baltrushaitis was silent, as always; but as we drew into Moscow, he suddenly said: 'Silly, wasn't it? Still, it was good that we went'. I think those were the best years of his life. (In 1921 he became Lithuanian ambassador to Moscow. He wanted to go on seeing his fellow-writers, but he was regarded as a diplomat and diplomatically avoided. He continued to write gloomy poems, some of them in Lithuanian. His life did not make much sense, but he was not surprised: he had known from childhood what it is to live in a desert.)

I remember a lighted window in Zubovsky Boulevard: the poet Vyacheslav Ivanov lived there. I thought of him as of an ancient sage (he was then fifty-two years old). He looked like a pastor out of Ibsen, in his old-fashioned clothes and gold-rimmed spectacles. He was a man of great culture; his writings were complex and charged with emotion; people called him Vyacheslav the Magnificent. I listened to him reading highly-polished sonnets in an excited voice, as though improvising, and two opposing feelings – reverence and pity – fought within me: time had made a leap forward, leaving behind the eccentric of Zubovsky Boulevard with his nineteenth-century clothes, his maenads, his Isolde, his Oriental roses and his psalms. Stoves called *bourjooikas*, on which we cooked millet gruel, appeared in every house, but Vyacheslav Ivanov wrote: 'Put down your bundle of food by the fireplace, cook your millet, and the hour is yours. Oh, deep is the grave of eternity!' He spoke very well about ancient Greece, but when events forced themselves into his study, however briefly, he was disconcerted. He wrote to G. I. Chulkov: 'Yes, we lit this bonfire, our conscience speaks the truth, but we were not mistaken when we sensed that it would burn our hearts'. I believe that Vyacheslav Ivanov's heart was not burning but slowly freezing during those years. (A few years later he went abroad to Italy, taught at a Catholic university, wrote sonnets as before, and died a very old man.)

Once I was walking back from a literary gathering with Mikhail Osipovich Gershenzon, who lived in one of the Arbat Lanes. I knew his books on Chaadayev and the Decembrists and thought that what he cared about most was saving those spiritual values of which Vyacheslav Ivanov talked. But Gershenzon, to my surprise, burst out laughing and, stopping by a snowdrift taller than himself, started counselling me: inner freedom was the most important thing; it was a waste of time crying over decayed vestments. He laughed, but his eyes were kind and sad. 'Why do you upset yourself? You're still a young man. Doesn't it make you happy to feel free of everything that once seemed eternal and unshakable? Look at me – I'm happy.' Gershenzon was not yet fifty at the time, but to me, of course, he seemed an old man. I could not understand then what he was happy about, but today, as I remember his words, I am full of admiration; he may have suffered from defective sight, but unlike many writers, including young ones, he was not myopic but long-sighted.

I shall speak later of Andrey Bely, whom I often met in Germany in 1922. During the years I am now describing he seemed to me like a ghost. He never sat in a chair like other people, but half-rose from it; one moment more, it seemed, and he would turn into a cloud; he did not address the person he was talking to, but an imaginary inhabitant of an imaginary planet. The word 'ether' has long become a technical term for people working on the Soviet radio – they say 'we're going on the ether (on the air)' even when referring to a talk about the prevention of stomach upsets. In those days, however, the word ether still had a mysterious ring: 'I shall carry you, free son of the ether, into the regions above the stars'. I had the impression that Andrey Bely's talk was directed exclusively into Lermontov's ether; he spoke of Russia and the Messiah, of building and destroying, of plunging into the abyss and soaring upwards. I admired him, but I thought: 'It's all very well for you, you don't sit in chairs, you are always on the wing; as for me, I don't know how to disembody myself or turn to vapour or talk like an oracle'.

Everything infuriated Balmont. One day we had to travel from Pokrovskiye Gate to the Arbat. Getting inside a tram was not easy; I jumped on the step and tried to force my way in, but Balmont began shouting: 'Make way, you dogs! Make way for the child of the sun'. This made not the slightest impression and Balmont announced that, since neither he nor I had money for a cab, we must walk: 'I cannot let my body touch these insensate amphibians'.

Ivan Bunin said that everything – the pillaging of his estate, the disappearance of sugar – was the fault of the Decadents. Once, at Alexey Tolstoy's, I read the poem on Pugachev's execution which I had written in Paris in 1915; it contained the lines: 'And all that will remain of our country will be lobster spawn, and, on a high pole, Pugachev's head'. Bunin got up, said to Tolstoy's wife: 'Excuse me, I cannot listen to such things', and went out. Someone made up a verse on that occasion, which I have come across in my notebook: 'Henceforth you are my friend, bandit and devil, Parisian snob in an enormous hat high as a snowdrift, you who frightened Ivan Bunin with a poem, not a gun. Henceforth I wish you may enjoy choice lobsters without spawn'.

Despite the inner disquiet that gripped Alexey Tolstoy, his house was always pleasant: he was able not only to enjoy himself, but even to fret with a kind of gusto. He always told funny stories and was always the first to laugh at them. One day, coming home from a rehearsal of one of his plays, he described how during the first days of the Revolution, at the Maly Theatre, some soldiers had found Jokanaan's head, which Salome mocks in Wilde's play; the soldiers took a liking to the head and started using it as a football. Another story he told was of a peasant woman in a village near Moscow who, during elections to the Constituent Assembly, picked up the wrong ballot paper from the table. The polling official said to her: 'That isn't your number, you know', to which she replied: 'I'm afraid of making a muck of it. With God's help we'll manage with this one'. Tolstoy roared with laughter, but, as I have already said, he felt anything but gay.

Amongst writers of the older generation whom I saw was Boris Zaitsev, baffled and ailing; he liked to remember Italy, but of what went on around him he used to say quite candidly: 'I don't understand anything'. Sometimes we went to see the poet Georgi Chulkov, who lived in Smolensky Boulevard. In his youth Chulkov had taken part in the revolutionary movement and had been imprisoned and exiled. Round about 1907 or 1908 he found himself at the centre of literary life; Blok and Andrey Bely argued over him. When I met him, he was ageing and depressed; he looked like a large, sickly bird. He no longer preached *sobornost* or 'mystical anarchism'; sometimes, after a silence, he would recite some lines of Tyutchev. Ivan Novikov preferred quoting Pushkin; he was a good host, generous to everyone; he had kind, calm eyes, and his house was run in the old style, with special cakes and coloured eggs at Easter.

The people who gathered at Kara-Murza's were mostly young; for them, Alexey Tolstoy was a classic. The poet Lipskerov read poems about the beauties of the Orient in a singsong voice. The poetess Vera Inber used to come. (I had met her in Paris; she had had to go to a mountain sanatorium in Switzerland and asked me to look after the publication of her first book, *Sorrowful Wine*. My friend the sculptor Zadkine illustrated the book.) She read flippant poems: 'Willie, dear Willie, tell me quick: have you ever loved anybody, pageboy Willie?' I made friends with V. G. Lidin. As a young man he was naïve and longed for romanticism. Ludmila Dzhalalova called him 'the pink marabou', and the nickname stuck.

In one of Mayakovsky's letters to Lily Brik I found the following lines: 'The café makes me sick. A second-rate bug-hole. Ehrenburg and Vera Inber still retain a faint resemblance to poets, but Kayransky has rightly summed up their activities thus: "Ehrenburg howls wildly, Inber approves his nonsense".' *Literary Inheritance* does not quote the end of the epigram: 'neither Moscow nor Petersburg can replace

Berdichev for them[1]. The critic Kayransky made up this rhyme at Kara-Murza's one night. There was much I did not foresee at that time, and so took no offence.

We amused ourselves as best we could. The sphinx set riddles for people which they could not solve and the sphinx devoured them. Oedipus knew that if he failed to solve the riddle, he would die; and yet I believe that whenever the sphinx left Oedipus in peace for a moment he tried to amuse himself.

Only Andrey Sobol laughed rarely, and his smile was melancholy. In his early youth he had been connected with the Socialist Revolutionary underground movement; as a youth of eighteen he had been sentenced to forced labour and exiled to the dread Zerentuy. He escaped and went abroad. I met him in the Italian village of Cavi di Lavagna, where for some reason Russian émigrés had chosen to settle, or rather to lead their unsettled existence. During the war Sobol returned to Russia on someone else's passport. I do not know why he was so sad: perhaps because he had seen so much trouble in his life, perhaps because reality was unlike the dreams of his adolescence; peasants were burning libraries on country estates, sailors held summary courts, and black marketeers, rather than Stepnyak-Kravchinsky's heroes, strode purposefully along Myasnitskaya. In 1923, an 'open letter' from Andrey Sobol was published in *Pravda*. 'During the stormy, tempestuous years which have passed before us, over us and through us, the whole of Russia made mistakes, stumbled and fell. Yes, I made mistakes, I know where, when and how, but my mistakes were an organic product of the vast complexity of life. Only hopeless fools or out-and-out scoundrels could regard themselves as without fault. Finding no stupidity and no iniquity in myself, I see no reason for remorse. Some recognize their mistakes sooner, others later. I have recognized mine later than many others, perhaps because I have always been and still remain a Socialist, and have always believed in that hour when, annihilating seas and oceans not only of water, but also of tears and blood, the Calcutta rickshaw-coolie will hold out his hand to Fedka Bespyaty from Nedoyelovka.' Sobol was a man of delicate health, kindly and gentle, with an intensely acute conscience. In 1926 he killed himself on a public bench in Tverskoy Boulevard.

The newspapers reported tremendous events: the German offensive,

[1] Berdichev was a town with a large Jewish population.

the Brest-Litovsk peace, the transfer of the government to Moscow, the revolt of the Left Socialist Revolutionaries, the beginning of civil war on the Don. Shooting kept breaking out in Moscow. Anarchist headquarters sprang up in practically every house along Povarskaya. At the Poets' Café, I often saw a Mauser beside a plate of cakes on a table. Bandits attacked pedestrians at night. Speakers at meetings kept saying: the Socialist motherland is in danger! The forming of an Extraordinary Commission for Combating Counter-Revolution, Speculation and Sabotage (the Cheka) was announced.

And yet life went on. I met the poet Mikhail Gerasimov; he took me to a Proletkult meeting where the Futurists were mocked at. Mayakovsky called the Proletkult poems 'stale goods'. Tolstoy said that the thing to do was to go to Paris. Bunin called Tolstoy a 'semi-Bolshevik'.

The sphinx insisted on an answer. But we still went to Kara-Murza's, joked, made up parodies, bought tobacco in Sukharevka, quarrelled with one another, fell in love.

I went to a 'Jack of Diamonds' exhibition; it included pictures by Suprematists and salon stylizers as well as by members of the 'Jack of Diamonds': the title was deceptive. But the works of those artists who, in the past, had really been the organizers of the 'Jack of Diamonds' group appealed to me. For some reason I had believed (as many people still do to this day) that they were blind imitators of the French. Certainly they admired Cézanne and knew Matisse, but they added something of their own to the experience of the French masters. In the early paintings of Lentulov, Mashkov, Konchalovsky, Larionov, Chagall and even Malevich (before his Suprematist period) there is something of the barber's, greengrocer's and tobacconist's shop-signs which were the real folk art in provincial Russian towns before the Revolution.

I was also interested in the theatre. According to my notebook, I saw within a single month *Three Sisters* and *The Village of Stepanchikovo* at the Art Theatre, Innokenty Annensky's *Thamira Kifared* at the Kamerny, and Merezhkovksy's *Paul* at the Dramatichesky. I also saw a play called *The Deluge* at the Art Theatre workshop. There was a café on the stage, and people called the waiter and ordered brandy. The art critic Y. A. Tugenhold, who had recently returned from Paris, was sitting next to me. When the curtain fell he put his hand in his pocket to fetch out some money: he thought he was in a

68

café and must pay for his drinks. I laughed, although the play was rather depressing: the naturalism of the production struck me as funny. The people on the stage really drank something or other, and everything was 'as in real life'. In Paris in 1909 I had not thought the tragedian Mounet-Sully realistic enough in the role of Oedipus Rex; now, the unreality of excessive realism seemed absurd to me.

Art beckoned, but I still thought about the riddles of the sphinx. Life was becoming outwardly more and more difficult; everyone went hungry. There was talk of gun fights, rationing and typhus. I was able to stand privations better than many of my new friends: I had gone through the school of hunger in Paris.

Once a letter arrived from Chantal, delivered by someone from abroad; she wrote that she was waiting for me. For a moment I saw Paris before my eyes. The Seine, the chestnut trees, my friends and the tiny side street, Cour de Rohan, where Chantal lived. I took a long time composing an answer; I wanted to explain that the war was still going on, that I had no money, and that – above all – I could not leave Russia before I had understood what was going on. It turned out a silly letter, and I tore it up.

9

My mother died in Poltava in the autumn of 1918. I knew she was gravely ill and I hurried to reach her. When I got to my uncle's house, my father was sitting in the hall, his shoulders hunched: he had just come back from the cemetery. I came two days too late to say goodbye to my mother. A mother's death makes many changes in a man's life. From the age of seventeen I had lived far from my parents, and yet I now felt an orphan. A cold rain fell. The flowers on the grave soon turned black in the early frosts. I did not know what to say to my father; we both kept silent. I spent two or three weeks with him. One could say a good deal about those weeks, or nothing at all.

Once I saw V. G. Korolenko in the street. He stooped as he walked; the kindness and the melancholy in his face were striking. One felt that here was the last representative of the past century's intelligentsia. (Ushakov's dictionary gives the following meaning, among others, for the term *intellighent* – member of the intelligentsia: 'A person whose social behaviour is characterized by the absence of will power, and by hesitations and doubts'. Yet the Russian intelligentsia of the nineteenth century was not devoid of will power; it knew how to pay the price of hardship, prison, forced labour for its ideas. Its doubts often sprang not from timidity but from a high degree of conscience. Korolenko, too, was precisely that: a man of conscience.) I remembered how kind he had been to me, a novice poet in a strange land. A student I knew who used to go to his house said: 'I'll introduce you if you like'. I knew that Korolenko was unwell, troubled by the events and worried about his son-in-law who had been arrested by the Germans. I knew I should not dare to ask him any questions. And I was too shy simply to go up to him and thank him for the fact that he was alive. So I never spoke to him.

I chose a bad time to come to Kiev. I want to describe how I lived there and what I saw. But first let me say something about Kiev itself. As a boy I had often been there to stay with my grandfather; later, I came to Kiev after my imprisonment, illegally, without a roof over my head. Two cities – Moscow and Paris – have been the scene of my life.

70

But I could never forget that Kiev was where I came from. I suppose that it is a matter of the power of words and the force of imagination. I do not know when my ancestors found themselves in the Ukraine and what winds of history carried them there; perhaps they came from Cordova or Granada. My grandfather arrived in Kiev from the ancient town of Novgorod-Seversk, a district centre in Chernigov province, and, of course, this was not in the time of Prince Igor but fairly recently, under the reign of Alexander II. Where did fine gentlemen pull his side-curls – was it in Novgorod-Seversk, in Kiev, or perhaps in that Berdichev which supplied Kayransky with his sarcastic rhyme? I shall never know. I cannot prove that I am a true, hereditary citizen of Kiev. But the heart has its own laws, and I always think of the place as my home town. In the autumn of 1941 we were losing one city after another, but I shall never forget the 20th September when I heard at the offices of *Red Star* that German divisions were marching down Kreshchatik. 'Kiev, Kiev! the wires repeated. Grief calling. Disaster speaking. Kiev, Kiev, my home!'

I remember how, when I was a boy, the train would begin to approach Kiev. It stopped at every station; it took its time (I was the one in a hurry). The names of the stations were queer: Bobrik, Bobrovitsa, Brovary. Then the sands began; I thought them a Sahara. I would lean out of the window. Kiev would appear suddenly: the domes of the Lavra, the gardens, the immensely broad Dnieper and its little islands dotted with green trees. But the train still went on for a long time clattering across the bridge.

Kiev had vast gardens, where chestnut trees grew; for a Moscow boy they were as exotic as palms. In the spring the trees sparkled with their chandeliers of blossom; in the autumn I collected shiny, polished-looking chestnuts. Everywhere there were gardens: in Institutskaya, in Mariinsko-Blagoveshchenskaya, in Zhitomirskaya, in Alexandrovskaya; as for Lukyanovka, where my aunt Masha lived amongst her pears and her chickens, it seemed to me an earthly paradise. In Kreshchatik there was Chernukha's, the stationer's, where they sold exercise books in shiny, coloured covers; in such an exercise book even a compound-interest problem looked brighter. There was Balabukha's, the confectioner's, where they sold preserves; you opened the box and there lay a sweet shaped like a rose, smelling of scent. In Kiev I ate cherry dumplings and garlic rolls. People in the streets had smiling faces. In summer, in Kreshchatik, they sat outside the cafés, drinking coffee or eating ice cream. I gazed upon the scene with envy and admiration.

Later, whenever I came to Kiev, I was struck by the ease, the friendliness, the liveliness of the people. Every country, I suppose, has its North and its South. The Italians regard the people of Turin as northerners; they are dry, reserved and businesslike. The Gascons live on the same latitude as the people of Turin, but Gascony is the South of France, and the word Gascon in French suggests a braggart, a card, a wag. For a Spaniard, the people of Barcelona are northerners, but if you travel north from Barcelona and cross the frontier, you soon reach Tartarin's Tarascon.

In the North, a man will sometimes smile because he has remembered something pleasant. Why does a southerner smile? Probably because he feels like it. Ukrainian imagination, Ukrainian humour warmed the stern face of old Russia. Gogol was a sick man with a terribly melancholy disposition, but how many people have felt better after reading his books! I know that Gogol is a 'great realist', it says so in every textbook, and as a schoolboy I had to learn by heart: 'Splendid is the Dnieper in calm weather'. In that passage it says: 'Rare is the bird that can fly as far as the middle of the Dnieper'. Birds fly across oceans, but Gogol was right: the Dnieper is wide, and so is art.

After the Revolution, colourful, impetuous, witty and romantic southerners entered Russian literature to dazzle, amuse and inspire us: Babel, Bagritsky, Paustovsky, Katayev, Svetlov, Zoshchenko, Ilf, Petrov, Olesha.

As a boy I used to stay with Auntie Masha. She rented a small farm near Borispol, where I heard blind men sing ancient songs on market-day. Many years later I heard M. F. Rylsky read his poems; something in them was familiar to me: the sly and tender music of Ukrainian speech.

I have spent many hours in Kiev's St Sophia. Byzantine art is often contrasted with Hellenic art. Christos Pantokrator, the stern and demanding, who derives not only from the blue skies of Greece but also from the fanatical police-state structure of the great Byzantine Empire, is, of course, a stranger to the world of centaurs and nymphs. And yet Byzantium kept something of the harmony of Hellas, and its echoes reached as far as ancient Kiev. In St Sophia I felt not only the burden of centuries, but also the lightness, the wings of art.

I love the baroque of Kiev; its complexity is softened by a kind of natural good humour; it is a smile, not a grimace. I am sorry they pulled down Mikhailovsky Monastery, it looked good standing there, and the courtyard was charming; Andreyevskaya church is finer, of course, but it is a pity all the same. (The Futurists were accused of disrespecting the past, but the Futurists' weapons were pens, not picks and shovels. When forests were cut down in the thirties it was not only chips that flew but sometimes age-old stones. In Archangel in 1934 I saw them blow up the customs house built in the time of Peter the Great; when I asked why, I was told: 'it interferes with the traffic'; yet in those days you could count the cars in Archangel on the fingers of two hands.)

The war inflicted many wounds on Kiev. The Germans blew up Lavra Cathedral. Kreshchatik ceased to exist. Later, pavements were laid, flower urns installed and militiamen posted; finally, the street was rebuilt. There were no ancient monuments in old Kreshchatik and memory alone makes it dear to me. In Moscow I live in Gorky Street, and my eye has become accustomed to the architecture now called 'decorative' although it is incapable of decorating anything. On the other hand, I was delighted to see the new avenues above the Dnieper: Kiev can now sit down on a seat (in calm weather, of course) and see for itself how splendid is the Dnieper. Green Lipki has become more beautiful. The outcast's brand has been removed from the Podol.

No, Kiev is not a stranger to me. My first memories are of a large courtyard, chickens, a white-and-ginger cat, and, across the road (in Alexandrovskaya), a row of pretty lanterns: a place of amusement, known as the *Château des Fleurs*, was open there in summer.

Many events in my life are bound up with Kiev. In 1918–19 there was a Kiev art school run by Alexandra Alexandrovna Ekster, a 'Left' artist who used to exhibit in Moscow with the 'Jack of Diamonds' group and who produced plays at the Kamerny Theatre. The students at this school included a dozen young girls and a few boys. I shall say more about this in a later chapter, but now I am speaking not of art but of myself. Among Mme Ekster's pupils there was a girl of eighteen called Lyuba Kozintseva. She became interested in me when she heard that I knew Picasso; as for me, I became interested in her although she only knew Mme Ekster. I started going to Dr Kozintsev's house in Mariinsko-Blagoveshchenskaya. My reputation was, of course, shaky, but then everything was shaky in those days. The Hetman was replaced by Petlyura, and Petlyura in his turn was ousted by the Red Army. Lyuba and her fellow-pupils decorated an *Agitparokhod*, or propaganda boat. The doorman at the 'Literary and Artistic Club' philosophized: 'Upside down today, out on your ear tomorrow'. I still wrote poetry, but when asked my profession in numerous question-naires I did not now put 'poet' but 'employee': I was working in several Soviet institutions. But all that is beside the point. Lyuba used to come and see me on the quiet (I was renting a room in Reitorskaya at the time). A few months later, without warning anyone, picking our way over the bodies of sleeping Red Army men and bales requisitioned by the Prodkom (Food Commissariat), we went off to the registry office.

In October 1943, together with other *Red Star* correspondents, I stayed in the burnt-out village of Lyotki on the Desna, waiting for the liberation of Kiev. Tall rushes whispered all round us. Sometimes we would drive to Darnitsa, from where it was possible to see Kiev. Sometimes we would cross to the right bank of the Dnieper. The waiting was hard. The poet Semyon Gudzenko wrote later: 'Yet in the snows of the Moscow country as in the Byelorussian marsh, Kiev was my first love, never to be forgotten'.

I saw the sands of Babiy Yar where the Nazis killed seventy thousand Jews. I was shown a proclamation: 'Jews of Kiev and surrounding districts. On Monday 29th September at 7 a.m. you are to report in Dorogozhitskaya Street near the Jewish Cemetery bringing your belongings, documents and warm clothing. Failure to report will be punished by death'. A procession of the doomed marched along endless Lvovskaya; mothers carried their babies; the paralysed were pulled along in handcarts. Then these people were made to strip and were killed. There were no relations of mine among those who lost their lives, but nowhere, I think, have I felt so wretched, so orphaned as on the sands of Babiy Yar. Here and there a pile of ashes and charred bones made a black patch (before they retreated, the Germans ordered prisoners of war to dig up the bodies of the victims and burn them). Somehow I had the feeling that my relatives, friends, childhood playmates had perished here, friends whom forty years earlier I had watched at their games in the murky streets of Podol and Demievka.

Many Jews lived in Kiev. When I was still a boy, my student cousin pointed out a man with glasses and long hair in Kreshchatik and ex-plained reverently that this was Sholem Aleichem. At that time I had not heard of this writer and I thought him just another of those learned eccentrics who pore over a book issuing meaningful sighs. Much later I read Aleichem's books and I myself sighed and laughed, trying to recall the face of the learned eccentric I had glimpsed in Kreshchatik. Sholem Aleichem called Kiev 'Yegupets', and its townspeople fill his books. Their children and grandchildren bade farewell to Yegupets on the sands of Babiy Yar.

In Kiev I saw a pogrom. The story by the Ukrainian writer Kotsyubinsky is doubly dear to me, both because I can understand the sufferings of Esterka and because, for me, the narrator is not the butcher Abrum but Mikhail Mikhailovich, son of Mikhail Matveyevich and Glikeria Maksimovna.

I have had many experiences in Kiev, but that is not the point. They say that one's place of birth may be accidental, a railway junction or a far-off country where fate had happened to deposit one's parents for a month or a year. Well, I claim that in such a case the railway junction ceases to be a mere point on the map and the far-off country becomes near to you forever.

'Kiev, Kiev, my home . . .'

Every time I come to Kiev I make a point of climbing one of its steep streets alone. As a boy I used to run up quickly; now I have aged and I am soon out of breath. I climb, and it seems to me as though it is only from Lipki or from Pechersk that I can survey the years, the decades, the lifetime behind me.

All this, if you like, is in the nature of a prelude. I lived in Kiev from the autumn of 1918 until November 1919: a year. Governments, regulations, flags, even shop-signs were changing. The town was a battlefield in the Civil War. Pillaging, murders and executions went on. That is the grim story I have to tell. The reason why I began with a lyrical digression is that almost all proverbs are lies (or rather, they are the obverse of the truth) and this goes also for the classical proverbs of the ancient Romans, who used to say *Ubi bene, ibi patria*: where it is good, there is your motherland. In reality, your motherland is even where it is very, very bad.

75

10

IN PARIS we had repeated dismally: 'The Germans are at Noyan'. Now I was to see the Germans in Kreshchatik. A tall officer with a moustache like the Kaiser's walked towards me. German sentries in jackboots stood outside the Duma beating a tattoo with their wooden soles. At one of the stations on the Kiev railway I saw one-half of the restaurant – the cleaner half – roped off and labelled: 'For German officers only'.

The newspapers said that the Ukraine was being ruled by Hetman Skoropadsky. The name was unfortunate; governments at this time fell too often[1]. I never saw him, and for all I know he may have looked all right. Petlyura's men came near Kiev, the Hetman departed for Germany; however, youthful volunteers continued to stand outside the house where he had lived, convinced that they were guarding the Head of State. The townspeople, laughing, said that the Hetman had been a bit too quick. Well, he was less hasty about dying: he spent almost thirty years in emigration, became an admirer of Hitler and witnessed Germany's second collapse. A German has told me that Skoropadsky was addressed as 'Herr Hetman' until his death; I expect he got used to the role as time went on, but in 1918 his acting was poor, like a beginner's. He was supposed to champion the independence of the Ukraine, but being an officer of the Tsarist army he obviously preferred Petersburg guardsmen to Ukrainian freebooters. The Germans made him Hetman, and so it is natural that he swore eternal love to them; but the Allies launched a big counter-offensive in France, and Skoropadsky sent one of his trusted men to Odessa, where the Allies' representative, the French consul Monsieur Hainaut, had his being.

Demobilized soldiers in ragged greatcoats sold crystal chandeliers and rifles in the open-air market. People sang: 'O my bread-bearing Ukraine, you've given your bread to the Germans, now you must go hungry'.

---

[1] 'skoro' = quickly, 'padat' = to fall.

The Germans showed no lack of appetite. They ate everywhere: in restaurants, in cafés, at the markets; they ate Vienna *schnitzels*, rich cakes, *shashlyks* and sour cream.

The Germans were cheerful and pleased with life: the Kiev pie-shops were a good deal more comfortable than the Chemin-des-Dames or Verdun. They looked like figures on one of those monuments that are put up in Germany to celebrate military victories. They believed that they would become masters of the world. (Twenty years later I saw the sons of the Germans who had once strolled down Kresh-chatik march along the Paris boulevards; the children resembled the fathers: they were always eating, and they had a blind faith in their own superiority.)

Kiev was like a down-at-heel, overcrowded holiday resort. Kiev people were heavily outnumbered by the multitude of refugees from the North. Kreshchatik was the first halt of the Russian emigration: before the Odessa quays, before the Turkish islands, before the Berlin boarding-houses and the Paris attics. How many future Paris taxi-drivers were strolling down Kreshchatik in those days! There were high-ranking Petrograd officials, slick journalists, chorus girls, owners of remunerative property, ordinary citizens; the north wind swept them along like leaves in autumn.

New restaurants, pie-shops, *shashlyk* bars opened every day; after a life of 'drought and famine', the northerners grew fat under one's very eyes. Gambling casinos, miniature theatres and cabarets opened too. At a small theatre well known to the Petrograd public, the performers, cavorting merrily, sang little ditties written by Agnivtsev: 'Ten governments there were, but none stayed long enough to hang us'.

An astonishing number of commission shops sprang up. This was a novelty and aroused much interest; the goods included furs, cruci-fixes, icons in valuable frames, silver tableware, ear-rings, tartan rugs, lace – in short, everything that people had managed to take away with them from Moscow and Petrograd. All kinds of currency were used – Tsarist money, *kerenkas*, *ukrainkas* – and no one knew which was the worst. Speculators peddled German marks, Austrian crowns, dollars and pounds sterling outside the Duma. When news came of German defeats in France, the mark fell and the pound rose. Dollars were particularly attractive to buyers, and the speculators, whether fired by imagination or in the hope of making a little more profit, divided the dollar notes into categories and charged the highest prices for those 'with bulls on'.

Officers, too, fell into different categories: there were supporters of Denikin, supporters of Krasnov, members of the Kuban army and even of the Astrakhan army. All, I believe, formed part of the 'special Russian corps', but they quarrelled among themselves. All, however, cursed the Bolsheviks, the Ukrainian nationalists and the Jews. It was in Kreshchatik that I first heard the war cry: 'Kill the Jews, save Russia'. They killed plenty of Jews, but they did not save their old Russia for all that.

Rumours began to spread: the Allies had beaten the Germans; there were disturbances in Germany; some kind of a German Kerensky, called Max von Baden, headed the new government. The White officers did not know whether to be glad or sorry; on the one hand they swore loyalty to the Allies and cursed the Brest-Litovsk peace, on the other they fully realized that if the Germans withdrew, Kiev would be taken by 'bandits', as they called Petlyura's men.

The Germans packed their bags efficiently and without haste. The Kaiser went off to Holland. Fighting in the West came to an end. The newspapers announced that a German 'Soviet of Soldiers' Deputies' had been formed in Kiev. I do not know what this Soviet did. At all events the German officers' and soldiers' efforts were directed towards taking as much booty home with them as possible: bacon, butter, sugar.

The S.R.s and Kadets of the municipal Duma were considering whether they should announce that they were taking power into their hands as the 'people's democratic choice'. But an emissary from Monsieur Hainaut in Odessa arrived declaring that the Allies had ordered 'the democratic forces' of Kiev to support Hetman Skoropadsky.

Pyotr Pilsky, who before the war had been known for ridiculing the Symbolist poets, was now publishing a humorous journal in Kiev called *The Devil's Pepperpot*. There was no shortage of things to laugh at: the Hetman installed by the Germans was hurriedly memorizing the *Marseillaise*; Monsieur Hainaut said he was for the Hetman, and offered to supply the National Directory with arms; the government of the new German Republic called itself Socialist, but negotiated with French generals for a campaign against Soviet Russia. Not a word about any of this appeared in *The Devil's Pepperpot*: the pepper was not ground by a devil but by a Petrograd literary gentleman conscious of the fact that he would soon be applying for a French or German visa.

Trains going to Odessa were taken by storm; everyone said that Odessa was where the Allied armies would land; they would land too late to preserve Kiev from Petlyura's men or the Bolsheviks, but Odessa was heaven, a fortress, a quiet life. Sceptics added that even if French *poilus* failed to reach Odessa from Marseilles, refugees would always be able to go from Odessa to Marseilles: the sea was the sea.

I have already said that tall stories are never so abundant as at the beginning of a war. The Civil War went on for a long time, but the opponents of Soviet power kept changing, and all of them let their imaginations soar as usually happens only at the very beginning of a war. Various 'well-informed' people swore that the Allies had ultra-violet rays by means of which they could destroy both the 'Reds' and the 'Nationalists' within a few hours.

There was much talk of 'gangs of bandits'. There were many rebel groups: outwardly they resembled each other, but they included people with very varied ideas; some believed in the Directory, others thought that the bourgeois should be wiped out, and meanwhile robbed the peasants; there were also some who just enjoyed looting, unrepentant louts whose early training had been the Jewish pogroms. I cannot remember when the various 'Fathers' appeared on the scene – was it in 1918 or in 1919? – but within that year I heard enough tales about Stryuk, Tyutyunik, Angel, Zelyony, Zabolotny and, of course, the most famous of them all, 'Father' Makhno.

The Directory troops stood outside Kiev. To finish up, the White officers emptied the wine cellars, drank, sang, swore, wept and shot 'suspects'.

When troops enter a town their spirits are high; when they evacuate it, they are filled with anger and it is best to keep out of their way. There were three phrases which I heard often that year: 'to Dukhonin's H.Q.', 'excesses', and 'slam the door'.

Petlyura's men marched down Kreshchatik gaily, molesting no one. Moscow ladies who had not had time to scramble off to Odessa were delighted: 'What nice boys!' The White officers were rounded up and locked in the Pedagogical Museum (this was, I rather fancy, a matter of the size of the building, not of educational aims). I remember a great scare: a big bang was heard and a lot of windows broke. The townspeople hurriedly began filling bathtubs with water – the water supply might be cut off – and burning Petlyurist newspapers. It turned out that someone had thrown a bomb at the Pedagogical Museum.

The names of newspapers changed. Yellow and sky-blue flags were hung out. Shopkeepers were ordered to alter their signs: everywhere one saw painters on ladders altering the Russian to the Ukrainian 'i'.

Coats of arms, British and French, appeared on two houses in Lipki. The papers announced that Monsieur Hainaut had promised to protect the independence of the Ukraine from both the Reds and the Whites.

Sometimes I felt as if I were watching a film and could not understand who was chasing whom; the pictures flashed by so quickly that it was impossible to see them properly, let alone think about them. The Petlyurists conducted negotiations with the Bolsheviks and with Denikin's men, with the Germans and with Monsieur Hainaut. The Directory troops entered Kiev in December and stayed only a short time: six weeks.

No one knew who would be arrested tomorrow, whose portrait it was best to hang on the wall and whose to hide, which currency to accept and which to try and pass on to some simpleton. Life, however, went on. For a long time I was without a room of my own, and I slept on a sofa in the house of my cousin, a professor of medicine specializing in venereal diseases. Sometimes there would be firing in the morning, but downcast patients would already be sitting in the waiting-room; they invariably looked away from each other, and some tried to hide their faces behind newspapers. The names of the newspapers changed and what they said was quite different from what they had said the day before, but this did not worry the patients.

There was a house in Lipki where arrested persons were interrogated. With every retreat, papers were burned and window-panes smashed. New authorities arrived, replaced the glass, brought fresh piles of paper and started questioning a new batch of arrested persons.

I have already mentioned the 'Literary and Artistic Club'; it was located in Nikolayevskaya and bore the unmelodious name of *Klak* (*Kievsky Literaturno-Artistichesky Klub*). During the months of Soviet power it was renamed *Khlam*[1], not as a mark of disrespect for the arts

[1] Khlam: rubbish.

but because everybody renamed everything; *Khlam* stood for 'Painters, literary men, actors, musicians' (*Khudozhniki, literatory, aktyory, musykanty*). I went there often. After every change of government certain regulars would disappear; either they left with the retreating army or, as the philosophical doorman used to say, they found themselves 'out on their ear'. Those who remained went on singing songs or listening to songs sung by others, reciting poetry and eating rissoles.

When, in February, the Red Army marched in from the left bank, almost everyone was glad. I remember one of the visitors to the Club, a bald-headed Moscow lawyer; he shouted in a state of great excitement: 'I'm against their ideas, but at least they've got ideas, and the way we've been living here is unspeakable'.

Some, of course, were irreconcilable; those who believed that Gorodskoy Sad (the City Park) would become Kupechesky Sad (Merchants' Park) once more, and that their beloved *Kievlyanin* would start coming out again. Hadn't Monsieur Hainaut promised that the Allies would land at Odessa, at Sevastopol, at Novorossisk, and their first action would be to free the 'mother of Russian cities' from the Bolsheviks?

The sociable Monsieur Hainaut seemed to have reached an understanding with practically everybody. 'Death battalions' and detachments loyal to various *atamans* prowled round Kiev. Houses burned, and feathers flew from slashed feather beds. Every day there were tales of fresh pogroms, of girls raped and old men with slit bellies. The Allies were meeting in Paris; inspired by the Romanticism of Venice in the time of the doges, they organized a Council of Ten; this 'council' (or 'Soviet') negotiated with Denikin. Monsieur Hainaut promised rifles to 'Father' Zelyony. People died of hunger, stray bullets, pogroms and typhus-carrying lice.

During Petlyura's time someone brought a copy of the French paper *Le Matin* to the *Klak*. I learned that a new fashion had sprung up in Paris: men now wore extremely tight-waisted coats, so that those who had defeated the Kaiser looked like elegant ladies. The item on fashions was followed by an article explaining that the Allies in Russia were defending freedom, civil rights and lofty human values.

I have said that Skoropadsky lived to a ripe old age on German bounty. Petlyura was shot in Paris by a watchmaker called

Schwarzbard. I do not know what became of Monsieur Hainaut; he was a little man and the historians are not interested in him. Yet often, as I put down my paper with its news of events in Guatemala or the Congo, in Iran or in Cuba, I remember the year 1919, ravaged Kiev and the shadow of the mysterious Monsieur Hainaut.

11

THE Red Army came in February 1919, and in August Kiev was occupied by the Whites. Those six months were full of life and colour. For Kiev this was the season of hopes and impulses, of extremes, of bewilderment, a season of spring storms.

Let me begin by talking about myself. I have already said that I became a Soviet official. In Paris I had been a guide; later I had unloaded trucks at a goods station and written articles which were published in the *Birzhevka*. None of this, including the newspaper work, needed much qualification. But the next page of my employment record is mysterious indeed: I was put in charge of the 'section of aesthetic education for mofective children' in the Kiev Department of Social Welfare. The reader will smile. It makes me smile too. No one until then had known what 'mofective children' were. I daresay the reader does not know either. Cryptic terms were popular in the first years of the Revolution. 'Mofective' meant morally defective, the concept included juvenile delinquents as well as ordinary 'difficult' children. (When a lean Froebel lady was explaining all this to me, I realized that as a child I had been ultra-mofective. Why was I entrusted with the aesthetic education of children, and abnormal children at that? I do not know. I had no connection whatsoever with education, and when my little daughter in Paris was naughty I knew only one way of pacifying her, which had no educational value whatever: I would buy her an emerald or crimson lollipop for two sous.)

However, many people in those days had jobs far removed from their real professions. The writer Marietta Shaginyan, who had been a lecturer in aesthetics, began giving classes in sheep-breeding and weaving. Ilya Selvinsky, the poet, who had graduated from the Law Faculty and completed a course in Marxism-Leninism for professors, became an instructor in fur selection.

A young man who had accidentally escaped the attention of the criminal police was employed at the 'mofective section' for two or three months: he traded in dollars, aspirin and sugar. He also wrote

83

poems of a totally illiterate kind (he used to say 'I'm sorry, but they're awfully erotic'). Many features of the hero of *Rvach* (The Grabber), a novel which I wrote in 1924, were taken from the biography of this colleague of mine. He knew even less than I about education, but being self-confident and cocky he always joined in the discussions of teachers and doctors. I remember a meeting at which the effect of albumen, fats and carbohydrates on the nervous system of children was discussed. The young author of 'awfully erotic' poems suddenly interrupted an elderly professor to say: 'Oh, come off it! I was pretty nervous myself as a kid. If you get down to it, fats can't do any harm, and white of egg's just the thing too'.

I warned the teachers and psychiatrists that I was a complete ignoramus, but they said I was doing good work. A reputation was established: Ehrenburg was a specialist in the aesthetic education of children; and in the autumn of 1920, when I returned to Moscow, V. E. Meyerhold offered to put me in charge of the Republic's children's theatres.

We spent a long time working out a project for an 'experimental pilot colony' where juvenile law-breakers would be educated in a spirit of 'creative work' and 'all-round development'. It was a great time for projects. In every institution in Kiev, it seemed, grey-haired eccentrics and young enthusiasts were drafting projects for a heavenly life on earth. We discussed the effect of excessively bright colours on excessively nervous children and wondered whether choral declamation influenced the collective consciousness and whether eurhythmics could be helpful in the suppression of juvenile prostitution.

The discrepancy between our discussions and reality was staggering. I began investigating reform schools, orphanages and dosshouses where the *besprizornye* (lost children) were to be found. The reports I drafted spoke not of eurhythmics but of bread and cloth. The boys ran away to join various 'Fathers'; the girls solicited prisoners of war returning from Germany.

A young painter called Panya Pastukhov, an exceedingly shy creature, was working in my section. One day I sent him to have a look at a home for refugee girls that had been set up in 1915. Pastukhov came back shaken to the core. It appeared that the girls were by this time quite big; abandoned to their fate as a result of various government changes, they had begun to earn their living, and now several had babies at the breast. When Pastukhov had tried to talk to them of the benefits of learning, one of the girls had playfully replied: 'A fag would be more to the point, big boy'.

Our institution was housed in a villa in Lipki. I remember a large Empire desk in the big main room with an enormous label that had been stuck on it at the time of requisitioning. One morning I found a new-born baby on top of this desk; someone had dumped it there during the night. The local Cheka was in the villa next door and cars kept driving up to it. The garden turned green all of a sudden; I listened to arguments about the Dalcroze method and gazed through the window. The acacias were in bloom.

At that time many people worked in several institutions at once. Besides working in the 'mofective section', I did a great many other things, such as taking part in meetings of the 'applied art section'. The times, one would have thought, were not favourable to the arts; there was frequent firing in the streets; Monsieur Hainaut was losing no time, and Kiev was surrounded by gangs of all kinds; homespun strategists argued about who would storm the city first, Petlyura's or Denikin's men. Yet the 'applied art section' got a lot done. I am not speaking about myself – I was, if not a layman, certainly only an amateur in the subject – but the section included some fine specialists from among the Kiev artists, such as V. Meller, Pribylskaya, Margarita Genke, Spasskaya. We held exhibitions of folk art and set up embroidery and pottery workshops. I met a talented peasant woman called Gapa Sobachka, who had an extraordinary sense of colour. Enormous panels with Ukrainian ornamental designs on them appeared in Kreshchatik.

I saw clay animals modelled by Ivan Gonchar, one of the last practitioners of traditional folk art. In those years his animals were not rams, or dogs, or lions, but belonged to a species unknown to zoologists; each was unique. (Folk art finds inspiration in nature but never copies it; the reason why the lacemakers of Vologda studied the hoar-frost designs on their windows was precisely that hoar-frost looks like the jungle, like a starry sky, like the letters of a non-existent alphabet.)

In Kiev I met the authoress S. Z. Fedorchenko, who had written an interesting book called *People at War*; she had worked as a nurse in a military hospital and recorded the soldiers' conversations. I copied out one soldier's reflections on art: 'There's a volunteer in our unit who goes in for drawing, and what he draws is exactly like the real

85

thing, just like it, so that it's quite dreary to look at'. All kinds of literary manifestos and artistic 'isms' have become outdated in the meantime, but the soldier's remark made casually in 1915 seems to me not only alive but topical today.

I also worked in a 'literary workshop' where I taught versification to beginners. (Although I was then writing disjointed 'free verse', I was nevertheless able to distinguish iambics from trochees.) Bryusov had tried to persuade me at great length that anyone with a modicum of ability could be taught to write good verse; Gumilev, who shared this view, used to say that he had turned even Otsup into a good poet. I, however, did not and do not believe that poetry can be taught. All that can be done at a school, whatever its name – institute, academy or workshop – is to teach the students to read poetry, that is to say, to raise the level of their aesthetic standards.

Among the pupils at the workshop there was a shy, polite youth called N. N. Ushakov. I am glad that my brief career as a poetry teacher has not prevented him from becoming a poet. I have met him on later occasions and have reassured myself that he bears me no ill-will.

The house in Nikolayevskaya sheltered the Writers' Union, the Art Workers' Union, the literary workshop and much else. Futurism was discussed, streets were allocated to painters for decorating, lectures on Marxism were delivered, safe-conducts and all kinds of certificates were issued.

Downstairs, in the cellar, was the *Khlam* (formerly *Klak*). There I used to see the local poet Vladimir Makkaveysky, who had recently published a collection of sonnets called *Alexandrian Stylos*. He had an excellent knowledge of Greek mythology, quoted Lucian and Asclepiades, Mallarmé and Rilke, in short he was the Vyacheslav Ivanov of Kiev. I have now had another look at his book and have found only one comprehensible line: 'Hellas, a mummy, lay down in the Alexandrian sarcophagus'. Makkaveysky badly wanted to be an Alexandrian, but the times did not allow it.

Another Kiev poet – less parochial, it is true – was called Benedikt Livshits. I remembered his outrageous contributions to the early Futurist collections; when I met him, I was surprised to find a quiet, highly cultured man who abused no one and whose youthful enthusiasms had obviously cooled down. He loved and understood art, and we talked mostly about painting. He wrote little and thought a great deal; doubtless, like myself and many others, he wanted to understand the meaning of what was happening.

Osip Mandelstam, already known for his book *Stone*, was prominent among the 'Northerners' in *Khlam*. I shall speak of him later; I got to know him far better at Koktebel in 1920. I remember him reading, in *Khlam*, a marvellous poem beginning 'I have studied the science of parting'.

V. B. Shklovsky flashed by like a meteor; he gave a brilliant, involved lecture at Mme Ekster's studio, smiled slyly, and criticized absolutely everyone mercilessly but with affection.

Also at *Khlam* I met the dreamy, curly-headed L. V. Nikulin; once he read us some very sad poems, all about coffins.

Natan Vengrov wrote poems for children. He organized a 'Children's Books Day': huge panels appeared in Kreshchatik, and bear-cubs, elephants and crocodiles filled the street. Vengrov tried to convince me that I was really a children's poet and merely happened to be doing a job not my own. (I have tried my hand at many things, but never have I written for children.)

The well-known actress Vera Yureneva used to come to *Khlam*; she was often accompanied by a young man, almost an adolescent, with a permanently scornful expression. When we were introduced, he muttered 'Misha Koltsov'.

The most boisterous among the Ukrainian poets was the Futurist Semenko. He was short, but had a powerful voice, rejected all authority and respected no one but Mayakovsky. I also met P. G. Tychina, taciturn and dreamy; one had the impression that he was listening for something all the time; he was gentle almost to the point of awkwardness. As soon as I saw him I felt that here was a real poet.

Feverish work was going on in the Jewish writers' section; they knew they had to fit their thinking, writing and publishing into the short period between Petlyura and Denikin. Bergelson, Kvitko, Dobrushin and Markisch were in Kiev at that time. If I succeed in writing the later volumes of this book, I shall try to recreate the image of Peretz Markish, whom I was to meet later in Paris and Moscow. That year in Kiev he was a handsome youth, with a great shock of hair always standing on end and eyes that were both sarcastic and sad. Everyone called him a 'rebel', saying that he was out to destroy the classics, to overthow idols; but at our first meeting I was reminded above all of an itinerant Jewish fiddler who plays melancholy songs at other men's weddings.

I met many artists in Kiev. Mme Ekster had spent a great deal of her life in Paris, where she was a friend of Léger and was regarded as a Cubist. Her work, however, was infinitely remote from Léger's urbanistic visions; her chief interest was the theatre (she had worked at the Kamerny in Moscow and at various Kiev theatres). I do not know why it was, but the same passion for the theatre and spectacles of all descriptions was felt among her pupils and among the young artists of her circle. Almost all the painters whom I met in Kiev at that time became theatre artists: Tyshler, Rabinovich, Shifrin, Meller, Petritsky.

'Passion for the theatre': as I write these words I cannot help thinking of Alex Tyshler, a twenty-year old student of Mme Ekster's. His story provides the best illustration of the passion for the theatre characteristic of Kiev artists. It is not a question of whether X, Y or Z worked for the theatre: almost all Soviet artists did so, if only because there have been periods when richness of colour, imagination and skill were more acceptable on the stage than in the picture galley. Alexander Tyshler is best known to Muscovites through his stage designs. His sets for *King Lear* had the realism-within-a-convention of Shakespeare's own verse. But the surprising thing is that even Tyshler's easel paintings retain the theatrical view of the world. I remember one of his pictures which showed soldiers shooting down a carrier pigeon, painted twenty years before Picasso's dove. Only an artist capable of seeing Tyutchev's 'world of the sky-dwellers' as a fantastic tragedy could have tackled such a subject in the thirties of the twentieth century.

The first years of the Revolution saw not only a flowering of dramatic art, but also an enthusiasm for the theatre amounting almost to an epidemic. In small Ukrainian towns, itinerant actors longing for a good meal enthralled their audiences, making them forget inadequate rations, unheated houses, nightly street firing. But Kiev was lucky: it got Konstantin Mardzhanov. He was a man bursting with excitement, with bold plans, a man of gentle but uncompromising spirit. I remember him saying heatedly as we sat in a canteen drinking bad tea (I was telling him about Spain; he was going to produce a play by Lope de Vega): 'The theatre is the theatre. I told them at the City Executive Committee that a City Executive Committee is a City Executive Committee. They want people on the stage to drink real tea. Well, what would they say if people drinking tea in the City Executive Committee's canteen started reciting soliloquies, raising their arms to heaven and talking in hexameters about the municipal economy?' Kiev saw *Fuente Ovejuna*, and a wind swept through the hall of the old Solovtsy Theatre. We stood there for a long time, clapping and refusing to go home.

Mardzhanov liked *Blanche's Chemise*, the play I had written with Alexey Tolstoy, and he decided to put it on. N. A. Shifrin did the sets. It was after the second or third performance, I think, that Denikin's men stormed the town.

I often met two juvenile (but not 'mofective') admirers of Mardzhanov, inseparable friends, Grisha Kozintsev – Lyuba's brother – and Seryozha Yutkevich. They invited me to the former premises of 'One-Eyed Jimmy', where they organized a 'popular fairground show', that is, one of those eccentric spectacles that amused the public in the cold and hungry years.

In Sofiyskaya Street, near Dumskaya Square, there was a dirty little café kept by an emaciated Greek with the long, passionate face of an El Greco. In the window there was a sign which said 'Genuine Fresh Sour Cream'. The Greek brewed fragrant Turkish coffee and we often gathered at his place – poets, painters, actors. This café is bound up for me with the later course of my life. I used sometimes to talk there to Lyuba, to Yadviga – a young student at the Pedagogical Institute – and to Nadya Khazina, who later became Osip Mandelstam's wife, about my adventures in foreign lands. I made up stories about what a good French bourgeois or a Roman *lazzarone* would do if they found themselves in revolutionary Russia. And so the characters of *Julio Jurenito*, which I wrote two years later, came into being.

I went on writing poetry; it did not become any better, but the tone changed. I still could not understand the full meaning of events but, despite the many various troubles of the period, I felt elated. 'Our grandchildren will muse as they turn the pages of the textbooks: "Nineteen fourteen – seventeen – nineteen ... However did they manage? Poor dears, poor dears!" The children of the new age will read of the battles, learn the names of the leaders and orators, the numbers of dead and the dates. They will never know how sweet the roses smelt on the field of battle, how blackbirds sang amid the voices of the guns, how beautiful life was in those years.'

If one thinks deeply about what happened long ago, many things

89

reveal themselves. Outwardly, life had a strange look. Gangs prowled about the city; every day there were new stories of pogroms and killings. Car brakes screeched alarmingly. Denikin and Petlyura raced to get to Kiev first. I often heard vicious murmurs: 'This lot won't be here much longer'. Meanwhile we sat over our various projects, discussing the publishing date of the third volume of Chekhov or Kotsyubinsky and the best place for a monument to the Revolution. We read poetry and looked at paintings, and the inner gaiety of which I speak shone in our eyes, not only in the eyes of fourteen-year-old Grisha Kozintsev but also in those of Konstantin Mardzhanov, who was then nearly fifty. It was not a matter of age – it was, if you like, a matter of the age of the Revolution. By the Moscow calendar it was then two years old; by the local one, a few months.

12

THERE are memories which gratify and inspire, reminding one of fine impulses, goodness and courage. And there are memories of another kind. It is wrong to say that time heals everything. It is true that scars form over old wounds, but suddenly the old wounds begin to ache, and they die only with oneself.

I must now speak of evil things. Two centuries before our era, Plautus amused the Romans with his plays. All that has remained of them in our memory are four words: *Homo homini lupus est*. When we speak of the ethics of social systems based on self-interest and on the struggle for a share in the spoils, we often say: Man is wolf to man. Plautus was wrong to bring wolves into it. L. A. Manteufel who has studied wolves told me that they rarely fight among themselves and that they attack human beings only when driven mad by hunger. In my own life I have often seen human beings persecute, torment and kill other human beings without the least necessity. If animals could meditate and invent aphorisms, some grey wolf attacked by one of his fellows would doubtless bark: 'Wolf is man to wolf'.

What can I say about the Kiev pogrom? Today nobody is surprised at anything. Women, old men, children screamed all night long in the black houses; one had the feeling that the houses themselves were screaming, the streets, the whole town.

In those years, Peretz Markisch wrote a long poem about the pogrom in Gorodishche. Five hundred Jews were killed there. More than seventy thousand were killed in Babiy Yar, six million in the whole of Europe. I catch myself making this comparison. Recently I listened to a machine which can compose music. Well, it seems to me that it is a machine, not the heart, that makes one think of these figures. Yes, it is true, the hangmen of 1919 had not yet thought of gas chambers. Their atrocities were of a rough and ready kind: carving a five-cornered star on a forehead, raping a little girl, throwing a baby out of a window.

An old man lay on his back in the courtyard staring at the empty autumn sky with empty eyes. Was this perhaps the milkman Tevye or his brother-in-law, an old inhabitant of doomed Yegupets? Round him was a puddle, not of milk, but blood. And the wind stirred his beard restlessly.

As in every tragedy, there were some farcical scenes. A tall fellow in officer's uniform burst into the flat of my father-in-law, Dr Kozintsev, and bawled: 'You've crucified Christ, you've sold Russia!' Then he caught sight of a cigar-box on the table and inquired in the calmest, most businesslike manner imaginable: 'Silver, is it?'

I decided to try and make my way to Voloshin's at Koktebel; his house seemed a refuge to me. It took us a week to get to Kharkov. Officers or Cossacks burst into the carriages at the stations: 'Jews, Communists and commissars, out!' The painter I. Rabinovich was taken out of our goods truck at one of the stations in this way.

Kharkov, then Rostov, then Mariupol, Kerch, Feodosia: we travelled for a good (no, a bad) month, digging ourselves into the darkest corners of goods trucks, lying hidden in ships' holds among people sick and dying of typhus; we lay there covered with a thick layer of lice. Again and again we heard the monotonous cry: 'Any yids in there?' Lice and blood, blood and lice.

Portraits of Denikin, Kolchak, Kutepov, May-Mayevsky and Shkuro on dirty fences. Drunken Kuban army men checking papers in the streets. Someone shouting 'Hold that man, he's a commissar!' The Palace Hotel in Kharkov housed the counter-intelligence; pedestrians made a big detour round this building. In the cafés, French officers sat at one table, black marketeers at another, all drinking coffee in the Warsaw style. Posters put up by *Osvag*, the Whites' propaganda organization, were everywhere: 'Forward to Moscow!': St George's horse trampling a hook-nosed Jew under its hoofs.

Moscow lawyers, Petrograd literary men, aristocratic ladies wrapped in countless shawls and carrying hatboxes crammed with food, actors, governesses and *besprizornye* scurried from town to town. A wit, adapting a well-known tag, declaimed in a wrecked, filthy hotel: 'To flee? For a short time it's not worth the trouble, to flee forever is impossible'. A demented old woman wearing a soldier's greatcoat and a hat trimmed with violet feathers muttered: 'No, Clemenceau will never abandon us to our fate'. Groups of drunken officers coming out of night clubs sang 'Shkuro is our general, we sneeze at Europe, we'll stick a feather . . .' the rest was unprintable.

(In 1925 I saw a poster on the walls of Paris: the 'Buffalo' circus was advertising a new turn – Cossack trick-riding under the direction of the 'celebrated General Shkuro'. The one-time hero of the pogrom ended his career in the circus ring.)

Townspeople going to market in the morning kept their ears open for the sound of shooting. They had all been through it, and no one believed anything that was said. The Civil War awakened feelings of hatred, courage and fortitude in people of spirit who knew what they were fighting for. But the snug and stuffy little houses crawled with frightened little people who wanted to save neither the old Russia nor the Revolution but only themselves. Out of fear they would report now to the Cheka, now to the White counter-intelligence that a neighbour's nephew was a member of a Food Detachment, or that another neighbour had married off his daughter to a White officer. They were afraid of the sound of footsteps on the stairs, a creaking door, a whisper at the gate. The most cunning among them hid *pyatakovkas*[1] and portraits of Karl Marx under floorboards, ready to replace them a month later with a portrait of May-Mayevsky, Tsarist money or even an icon of St Nicholas.

At the railways stations one had to step over bodies: typhus sufferers, refugees, travelling black marketeers lay on the platforms.

Here was a curly-headed lad who only yesterday had been singing: 'Boldly we'll go into battle for the power of the Soviets'. Today he was roaring out: 'Boldly we'll go into battle for Holy Russia, and will wipe out all the Jews'. He had not and had never had the slightest intention of going into any battle; he did a brisk trade in felt boots stolen from a warehouse.

The Cossacks were ferocious: it was the outcome of tradition, of anger over their own wrecked and uprooted lives, of utter perplexity.

In the White Army there were men of the Black Hundreds, former members of the Okhrana (Tsarist secret police), gendarmes, hangmen. They occupied important posts in the administration, the counter-intelligence and the *Osvag*. They preached (and possibly believed) that the Russian people had been deceived by the Communists, the Jews, the Latvians; that what they needed was a good flogging, after which they should be chained up like dogs.

Many years later, in Paris, I bought a collection of verse written by a certain Posazhnoy, who proclaimed himself a 'Black hussar'. He worked at Renault's, cursed the 'frogs' and lamented the magnificence

---

[1] The latest Soviet paper currency.

of bygone days; here is how he remembered his war-horse: 'Pegasus entered the dining-room and had a drink of Kakhetinsky wine, ate a bunch of white roses and shat politely on a tray. It was a time for gentlemen, the audience cried hurrah, Caucasian musicians played loudly on their instruments. Memory, be silent!' And this is how he expressed his ideals: 'Those who are Red today shall perish. They have long been due to go to the devil. And once again the wine shall foam in the goblets of those who once were Junkers'. Reading these magic spells in 1929 I laughed, but in 1919 such men as Posazhnoy would burst into a goods truck, hit you across the face, then shoot you.

The majority of the Whites, however, were people who had lost their heads; their bodies were raw with louse bites, their hearts raw with grievances suffered and anticipated, with massacres, arrests, shootings, with the weeping of cities that constantly changed hands, with the knowledge that tomorrow they would be put up against the same filthy wall to which they were dragging the latest batch of 'suspects' today.

Leonhard Frank called one of his books *Man is Good*. But man is neither good nor evil; he can be good, and he can be very evil indeed. Not all the Whites were sadists, of course; many were ordinary men of quite good disposition who had never before hurt anyone; but they had been obliged to abandon their good nature together with the bric-à-brac of their cosy homes. Evil was dictated by despair. Not even in the autumn of 1919, when the Whites took Orel, did they feel like conquerors. They advanced as if across strange country, seeing enemies everywhere. In the night clubs, White officers wanted to hear a song then in fashion which went: 'You'll be the first. Don't get flustered. The stronger the nerves, the nearer the goal'. Drinking parties frequently ended in shooting at fellow-customers, at mirrors, or in the air: the officers saw partisans, underground workers and Bolsheviks everywhere. The more they shouted about their strong nerves, the more clear it was that their nerves were giving way; and the goal was vanishing behind a fog of alcohol, hatred, fear and blood.

A few of the 'volunteers' were men who had been drawn into the thing by chance, innocent romantics or weak-willed creatures who had given in to their friends' persuasions or had been hypnotized by talk of 'loyalty', 'honour' and 'the oath'. Seryozha Efron, Marina Tsvetayeva's husband, was one of those.

I, too, met one of these 'lost souls' – a second lieutenant with a liking for Blok's poems. God alone knows how he happened to be in the White army. He saved my life, and it is a bitter thing for me to have to admit that I do not remember his name. It was between Mariupol and Feodosia. We were on board ship for a long time; first there was a fire; then the tiny vessel found itself in the ice-bound sea of Azov. There was no bread. People with typhus crawled along the ice. On one of the last nights, a huge officer in a cossack hat dragged me on to the icy deck. Everyone was asleep. The fellow was much stronger than I, but he had had too much to drink. We struggled. He kept repeating thickly: 'I'll baptize you in a minute', and pushing me towards the rails. I remember thinking: it's a good thing we're going to fall in together. Yadviga, who was travelling with us, heard the shouting and ran to the wardroom to find the second lieutenant whose name I have forgotten. He came up on deck at once: 'Stop or I fire!' On seeing the revolver, my 'godfather' slackened his embrace.

In Feodosia the same portraits were up, and General Shkuro smiled dashingly. I saw the well-scrubbed, clean-shaven English. Hungry children crowded round their field-kitchen: the Whites had forcibly evacuated a large group of railwaymen and their families, I cannot remember whether it was from Orel or from Kursk. These evacuees sheltered in pitiful shacks in Karantinnaya village. The English gazed despondently at the hungry, ragged people around them. They were only on the sidelines; they had been sent there as they might have been sent to Nairobi or Karachi; they were carrying out orders. They knew nothing, of course, about oil shares, or slit bellies, or the future fate of the children avidly sniffing the air: there was a smell of meat.

Voloshin received me kindly; I gave him an incoherent account of our travelling adventures. His eyes were friendly and remote as always. He started talking about Russia's destiny as the predictions of the prophet Ezekiel. His mother, whom everyone called Pra, came in and interrupted him: 'Max, that'll do! They're too hungry to listen to your stories'. And she produced a frying-pan full of potatoes.

13

MY DAUGHTER sometimes spends her holidays at Koktebel, sunbathing on the beach where there are many pretty pebbles, swimming, climbing. When she tells me about it afterwards I remember the distant past: it is difficult for me to imagine that Koktebel is a place where one can have a holiday. I, too, used to wander on the beach there, not collecting pebbles but pieces of wood washed up by the sea; I used these to burn in our stove, or *mangalka* as these stoves are called in the Crimea. Once I found a dead seagull which I gutted and boiled; it stank of rotten fish, but we ate it.

Soon after our arrival I swapped my ragged Parisian jacket for some firewood; it was a hard winter and an icy north-east wind was always blowing. I kept the stove going and we were not cold indoors. But I do not think I have ever experienced such constant, unremitting hunger as at Koktebel. Often I would make soup out of peppers.

We spent nine months at Koktebel, but looking back it seems like several long years. At first it was very cold, then very hot. Lyuba's mother had given her some of her brooches and rings. We sold them. Then there was nothing more to sell. To think of making any money by writing was silly. In the spring I had the idea of organizing a playground for the peasants' children; the Froebel ladies of Kiev had convinced me, it seems, of my pedagogical gifts.

There were Bulgarians living in the village, most of them kulaks. They did not think too highly of the Whites, who requisitioned foodstuffs and sometimes grabbed a pig or a barrel of wine without leaving any kind of receipt at all, but more than anything they feared the coming of the Bolsheviks. It is true that I found one Bulgarian family who helped the underground workers and hated the White Guards. They were the Stamovs. They enjoyed the respect of the other peasants and were considered honest and industrious, but when the conversation turned to politics no one listened to them. There also lived in the village a Russian tailor; he was another who waited for the arrival of the Red Army. His comments on the Whites' military communiqués were ironic: 'They've "occupied more favourable positions"

Boris Pasternak

Portrait of Lenin by N. Altman, 1920

Lenin: drawing by N. Altman, 1920

Vladimir Mayakovsky, 1924

Portrait of Valery Bryusov by Vrubel

Portrait of Meyerhold by Konchalovsky

near Uman, that means you couldn't see them for dust'. But this tailor was a 'foreigner' and was afraid, with justification, of being denounced.

The peasants wanted me to teach their children city manners, but I read them Chukovsky's *Crocodile*; at home, they recited 'urchins cocked snooks at him', which the parents did not like at all. I wanted to introduce the children to the arts, develop their imagination, tell them about Hans Andersen's nightingale. We decided to put on a play. There were no written parts. The little boy who took the part of the nightingale had to invent for himself how to delight the Chinese Emperor. At the end of the play the Emperor lay on his deathbed and his memories of good and bad deeds surrounded him. Some children repeated what they had heard at home: 'Do you remember how you stole the old woman's goose?' or 'Do you remember when you gave twenty gold roubles to that mandarin on his wedding day?' Others invented more complicated stories, some of which I wrote down. I remember one little girl who asked severely: 'Tell me, Emperor, do you remember when you invited that actress to come to China? She sang almost like a nightingale and you gave her a big medal and fed her on goldfish. And then she sang another song and you got angry. Why did you get angry, Emperor? She fell in love with a strange soldier. Was that so wicked? They searched the soldier's house and found a book. You said it was a bad book, and so they locked up the actress in a shed and asked her questions from morning till night, they gave her nothing to eat and beat her with Chinese rods, and she died very young. And now you want the nightingale to come back to you. No, Emperor, it'll never come back; it's got wings, you can't lock it up in a shed; when it flies away no one can catch it again.' We rehearsed the play for a long time. At last we fixed the date for the performance and invited the parents. After this the rumour spread round the village that I was a Red. Some of the parents forbade their children to come to the playground.

What proved fatal, however, was the modelling class. Here, too, I did not want to inhibit the children's imagination; they took home all kinds of strange beasts and people with huge heads; one little boy made a devil with horns. That was when the village priest stepped in. He went from house to house, saying: 'This man's a Jew and a Bolshevik, he wants to convert the children to the devil's faith'. The playground had to be closed down. It had lasted for three or four months. I do not know whether the children got anything out of it; I, at any rate, sometimes took home a bottle of milk or a few eggs. Payment was supposed to be in kind, but it was not laid down when or how much I was to be paid. Some parents gave nothing. The children turned up with their own food and I found it quite hard to watch them eat: I was afraid of betraying my own hunger. One little fellow, putting away large hunks of bread and bacon followed by cheese cake, announced: 'My Dad said not to give you anything'.

But now it had turned warm. I walked about barefooted, wearing a pair of pyjamas brought from Paris. Once I went into the village hoping to buy some milk or curds. I happened to go into a kulak's courtyard. He set the dog on me; it bit me in the calf. The bite did not matter, but the dog had torn my trouser-leg into shreds. I had to cut the other leg off as well. From then on I walked about in shorts. It may have made me look younger, I don't know; judging by photographs my appearance was rather frightening: I had lost a lot of weight. I skipped about with the children in a costume that Raymond Duncan – that lover of antique simplicity – might have envied. But, when all is said and done, is there any limit to the things a man may have to do, particularly in times known as historic?

Sometimes I would escape for an hour or two into the hills. The country round Koktebel has a beauty that is not easy for the human eye, like Aragon or Old Castile: purplish or rust-coloured slopes, not a house nor a tree anywhere, a rough model of the cruel world that once inspired El Greco. It may be, however, that Koktebel appeared to me in that light because of the things happening all about me.

When I first re-entered Voloshin's workroom I was reminded of Paris: the same Princess Tayah, the same shelves laden with books, French ones by preference. Max was rather subdued; his former frivolity had vanished; even so, he often played the fool and mystified us all; it was funny, but I did not laugh. Sometimes we had long talks which were like continuations of those in Rivera's studio or at the Rotonde. The reason why we talked was not, however, that the subjects which had excited us five years earlier were still live issues to us, but that we wanted to escape into the past for a few hours.

Maya Kudasheva was living in Voloshin's house with her French mother. Her father was Russian and she had been born in Russia, but she rolled her 'r's' like a Parisian and wrote poetry in French. This is how Voloshin described her appearance: 'Your forehead is covered by a cascade of straight, shining hair, a radiance rises like a whirlwind above your head. Your childlike glance is narrowed by a smile, your mouth is narrowed by unchildlike sadness, and sweat stands on your brow like a chain of small pearls'. In Moscow, where Maya had come from, she had moved in literary circles; she had known Vyacheslav Ivanov and Andrey Bely and had been a friend of Tsvetayeva. Her mother was dispirited by the events which would not conform with her ideas of decent behaviour or with Rostand's plays. But Maya, despite the cold, the hunger and all the other troubles, lived her own life. This is what happened to her afterwards: she began exchanging letters with Romain Rolland, went to Switzerland to join him and became his wife. A few years ago we met again in Paris. Maria Pavlovna – that is, Maya – was busy organizing the Rolland museum, and asked me to help by sending some Russian exhibits. We did not mention Koktebel, although there were many things we might have recalled together.

Here is what the author Veresayev wrote about the three years he spent at Koktebel: 'During that period the Crimea changed hands several times and we went through many hardships; six times I was robbed; for half an hour, ill and with a temperature of 104 degrees, I lay with the revolver of a drunken Red Army man pointing at me (he was shot two days later); I was arrested by the Whites; I had scurvy.' At the beginning of 1920 Veresayev went through a particularly difficult time. His medical practice helped a little. He told me, laughing, that at first the peasants did not believe he was a doctor: someone had told them that he wrote books. Typhus was raging in the nearby villages. Once, after examining a patient, Veresayev calculated when the crisis must occur; the temperature went down at the time he had predicted, and the peasants were convinced. They paid him in eggs and lard. He had a bicycle, but his clothes were completely worn out. I owned a queer object, Dr Kozintsev's nightshirt which he had given to me in Kiev. We presented Veresayev with this garment and in it he made his rounds on his bicycle.

When Lyuba contracted typhus, Veresayev often came to see her and I had many long talks with him. I had read some of his books and thought he was a man of simple commonsense; in reality, he adored the arts, translated the ancient Greek poets, and was caused torments by everything primitive and coarse. In the struggle against the White Guards all his sympathies were naturally on the side of Moscow, but there was much he could not understand or accept. Later I read his novel *The Deadlock* where he describes the life of the Russian intelligentsia during the early years of the Revolution. I recognized Veresayev's own thoughts expressed now by the democratically-minded scholar, now by his Bolshevik daughter. Veresayev was seven years younger than Chekhov but he must, of course, be regarded as belonging to the same generation. In a way, his character, too, was reminiscent of Chekhov's: he was indulgent towards other men's weaknesses, made a cult of goodness and was filled with a calm and constant sadness caused not so much by circumstances as by his profound knowledge of human beings. In the novel Katya says bitterly to her father, an old Russian intellectual: 'My dear beloved one, your honesty, your nobility, your love of the people, none, none of that is needed by anyone'. Many young people argued like that in 1920. In 1960, their children and grandchildren have realized that they desperately need the honesty, the nobility and the love of the people which once inspired Chekhov and his kindred spirits.

I shall speak about Osip Mandelstam in the next chapter. With him came his brother, Alexander Emilyevich, a kindly and entirely realistic person, who more than once helped his brother and us. The literary scholar D. D. Blagoy and his wife, a doctor, also lived at Koktebel. Andrey Sobol's wife, Rakhil Saulovna, was a doctor too; she was nursing her year-old son, Mark. (In 1949 the poet Mark Sobol gave me a book of mine in which Andrey Sobol had written his name, and Mark wrote a poem ending 'A quarter of century has passed, and the son writes words of love under the father's signature'.)

Typhus is a foul disease at the best of times, and under 1920 conditions it was no easy thing to nurse a patient through it. Yadviga helped me to look after Lyuba, but she herself was a frail girl of twenty. The patient took a turn for the worse. The doctor wanted to inject camphor, but there was no syringe. Alexander Emilyevich rode on horseback to Feodosia, obtained a syringe with difficulty, and broke it while hurrying home; he had to go to the town a second time. Surgical spirit was also needed. I called at the houses where my pupils lived asking for vodka and was told that the Whites had drunk it all. At one house a wedding was being celebrated; seeing large bottles on the table I rejoiced, but the master of the house said: 'If you want a drink, sit down and we'll pour you one, but there's none for taking away'. Veresayev told me to keep checking Lyuba's pulse. One night the pulse disappeared. Unfortunately Veresayev had gone off to another village. I ran to consult Blagoy's wife and Sobol's; they were very nervous and said that Lyuba's condition was hopeless and it was useless tormenting her; still, I made them inject her with strychnine.

After Lyuba's temperature had gone down, a complication arose: she was convinced that she had died and that we were for some reason forcing a life after death upon her. With the greatest difficulty I got food for her and cooked it, my mouth watering, while she repeated: 'Why should I eat? I'm dead, aren't I?' One can easily imagine the effect this had on me; yet I had to go to the playground and play ring-a-ring-o'-roses with the children.

Then we got hold of some sheep-shears which Veresayev used to crop Lyuba's hair. Fortunately, Voloshin began dropping in at our little house about this time, and he adored sophisticated talk. Lyuba said that she saw everything as through a wall; Max liked this very much. Mandelstam used to take off Symbolist conversations: 'Well, how are you, Ivan Ivanovich? Not too bad, thank you, Pyotr Petrovich, I am living in anticipation of death'. Despite the tragedy of the situation, Max could not shake off his love of everything other-wordly. He genuinely enjoyed his talks with Lyuba; meanwhile I wondered what would happen to me: would I go out of my mind, catch typhus or survive in the teeth of everything? Slim, dark-skinned Yadviga, who looked like the heroine of an Italian Neo-Realist film, washed bed-linen from morning till night.

I have said that I had people to talk to: Veresayev, Voloshin, Mandelstam. But the chief conversation partner that attended me from the day of my arrival at Koktebel was the sphinx who had set me those riddles to solve in Moscow, and who was still without an answer. The winter nights were long. Lyuba slept. The furious sea blustered under the windows. I sat and thought. I was beginning to understand many things; this, as it turned out, was not easy. Behind me lay poetry, faith and lack of faith, and I had to reconcile the rose glow of Florence, the fierce sermons of Léon Bloy and the prophecies of Modigliani with all that I had seen.

The chief thing was to understand the meaning of the passions and sufferings of people in what we call 'history', to convince myself that what was going on was not a terrible bloody riot, a gigantic Pugachev rebellion, but the birth of a new world with new concepts of human values: in other words, to step out of the nineteenth century – in which, without knowing it, I still continued to live – into the dark ante-room of a new age. I realized that the old world which I had exposed in my *Poems about the Eves* could not be changed by ancient spells nor by ultra-modern art. Of course I remained myself; I was frightened by the senseless sacrifices, by the ferocity with which human beings were treated and by the oversimplification of the complex world of the emotions; but I realized that my feelings were debatable: 'Born yesterday, I am addicted to yesterday's wisdom'.

I wrote a small book called *Reflections*, and I should like to quote a few lines from a poem dated January 1920. The verse is weak, but the poem expressed my thoughts, not only during that winter but also during the years that followed. 'You are swollen with hunger, blood seeps from your open wounds, and sorrowfully you are huddled on Mother Earth. O Russia, they have mistaken your childbed fever for the death agony; they spurn you, they who are well-fed and clean. Their womb is without fruit, their breasts are turning to stone. Who shall grasp the ancient inheritance? Who shall re-kindle and carry forward the half-extinguished torch of Prometheus? The birth is hard. The hour is great and terrible. Not in the foam of the sea, not in the sky's azure, but on a festering bed, washed with our blood, a great new age is born. For a short time a people is called to quench with its blood the earth's thirsty furrows. Your persecutors will come to you, Motherland, kissing the bloody traces in the snow.' The deliberately bookish language – festering bed, womb, furrows – now makes me wince. It is curious that after *Poems about the Eves* and after my enthusiasm for Cubism I should have strayed into the vocabulary of the Symbolists. However, the new-style vocabulary was no better; had I used it, I should have had to declare that I was 'adopting the Soviet platform'. What 'platform' could I possibly have adopted? Only the children's playground – and even that was closed down quite quickly.

Our life at Koktebel was by no means calm; soldiers and security men kept coming from Feodosia in search of underground workers, partisans, 'troublemakers'. Mandelstam was arrested. He was soon released again, but it was a toss-up – he might have been shot. Once they searched Voloshin's house. I looked up and down the road nervously. Many times in my life I have felt like hunter's prey, an ear cocked listening for footsteps on the staircase, or the sound of the lift coming up. It is a vile, humiliating feeling. But I comforted myself with the fact that I am, by nature, not a hunter, and have never myself stalked or arrested anyone.

Sometimes, at night, the characters of *Jurenito* haunted me; it was as though they were knocking at the door of the unwritten book; but I had not thought of sitting down to write a novel (I might add, to round off the joke, that I did not even have the paper for it; I wrote my poems on the backs of old bills). I was thinking of something else: how to get back to Moscow. It seemed as though the war would never end; Kolchak had been defeated, but now the Poles had launched their campaign. Once, in Feodosia, I found a few copies of some Paris newspapers. From these I learned that the right wing had been successful in the French elections, that the Allies would never abandon their bridgeheads in Russia, and that they were defending the 'free world'. (Phrases have a longer life than governments.) It is true that I saw many foreign officers in Feodosia. The port was very busy: guns and war material were being unloaded.

I rarely went to Feodosia; it was not easy to find a peasant who would, for a very modest payment, give a man a lift in his cart (made of four logs which kept slipping apart all the time); besides, I did not feel like tempting providence and the security service. The town was handsome and reminded me of Italy, possibly because of its arcades or the tiers of houses on the hillside; but life in Feodosia was bad. In its streets no one behaved normally; some shouted orders, others cringed.

Osip Mandelstam had many friends in Feodosia: liberal lawyers, Jewish businessmen, lovers of literature, young poets, port officials. He introduced me to a few; among them were some attractive people, but I had the impression that they were slightly nervous about meeting us.

The Mandelstams left, assisted, if I remember rightly, by the harbourmaster. I pestered Voloshin and my acquaintances in Feodosia with requests to help us to get away. At last Max said: 'I think there's a chance'. A long chapter – not of a book, but of my life – was coming to an end.

14

I HAVE already said that when Wrangel's men arrested Osip Mandelstam, Voloshin went off to Feodosia at once. He came back dispirited, saying that the Whites regarded Mandelstam as a dangerous criminal and swore that he was pretending to be mad: locked up in a cell, he began banging on the door, and when the warder came to find out what was wrong, Mandelstam said: 'You've got to let me out, I wasn't made for prison'. During his interrogation, he interrupted the investigator, saying: 'But please tell me, do you release innocent people or not?' I can see that to the counter-intelligence in 1919 such words had a fantastic ring and that a White officer may have taken them for feigned insanity; but if we think further and forget about tactics and even about strategy, was there not a profound human truth in Mandelstam's behaviour? He did not try to prove his innocence to the hangman, but asked frankly whether it was worth his while to speak at all; he told the warder that he was 'not made for prison'; this is childish and at the same time wise. 'It's out of step with the times,' Pra remarked sadly. Of course it was. Mandelstam wrote a poem about the times: 'The age like a wolf-hound leaps at my shoulders, but I am no wolf in my blood; push me rather, like a cap, up the sleeve of the warm fur-coat of the Siberian steppe'.

I met Mandelstam in Moscow; later we often met in Kiev, at the Greek café in Sofiyskaya. There he read me his poem on the Revolution. 'You are rising in the dark years, O sun, O people – judge.' I saw him on the day the Red Army was evacuating Kiev. (He described it later: 'Gipsy girls no longer tell the fortune of beautiful women, violins play no longer in Kupechesky Gardens, the horses have fallen in Kreshchatik, the gentry's Lipki smells of death. Red Army men were leaving the town with the last tram and a damp greatcoat shouted: "We're coming back, make no mistake about it!" ') Together we lived through the night of the pogrom. Together we suffered the wretchedness of Koktebel. Together we made our way from Tbilisi to Moscow. In the summer of 1934 I searched for him in Voronezh ('Let me go, give me back, Voronezh, you'll drop me or spill me, you'll let me fall or return me, Voronezh folly, Voronezh raven, Voronezh knife'). I saw him for the last time in Moscow in the spring of 1938.

We were born in the same year 1891; he was two weeks older than I. Often, listening to his poems, I felt that he was many years the older and the wiser. But in daily life he seemed to me a child, given to tantrums, quick to take offence, jumpy. 'How insufferable,' I would think for a brief moment, and immediately add: 'how terribly nice he is!' The unstable exterior concealed kindness, humanity, inspiration.

He was small and frail; he used to throw back his head with its little quiff of hair. He liked the image of the cock tearing apart the night with its song under the walls of the Acropolis; and, when he began to chant his solemn odes in that deep little voice of his, he was like a young cockerel himself.

He would sit on the edge of his chair and suddenly rush off; he dreamt of good dinners, made fantastic schemes, worked spells on editors. Once in Feodosia he gathered some rich 'liberals' and told them severely: 'At the Last Judgment you'll be asked whether you understood the poet Mandelstam, and you'll say no. You'll be asked whether you gave him to eat, and if you answer yes, much shall be forgiven you'. At the most tragic moments he would make us laugh with the rhymes he made up. 'Why d'you keep blowing that horn, young man? It were better you hadn't been born, young man.'

People who met Mandelstam for the first time in an editor's office or a café thought him the most frivolous of men, incapable of taking thought even for a moment. But Mandelstam knew how to work. He made up poetry, not at his desk but in the streets of Moscow and Leningrad, in the steppe, in the mountains of the Crimea, in Georgia and Armenia. He said of Dante: 'How many heels, how many ox-hide soles, how many sandals Alighieri wore out in the course of his poetic labour, treading the goat-paths of Italy'. These words apply to Mandelstam himself better than to anyone else. His poems were born out of a line, a single word; he altered everything hundreds of times: sometimes a poem which was clear at first would become more complex, almost unintelligible; sometimes, on the contrary, it would gain clarity. His gestation period for an eight-line poem was a long one – sometimes it took months – and he was always overwhelmed by the birth of a poem.

During the first years of the Revolution his vocabulary and his classic verse were regarded by many as archaisms: 'I have studied the science of parting on plaintive, bare-headed nights . . .' These lines seem entirely contemporary to me today, whilst Burlyuk's poems read like a tribute to a long-forgotten fashion. Mandelstam said: 'The ideal of perfect courage has been laid down by the style and practical demands of our epoch. Everything has become heavier and vaster'. That was not a canon nor a direction: 'There is no point in creating new schools. There is no point in inventing new poetics'. Later, Mandelstam's poetry liberated itself and became lighter, more transparent.

Some poets react to the world through the ear, others through the eye. Blok heard; Mayakovsky saw. Mandelstam lived in different elements. Remembering his childhood years, he wrote: 'I fell in love with Tchaikovsky at this time, with a painful nervous intensity like the desire of Dostoyevsky's Netochka Nezvanova to hear a violin concerto behind the scarlet flame of silken curtains. I caught the broad, measured, purely violin passages in Tchaikovsky from behind a thorny hedge, and more than once tore my clothes and scratched my hands scrambling through to the orchestra pit without paying.' A few lines on a still-life suffice to give an idea of his feeling for visual art (one recalls Konchalovsky's works): 'The artist has shown us the deep swoon of lilac, and has laid sonorous steps of colour like scabs on the canvas. One guesses at a swing, the veils are incompletely painted, and the bumble-bee has already taken over in this twilit scene of decay'. We often talked about painting; in the twenties, the artists who appealed to him most were the old Venetians, Tintoretto and Titian.

He had a good knowledge of French, Italian and German poetry; he could see countries where he had never been. 'I beg as I would for pity and mercy, France, for your soil and your honeysuckle, for the truth of your little doves and the untruth of your dwarf vine-tenders in their lint partitions. In a light December your cropped air grows frosty with money and injury.' I have lived in France many years; it is impossible to say anything better or more precise than this. Mandelstam's reflections on the wonderful 'childlikeness' of Italian phonetics astonished the Italians to whom I translated lines from the 'Conversation on Dante'.

But his greatest passion was the Russian language and Russian poetry. 'Because of a whole series of historical circumstances, the living forces of Hellenic culture, having abandoned the West to Latin influences and lingering but a short time in childless Byzantium, betook themselves into the lap of Russian speech, communicating to it the original secret of the Hellenistic view of the world, the secret of free incarnation, and that is precisely why the Russian language has become ringing and burning flesh.' He rejected Symbolism as a phenomenon foreign to Russian poetry. 'Balmont, the most un-Russian of poets, a foreign translator . . . foreign representative of a non-existent phonetic power . . .' Andrey Bely, for example, was to him an 'unhealthy and negative phenomenon in the life of the Russian language'. (Yet Mandelstam loved and respected Bely; after his death he wrote several wonderful poems. 'They crowned you with a tiara – the holy idiot's tall cap – turquoise teacher, tormentor, master, fool . . . Like snow over Moscow you started up a shindy, popinjay, obscure, understandable, unclear, intricate and light. Gatherer of space, fledgling with all your exams behind you, inventor of stories, young goldfinch, little student, student, tinkling bell.') He wrote with tender affection of the poets of Pushkin's galaxy as also of Blok and his own contemporaries, of the River Kama, the steppe, of hot, dry Armenia and of his native Leningrad. I remember many of his lines, I repeat them like incantations, and, looking back, I am happy that I once lived by his side.

I have mentioned the contradiction between Mandelstam's frivolity in everyday life and his seriousness in art. But perhaps there was no contradiction. At nineteen he wrote an article on François Villon in which he found a justification for the disreputable life of the poet of the cruel age: the 'poor scholar' defended the poet's dignity in his own way. This is how Mandelstam wrote of Dante: 'That which for us was the irreproachable hood and the so-called eagle profile was, from within, an awkwardness painfully overcome, a purely Pushkinesque struggle of the young courtier in revolt for the social dignity and public position of the poet'. Again, these words apply to Mandelstam himself: many apparently senseless, sometimes ridiculous actions were dictated by an 'awkwardness painfully overcome'.

Some critics thought him un-modern, a museum artist. There were worse charges, too. Before me is a volume of the *Literary Encyclopedia* published in 1932, which says: 'Mandelstam's work is the artistic expression of the consciousness of the big bourgeoisie during the period between two revolutions . . . Mandelstam's view of the world is characterized by extreme fatalism and the coldness of an inner indifference to all current happenings . . . This is nothing but a highly "sublimated" and coded ideological perpetuation of capitalism and its culture'. (The article was written by a young critic who came running to see me many times, enthusiastically showed me unpublished poems by Mandelstam, copied Mandelstam's works, had them bound and gave them to his friends.) It would be difficult to say anything more absurd about Mandelstam's poetry. Of all poets he was the one who least expressed the consciousness of the bourgeoisie, whether big, middle or petty. I have already described how, in 1918, his profound understanding of the grandeur of what was taking place astonished me: I mean the poem about the ship of time changing course. He never turned away from his century, even when the wolf-hound took him for what he was not. 'It's time you knew it: I, too, am a contemporary. I am a man of the Moskvoshvey[1] age. See how the shoulders of my coat bristle! See how I talk and how I walk! Try and tear me away from my century: I guarantee you'll break your neck over it.' Here is Mandelstam on the true nature of the age: 'The sonorous valour of years to come, the lofty breed of men . . .' On Leningrad: 'I have come back to my city familiar to the point of tears, to the hollow of my veins, to the swollen glands of childhood. You have come back: then swallow quickly the cod-liver oil of Leningrad's riverside lamps . . . Petersburg, I do not want to die yet; you have the numbers of my telephones, Petersburg, I still have the addresses where I shall find the voices of the dead . . .' This poem was published in the *Literary Gazette* in 1932. In 1945 I heard these lines spoken by a Leningrad woman who had come home.

Mandelstam deserves no reproach. Unless it be that both the weakness and the strength of any man is in his love of life. 'I'll give anything for life – I so need to be cared for – a sulphur match could warm me.' 'Eyelashes prickle, a tear boils up in the breast. I sense without fear that there'll be, there'll be a storm. Someone uncanny is hurrying me to forget something. It's stifling, and yet I am dying to live.'

In whose way can he have stood, this poet with a sickly body and verses so musical that they could people the night? An agronomist from Bryansk, V. Merkulov, came to see me at the beginning of 1952. He told me how, in 1940, Osip Mandelstam died ten thousand kilometres from his native city; already ill, he would read the sonnets of

[1] Moscow Clothing Trust.

108

Petrarch by the camp-fire. Yes, he was afraid to drink a glass of water that had not been boiled, but there was within him a true fortitude which stayed with him all his life, all the way to the sonnets by the camp-fire.

He wrote in 1936: 'Not as a mealy white butterfly shall I return my borrowed dust to the earth: I want this thinking body to be transformed into a street, a country; the vertebrate, charred body conscious of its own length'. His poems have remained, I hear them, others hear them; we are walking along a street where children play. That, I suppose, is what in solemn moments we term 'immortality'.

But in my memory there is the living Osip Mandelstam, the dear restless fidget. We embraced thrice when he came to say goodbye: he was leaving Koktebel at last. I quoted to myself: 'Who can tell, when the word "parting" is spoken, what kind of separation is before us . . .?'

15

THE salt lakes in the northern part of the Crimea serve as a source of common salt, and have done so since before the Revolution. I must have been taught this fact in my third or fourth year at school, but school knowledge is quickly forgotten. Besides, I was never interested in the origins of the salt I found on my table. Now, however, salt – Crimean salt – was to play an important part in my life.

At that time, the way from Feodosia to Moscow lay through Menshevik Georgia, which traded with White Crimea and where there was a Soviet embassy. Common salt, a valuable commodity, was sent to Georgia from Feodosia. When I say 'valuable' I am not joking in the least: salt was being sold in the markets by the glassful, as sugar was to be sold later.

A certain enterprising Feodosian decided to transport some salt to Poti. A big old barge was loaded with the stuff. The owner of the salt was to travel in the tug. After long and complicated negotiations, in the course of which my patrons spoke both of poetry and of roubles, the captain of the tug and the owner of the salt agreed to let me, Lyuba and Yadviga travel in the barge. Naturally the Whites examined all outgoing vessels, and we were told to get on the barge the day before and stay quietly in the airless hold – where the precious salt lay – until we were in the open sea. This was not the most pleasant spot to be in, but we were given bread and tomatoes (there was no shortage of salt to go with them) and did not grumble.

There were a few unpleasant moments when the boots of officers who had come to check whether the barge was carrying any passengers clattered overhead. I remembered Voloshin's line: 'To harden like salt . . .' and, I think, hardened into total immobility. The steps died away like a passing storm.

The tug took a southward course, as though we were going towards the Turkish coast. The reason was that Novorossisk was held by the Soviets and the owner of the salt was afraid that the Bolsheviks might seize his cargo. But the barge was meant only for short journeys along the coast; besides, as I have already said, its age was hardly suited for adventures.

It was the end of September, that is to say a season when storms frequently occur in the Black Sea. For a few hours our journey was idyllic: the sun shone, the white-crested waves were small and the barge rocked gently and lazily from side to side. We were happy to have got away from the Crimea, and ate bread and salt. The storm broke suddenly; when a high wave swamped the deck, we could not understand what had happened. We lay down in the most protected place we could find and covered ourselves with a tarpaulin. The storm grew stronger; a quick, southern night fell suddenly.

On the barge there were three or four sailors. They told us things were bad: we were far from the coast, water had got into the hold and the cargo had become too heavy. They cursed the captain of the tug, the owner of the salt, the Whites, the Reds, the Georgians and everything else.

We tried to sleep but it was impossible; despite the tarpaulin, we were constantly getting soaked; although, according to the crew, the barge was overloaded, the storm tossed it about like a tiny rowing boat. Meanwhile the waves grew taller. I did my best to remember all kinds of funny stories and our spirits remained high.

The worst, however, was still to come. The captain of the tug decided to abandon the barge, fearing that it might ram and smash the tug. This information was shouted to us through a megaphone, together with the suggestion that we should make our way to the tug hand-over-hand along the towing cable. We were not athletes but people who had grown very thin on a diet of pepper soup; Lyuba had had typhus not long before and so, naturally, we could not climb along the cable and decided to stay on the barge whatever happened.

I have noticed many times in the course of my life that fear is an unaccountable emotion, often quite dissociated from reason. My friend the writer O. G. Savich used to talk perfectly calmly about poetry under frightful bombardments in Spain, yet when we were travelling together from Belgium to France, I remember that he was terrified of the customs, although he was not carrying any contraband. I was in Toledo with the Spanish painter Fernando Gerassi who was at that time an officer and whose courage had often impressed other people. The Alcazar of Toledo was then held by the fascists, who used to fire at the anarchists indolently, from time to time, for the sake of form.

Fernando confessed to me that he did not like the idea of climbing on to the roof of the house with me; he was afraid; the front was one thing, but he had come to Toledo simply to keep me company, and here he was frightened. As for me, I did not experience any fear at the front, in Spain or during air-raids, but only in times of peace, waiting for a ring or a knock at the door, as I have already said. Neither I nor the two girls were in the least afraid at the thought that we should be abandoned on a leaking barge in the midst of a raging sea and would certainly sink together with the precious salt. We chatted and joked, and if we shivered it was not out of fear but because we had been soaked to the skin and were very cold.

In the end the captain did not abandon the barge. When we came alongside safely by the quay at Sukhumi, he told Lyuba that he had felt too sorry for her. I took that as an Oriental compliment. The owner of the salt was in the tug and he made sure that his goods were not lost.

Sukhumi appeared to us inexpressibly beautiful. It is indeed a fine town, but to us it was not just a matter of picturesqueness: on that bright, sunny morning we felt that life had been restored to us. It seemed to us as though all difficulties – not merely of the journey to Moscow, but of our entire lives – now lay behind. A Georgian offered to change our money, and presently we were sitting in a café by the side of the road, drinking coffee. Loud-voiced men with moustaches smiled at us. Warm golden grapes were hawked. It was hot, and we thought neither of the price of salt nor of the price of human life. We were having a good time. The combined ages of the three of us were less than my age today.

That night we slept on the barge again, but it was an ordinary quiet night: we were sailing along the coast to Poti. Then we took the train to Tbilisi. Where to go? Where was the embassy? Where Moscow? We felt a little confused in the strange city, without papers or money.

Occasionally those lucky accidents on which writers rely to provide a happy solution to a hopeless situation do occur in real life. Walking towards us along Golovinsky Prospect was Osip Mandelstam. We were delighted to see him, he was delighted to see us. He had already found his feet in Tbilisi, and announced in a business-like manner: 'Come along, we're going to see Tizian Tabidze, he'll take us to a marvellous tavern'.

16

MANDELSTAM told us about his misadventures. At Batumi there was a plague scare, and the quarter where he and his brother had rented a room was cordoned off. Mandelstam wondered whether he would die romantically of the plague or vulgarly of starvation. His speculations were interrupted by the Menshevik secret police, who took him off to prison. He tried in vain to explain once more that he was not made for prison life; this made no impression at all. He said that he was Osip Mandelstam, the author of a book called *Stone*, in answer to which he was told that he was an agent both of General Wrangel and of the Bolsheviks. A glance at Mandelstam was enough to show how very unlike an agent – even an ordinary agent, let alone a double one – he was. The secret police, however, had no time for thought; they were fulfilling, and possibly overfulfilling, a plan. (The author of even the silliest thriller takes care to ensure some degree of verisimilitude, but policemen never bother their heads, preferring to smash other people's.) Some Georgian poets arrived in Batumi by chance and happened to read in the paper that 'the double agent Osip Mandelstam' was passing himself off as a poet. They obtained his release.

Having told us this story, Mandelstam did not proceed to philosophize over the peculiarities of the age but led us off to see Tizian Tabidze, who exclaimed enthusiastically, embraced everybody, recited some poetry and then ran off to fetch his friend Paolo Yashvili. When we saw on the tavern table various dishes whose very existence we had forgotten, we were transfixed.

I had met Paolo Yashvili in Paris, at the Rotonde, in 1914. He was then a thin, impetuous youth of twenty, who kept asking me: 'Which was Verlaine's café? When will Picasso come? Is it true you do your writing in a café? I couldn't. Look at those two kissing over there! Shocking! It inspires me too much'. Meeting Paolo again I was as happy to see him as a soldier is to encounter a regimental comrade, even though our meeting in Paris had been casual and brief.

No sooner had we sat down then Tizian and Paolo explained to us that they were the founders of a poetic order called the Blue Horn.

I did not think this could have anything to do with the meal we were about to have; after all, there was the journal called the Blue Rider and exhibitions of the Blue Rose. The tavern keeper, however, brought along several enormous drinking horns. Into the one Paolo passed to me he poured a quart of wine. A drinking horn is not a tumbler – you cannot put it down on the table – and so, after holding it for a few moments, I drank the lot in desperation. Bearing in mind how little I had had to eat at Koktebel, you can easily imagine how all this ended for me. For some reason our Georgian friends dragged us off to a concert given by some famous virtuoso. I vaguely remember lying on the floor in one of the rooms of the Tbilisi Conservatoire, amidst harps and ribbons off festive wreaths.

The next morning I went with Mandelstam to the Soviet embassy. We were kindly received and promised transport to Russia; however, we should have to wait a week or two.

Paolo found us accommodation in a shabby old hotel. There was an acute shortage of rooms, and all of us – the Mandelstam brothers, Lyuba, Yadviga and I – had to sleep in one hotel room. Osip Mandelstam refused to sleep in the bed for fear of bedbugs and microbes, and slept on a high-legged table instead. At dawn I could see his profile above me; he slept on his back, and slept solemnly.

We spent two weeks in Tbilisi; they seemed to me a lyrical intermezzo.

We had lunch every day; more than that, we had dinner every day. Neither Paolo nor Tizian had any money, but they entertained us in the luxurious style of medieval princes, choosing the most famous taverns and pressing the most exquisite dishes upon us. Sometimes we would go from one tavern straight to another: lunch merged into dinner. The names of Georgian dishes sounded like lines of poetry: *sulguni, sotskhali, satsivi, lobi*. We ate trout, highly-seasoned soups, hot cheese, nut and rhubarb sauce, chicken livers and pigs' navels on a spit, not to mention every conceivable kind of *shashlyk*. At Persian eating places we were served pilau and lamb baked in earthenware dishes. We compared the quality of Teliani and Kvareli wines.

I had never been East before, and old Tbilisi seemed to me like a town out of the Arabian Nights. We walked through the unending Maidan, where turquoise in resin, hot pancakes, English coats, daggers, hookahs, gramophones, fragrant herbs, rifles, portraits of Queen

Tamara, dollars, old manuscripts and underpants were sold. The stall-keepers touted, haggled, lavished flowery compliments and swore on the lives of innumerable members of their families.

We went to the sulphur baths; an enormous bath attendant climbed on my back and smeared me all over with miracle-working mud, which destroyed all the vegetation on my body; Paolo assured me in dead earnest that I now resembled Narcissus.

We sipped wine in the Verii Gardens; the impatient Kura river played with red and yellow lights down below, while *tarkhun* and *kindza* gave off delicious smells on the table.

In the ancient temples we gazed at stone queens fondling snow leopards. Inside taverns we admired the paintings of Pirosmanishvili, the Georgian douanier Rousseau, a self-taught artist who decorated the walls of cellars in exchange for *shashlyks* and wine. He was simple and poignant; the skill of his compositions and the richness of his colours were astounding.

Tbilisi was a station at which the train of time had halted by chance for an instant. Noah Jordania, the head of the Menshevik government, in the past a contributor to various Marxist journals, invoked Kautsky one moment and Queen Tamara the next. Kautsky wrote that Menshevik Georgia was a State with a future, but the people from Petrograd and Moscow who had got held up at the 'station' packed their bags hastily: some were in a hurry to go North, others to go abroad. I met some of them. The actor N. N. Khodotov was hoping to go home to Petrograd. The poets Agnivtsev and Rafalovich waited for French visas. The inhabitants of Tbilisi spoke badly of the Mensheviks and said that their days were numbered.

Different centuries co-existed in that wonderful town. I saw 'Shakse-Vaksey', the festival of the Shiite Muslims. Faceless Persian women were carried on litters decorated with flowery carpets. Young men darted about, and riders in costume slashed them mercilessly with whips. These were followed by hundreds of half-naked men flagellating themselves with iron chains. There was a blare of music. The principal actors were men in loose white gowns who, swaying, shouted 'Shakse-Vaksey!' and struck themselves in the face with sabres. In the bright sun the blood looked like red paint. The self-torture was inflicted in commemoration of Husain, a Caliph's son killed in battle four hundred years previously.

Meanwhile, in the next street, industrial craftsmen read leaflets:

'The red banner of Soviet power has been hoisted over Baku. Any day now it will unfurl above Tbilisi'.

I was given a *Collection of Poems from the Tbilisi Poets' Workshop.* By chance, I still have this book. Among the authors there were many poetesses with poetic names: Nina Grazianskaya, Bel-Kon-Lyubomirskaya, Magdalina de Kaprelevich. The poets of the 'Tbilisi Workshop' wrote poems about Svarog, Eros, the Shulamite, Montfort and other personages equally close to the events of the day.

I must admit that I never opened the *Collection* at the time: I was spending every hour with my new friends Paolo Yashvili and Tizian Tabidze whom I learned to love at once.

They were bound together not only by poetic ideas held in common but also by a firm friendship, which proved more lasting than any poetic school. They also lost their lives together. Yet they were extraordinarily unlike each other. Paolo was tall and full of passion, extremely energetic, good at organizing things, whether a declaration by the Blue Horn or dining out. His poems were lively, intelligent and solidly constructed. Tizians's outstanding quality, on the other hand, was his gentle dreaminess. He was handsome and always wore a red carnation in his buttonhole; he recited poetry in a singsong voice and his eyes were as blue as mountain lakes. It is difficult to understand poetry in translation. I used to listen to the poems in Georgian as well as Russian. I remember Tizian telling me that poetry was an avalanche. Many years later I read, in translation, a poem of his containing the lines: 'I do not write my poems. Like a story, they write me, and the course of life accompanies them. What is a poem? A snowy avalanche. It breathes, and you are blown off your feet and buried alive. That's what a poem is'. In these lines, I believe, is the clue to Tizian, to his purity and his exaltation; he was a poet above all else.

Yashvili and Tabidze knew and loved Russian and French poetry, Pushkin and Baudelaire, Blok and Verlaine, Nekrasov and Rimbaud, Mayakovsky and Apollinaire. They smashed the old forms of Georgian versification. But it would be difficult, I think, to find two other poets who loved their country as much as they did. One could give them intense pleasure by saying that some Georgian word was expressive, or by remarking on a mountain flower or on the smile of a girl in Rustaveli Prospect. Any reference book today will tell you that they were very good poets. I should like to add that they were also real

116

people. I visited Tbilisi again in 1926; I came to see Tizian and Paolo. Later I saw them in Moscow: our friendship had stood the test of time.

At the end of 1937 I arrived in Tbilisi straight from Spain – from the area of Teruel – to attend the Rustaveli eighth centenary celebrations. Paolo and Tizian were not there. Let me tell what happened to them in the words of Guram Asatiani, the author of a book on Tizian Tabidze. 'Like his remarkable contemporaries, the well-known Soviet writers P. Yashvili, M. Dzhavakhishvili, N. Mitsishvili and others, Tabidze fell a victim to the criminal hands of inveterate enemies of the people.' I found in Tbilisi only the poet G. Leonidze whom I had met in 1926. He invited me to his house on New Year's Eve. Suddenly the toasts broke off: we raised our glasses and said nothing; Tizian and Paolo were before us. I often think of Yashvili's poems written several years before the tragic dénouement: 'Do not fear gossip. Silence is worse, when, seeping in furtively from the streets, it frightens like impending war and the nearness of the bullet meant for me'.

Many Russian poets loved Tizian and Paolo: Yesenin, Pasternak, Tikhonov, Zabolotsky, Antokolsky. But we were the first Soviet poets who found in Tbilisi not only spiritual rest but also a romantic experience, a sense of elation, a whiff of oxygen: I speak of both the mountains and the people, for it is impossible to separate Paolo and Tizian from the landscape surrounding them. After my voyage to Georgia in 1926 I wrote: 'Let us agree on this: mountains are not only the alpinist's asthma, not only the oh's! and ah's! of admirers of holiday beauty on return to the family circle. They are also a certain unrest of nature, its exigency, which profoundly corresponds to human nature. The beasts and vines of Ananur Monastery play, grow and live. Shepherds and stars gaze lovingly upon them. The *zurna*[1] weeps in the Verii Gardens like a beloved woman whose voice it is impossible not to recognize even after a thousand years. Let the poets of the Blue Horn admire Rimbaud and Lautréamont: ingenuous spirits recite their poems to trusting girls over Griboyedov's grave, when the astronomers' constellations, the lights of Sololaki and excited pupils of their eyes merge into one; while on the walls of Georgian restaurants the water melons painted by Niko Pirosmanishvili bleed to death.'

[1] Wind instrument, forerunner of the oboe.

In France, the Alps mean sport, tourism, sanatoria, skis, hotels, rucksacks and picture postcards. As for the Caucasus, it would be difficult to imagine Russian poetry without it: that is where its soul found rest, that was its launching platform.

At this moment, however, I am writing only of two short weeks in the autumn of 1920 when our Georgian friends welcomed and warmed us. Those friends are no more; it remains to salute the mountains of Georgia. Yashvili and Tabidze came with us as far as the first halt along the Georgian military highway, and Tizian's high, piercing voice rings in my ears to this day: 'Nocturnal darkness lies upon the Georgian hills; Aragva roars before me. I am sad, yet my heart is light; my sadness is bright; my sadness is full of thee'.

17

I HAVE already said that in the course of my life I have had many varied and unexpected occupations. I must now tell of the most improbable one of all. It was brief but tempestuous. The Soviet ambassador announced to me that I should travel from Tbilisi to Moscow as a diplomatic courier. This was neither an honorary sinecure nor a disguise intended to enable me to cross the frontier: no, I was to deliver a packet of mail and three huge bales adorned with an impressive number of seals.

I have often travelled abroad, and still do; if other comrades travel with me, one of them is invariably called 'the leader of the delegation'. But from Tbilisi I travelled with seven people; some of these were described in our travel document as 'accompanying' me (Lyuba, Yadviga, the Mandelstam brothers and a very serious comrade returning, I believe, from England); the others, a Red Navy man and a very young actor from the Art Theatre, were described as 'protecting' me. Thus I had made a career from the start in my new profession.

Nowadays I often meet diplomatic couriers on my air travels. They are calm, substantial persons used to their work; on long journeys there are always two of them: while one sleeps, the other keeps watch on the mail. As I look at them out of the corner of my eye I remember the distant past: they would never guess that I also had carried similar baggage, though not in a plane where air hostesses offer you sweets, but in a dilapidated railway carriage coupled to an armoured engine.

In the autumn of 1920 Soviet diplomats were mere beginners. Diplomatic relations existed only with Afghanistan, the newly created Baltic States and Menshevik Georgia. Everything was new, nothing had yet been tested. The Bolsheviks well remembered their heated discussions with the Mensheviks at illegal meetings; sometimes the police would appear and arrest everybody. Now the picture had changed: the Menshevik publicist A. Kostrov, also known as Noah Jordania, had become head of the Georgian government and his police had taken to putting the Mensheviks' recent discussion partners into Metekhskaya Prison. Of course, a diplomatic courier enjoys immunity and no one has any right to touch the baggage he is carrying. The ambassador was well aware of this, but he did not know whether the Mensheviks were also aware of it, and gave me strict instructions on no account to allow the parcel wrapped in brown paper and sealed with ten wax seals to be opened at the frontier. I held this parcel in my hands and refused to be parted from it for eight days, until I delivered it to the Narkomindel in Moscow.

At first the voyage was idyllic. We had supper at an inn and spent the night *en route*; all my companions, both 'accompanying' and 'protecting' me, slept peacefully while I stayed awake, clutching the precious parcel. In the morning we continued on our way. The snow sparkled, mountain streams roared below and flocks of sheep grazed on the mountain slopes.

We were approaching the frontier and I began to wonder what I should do if the Georgian frontier guards took it into their heads to open my parcel. The Red Navy man had a revolver, but when I raised the subject of the impending danger he replied indifferently that the parcel was my business; he personally was carrying nothing but fruit. The comrade returning from England was beautifully shaved, smelt of lavender water and gazed lightheartedly at the eternal snows through his field-glasses. Osip Mandelstam recited poetry to the girls.

The Georgian officer in charge of the frontier guards turned out to be a charming fellow. On hearing that my wife was a painter, he started asking her what Russian artists were doing; he wanted to go to Moscow and get into the *Vkhutemas*[1] ; would Lyuba put in a word for him?

We took a long time dragging the bales across the 'neutral strip'. The Soviet frontier guards were busy, having just caught three smugglers. We were promised cars for that evening. I began to protest: the mail was urgent, there was not an hour to be lost (those were the exact words the ambassador had used to me).

We drove into Vladikavkaz at night and were taken to an hotel where Denikin's men had stayed six months earlier. Everything was in a state of ruin and neglect. There was no glass in the windows and we were exposed to the cold wind. The town was like the front line. People going to work looked worried and on their guard; they could

---

[1] Institute for higher education in the applied arts.

not understand that the Civil War was nearing its end and out of habit tried guessing who would storm the town tomorrow.

I began to discuss with the representatives of the Town Soviet and the military command how we could get to Mineralnye Vody: there were no trains, and on the road there were skirmishes with small White detachments. We ate borshch in the canteen set aside for the top comrades, and were even issued three loaves of bread. At nightfall it was decided to send an armoured train to Mineralnye Vody. However, no armoured train was available, and two ordinary coaches were coupled to an armoured engine. The 'protection' this time was rather more impressive: it consisted of Red Army men with machine guns.

When we had travelled forty or fifty kilometres, the train stopped. We heard firing. One of our machine guns began to rattle away. The Red Army men told us that the Whites had dismantled the line and would attack our train; we must take up rifles and shoot. All this drove Osip Mandelstam frantic: he had an insurmountable horror of all forms of weapons. He evolved a fantastic plan: he and Lyuba would take to the mountains. Lyuba would not listen to his blandishments, and the Whites were driven off quite quickly.

People waited for weeks at a time at Mineralnye Vody station to get on a train. The Red Army men helped me to make my way through the crowd to a railway carriage; someone shouted 'Diplomatic courier!' but it did not help. It would have been just as effective to shout 'The Pope!' or 'Chaliapine!' I cannot remember how in the end we found ourselves inside an overfilled compartment. Here it was that my real tribulations began: the bales took up a great deal of room and everyone tried to sit down on them: I realized full well that nothing would be left of the wax seals, and yelled at the top of my voice: 'Keep off the diplomatic mail!' The words were less effective than my voice, which had the authentic ring of despair.

At first my Red Navy man helped me to repulse these attempts, but soon a misfortune occurred: at one of the stations he bought two large sacks of salt. So once again salt, that infernal stuff, was interfering with my life. Now the Red Navy man no longer guarded the diplomatic mail but only the salt and cynically drove everyone away from his sacks: 'There's diplomatic mail in there'. I looked like an impostor.

On the fourth or fifth day, fresh difficulties awaited us: somewhere between Rostov and Kharkov our train ran into Makhno's men. I already knew from experience what this meant. But now I had those bales, that precious parcel ... What was I to do? The comrade returning from England had hot tea in a thermos and some brandy in a hip flask; he kept saying to me: 'Have a drink, everything will turn out all right'.

In the end everything really did turn out all right. We got to Moscow. I clutched the parcel to my breast like a baby. The other passengers dispersed gradually, but I still stood over my bales. Towards evening, Alexander Mandelstam and the Red Navy man managed to hire a cart on which we loaded the luggage (I carried the parcel). We walked behind the cart. It looked just like a village funeral.

Osip Mandelstam had meanwhile contacted someone or other by telephone, had arranged accommodation for the night for his brother and himself and announced to us that in the evening we must come to the Press Club in Nikitsky Boulevard, where we would get sandwiches.

The Narkomindel offices were then in the Metropole building; the entrance was in the little square at the back. A guard on duty relieved me of the mail. He treated the small parcel respectfully and I rose again in my own estimation; the bales he dumped in a store room with evident disdain. I tried to explain to him that a hateful woman on the train had, despite all my vigilance, damaged one of the numerous seals; he replied indifferently: 'Oh, there's nothing in there but newspapers'.

A miracle happened. Remember that those were the early years of the Revolution, romantic years. Hearing that I had nowhere to go, the guard took pity on me, told someone over the telephone that a diplomatic courier had arrived from Tbilisi and began ringing up various hostels. I was given a slip of paper saying that Ehrenburg and wife were to be housed in the Narkomindel's Third Hostel. The Third Hostel turned out to be the former Knyazhi Dvor hotel where I had once stayed with my father. It was warm there, and I realized that I was in paradise.

In the evening we went to the Press Club. I met many friends. At the buffet one really did get tiny slices of black bread with red caviare and dried fish; in addition, one could get tea which gave out an aroma of apples or mint, one could not be sure which; there was, of course, no sugar. All this was rapture, and I plunged at once into a literary discussion on whether the Futurists or the Imaginists were closer to reality.

An incident involving Mandelstam, who was sitting in another corner of the room, cast a small shadow. Suddenly Blumkin leapt to his feet and began to shout: 'I'm going to shoot you!' training his revolver on Mandelstam, who cried out. The revolver was knocked out of Blumkin's hand and everything ended well.

We walked back through Arbat Square, past the little church of St Boris and St Gleb. It was very dark, but faint lights stirred in the windows. This was Moscow, the city which the whole world was watching. There was no bread and no coal, people were suffering great hardships, but they were stubborn and they had already won a war and made a breakthrough into history.

Those were my thoughts on my way back to the Third Hostel. I longed to do something, to write, above all to smash the past, smash it with a will: I knew now what the past smelt of.

18

THE WARDEN of the Narkomindel's Third Hostel was called Comrade Adam; but, speaking frankly, it was I who felt like Adam: I suddenly found myself in paradise, from which I might easily be expelled. I had to produce a certificate from my place of work, but although I had delivered the mail safely, there could be no hope of a diplomatic career for me. Comrade Adam gave us an unheated room; nevertheless, the Knyazhi Dvor was paradise. Rations were issued in the morning: less than half a pound of bread, a tiny lump of butter and two lumps of sugar. At midday we were given barley or millet gruel. The fare of the ancient princes[1] was certainly better, but in the Moscow of 1920 such rations were in truth princely.

I saw old friends, met some young poets and wrote a few poems. Lyuba looked up Madame Ekster and got into *Vkhutemas*. I was told to my surprise that Meyerhold wanted to see me to offer me an interesting job. I did not know what kind of a job it might be, but I felt as though I had been given wings.

A reading of my poetry was arranged at the Press Club. I read poems written at Koktebel and in Moscow. I was disreputably dressed, but no one paid any attention to such things at that time; and the poems were charged with feeling. For example, I addressed the man of the future who would one day chance upon a book of mine in a library: 'Amid the trumpery of the past, amid wretched words, amid the chronicles of distant troubles, you will behold a man dying on a threshold, his face turned towards you'. When I had finished reading, the audience made for the buffet as one man. The committee member on duty that night, the poet Vengrov, came up to me and whispered that two representatives of the Cheka were asking for me in the cloakroom downstairs. 'Don't worry,' he added amiably, 'it's obviously a mistake.'

Two young men were waiting for me by the coat-rack. They showed me a warrant. We walked to the square and got into a car which

[1] Knyazhi Dvor = Princes' Court.

took us to Lubyanka, to the premises of the former Russia Insurance Co. where the Cheka had its headquarters. This building has become part of history. Few people remember that Kirov Street used to be called Myasnitskaya, Kropotkinskaya Street Prechistenka or Gorky Street Tverskaya, but the word Lubyanka has remained.

They searched me and found a photograph of Lyuba and some reproductions of her paintings. The young men started asking me about the meaning of Cubism. However, I had other things on my mind: what was the meaning of my arrest? The lecture on art did not take place. The young men said that they would tell my wife what had happened to me (they really did go and see her with words of comfort – 'they're sure to let him out soon' – and many questions about modern painting). I was taken to a cell where there were already eight men, Red Navy officers, a likeable and manly crew; they made room for me and I lay down to sleep. Next morning it was explained to me that in our cell it was not done to talk about whatever unpleasantness had befallen one: each man talked about the subject on which he was an expert. First came a lecture about a submarine designed by Nalyotov, then a description of a sea voyage in the Indian Ocean. When my turn came I talked about Paris, the poetry of François Villon and Italian art. (A few months later I saw the companions of my brief captivity at the first night of *Princess Brambilla* at the Kamerny Theatre. We were delighted to meet again and immediately launched into a discussion on the relative merits of Meyerhold and Tairov.)

In the evening I was led off for interrogation through a series of long, winding corridors. The investigator greeted me as a friend and said that he had met me at the Rotonde. I did not remember him, but we had a chat about Paris. Then he said: 'You see, it's like this. We've been informed that you are a Wrangel agent. Prove that you're not'. My trouble is that all my life I cannot rid myself of certain arguments of Descartes; I know that man does not live by logic, and yet it is precisely logic that I always catch myself demanding from others. I replied that the informer must prove that I was a Wrangel agent; if I were told what his accusation was based on I should be able to disprove it. The investigator asked me to tell him how I had got to Moscow, sympathized with me over our difficulties *en route*, commented harshly on the owner of the salt and ended by saying: 'We'll talk again later'. I gave my cell companions a lecture on Spanish poetry and listened to one on the effect of the development of aviation on naval operations. Two days later the investigator sent for me again. 'Tell me, why were you chosen to deliver diplomatic mail to Moscow?' I replied that the question should be put to our ambassador in Tbilisi; for my part, I had simply asked the embassy to send me to Moscow. We swapped a few more reminiscences of Paris and I was taken back to my cell. I gave a talk on the architecture of Versailles and heard an analysis of submarine warfare in 1917–18. The third interrogation opened with the familiar words: 'Prove that you aren't a Wrangel agent'. The investigator was in a bad mood and told me I was being obstinate; this might well prove to be my downfall; the counter-revolution was refusing to give in, and the proletariat would not repeat the mistakes of the Commune. I came to the conclusion that I would certainly be shot. In the morning, however, I gave a lecture on Picasso's paintings, and was so carried away that I actually forgot all about the investigator's sinister hints.

Another day passed and, without warning, I was released.

What an extraordinary time that was! Fighting with Wrangel's army was still going on; various 'gangs' were still operating; the terrorists were still shooting. The struggle went on somewhere underground, in dark sappers' tunnels. Sometimes an arrested person would get shot. Those who were not shot were released.

I was released in the evening. I went to the Knyazhi Dvor, but was not allowed in: Comrade Adam, who, like God, was omnipotent, had expelled Eve – that is to say Lyuba – from paradise. I did not know where she was and did not know where I should go. It was extremely cold, and suddenly I thought with intense nostalgia of the stuffy cell: at least it had been warm there.

I betook myself to the Press Club. It was late, and I found only a clerk on duty. He explained to me at great length that no one was allowed to spend the night in the building, but, after a closer look at me, he was moved to compassion. 'Oh, very well. Let's go upstairs.' Upstairs were the rooms assigned to various literary groups. He put me up in the Proletarian Writers' Room, which contained a large sofa. Unfortunately, the first floor was not heated. My Parisian overcoat, which had seen me through three stormy years, resembled the battered overcoat of Gogol's Akaky Akakiyevich. I lay there and felt that I was freezing to death. In total darkness, I tore a piece of canvas off the wall and wrapped myself up in it; it did not make me any warmer, but fortunately I went off to sleep.

I was awakened by loud laughter: several Proletarian Writers, among them my Paris friend Misha Gerasimov, were standing over me, laughing their heads off. It turned out that I had wrapped myself up in a banner inscribed with the slogan 'All culture to the proletariat!' I had to laugh myself.

Re-reading what I have just written, I wonder why it is that in this volume of my reminiscences there are so many cheerful, almost frivolous pages. After all, the events I am describing were by no means pleasurable: the salt barge might easily have sunk; bandits would have thought nothing of finishing off a guileless diplomatic courier; and my chats with the investigator could have ended very differently. All that is true. But human beings can keep an inner gaiety in the hour of the hardest trials, just as they can pine and even despair when nothing is directly threatening them. I have written of my early youth with tenderness but also with bitterness. And in the forthcoming volumes of my book I shall have to talk about many things which no one could call gay. It is not danger that oppresses but inner wrongs, disillusionment, a feeling of impotence.

Both Hašek and Kafka were born in Prague in 1883, but they spoke in voices that were utterly unlike each other; you cannot insert one of the good soldier Schweik's soliloquies into a Kafka novel: the dissonance would be appalling. But life is not a writer; it cares nothing for unity of style; it writes one chapter with a smile and, in the next, it lacerates the hero's soul.

Let me return to my story. Gerasimov managed to get hold of a hunk of bread and some tea. We had breakfast. Young poets were already arguing about the future of the arts in the corridors of the Press Club and I went out to look for Lyuba.

19

As a boy I saw V. E. Meyerhold several times on the Art Theatre stage. I remember him as a mad old man in *Ivan the Terrible* and as an excitable, indignant youth in *The Seagull*.

Sitting at the Rotonde I often recalled the words of Chekhov's hero: 'When the curtain goes up and, under artificial light in a room with three walls, these great talents, high priests of holy art, portray how people eat, drink, love, walk and wear their coats; when they try to fish a moral out of vulgar pictures and phrases, a small moral easy to understand and handy for domestic use; when in a thousand variations I am offered the same thing, over and over and over again – then I run and run, as Maupassant ran from the Eiffel Tower, the vulgarity of which pressed on his brain . . . We need new forms. We need new forms and if we can't have them we had better have nothing.' (Chekhov wrote *The Seagull* in 1896; Maupassant died in 1893; the Eiffel Tower was built in 1889. In 1913, we accepted the Eiffel Tower and rejected Maupassant, but the words about 'new forms' still held life and meaning for me.)

I missed my chance of meeting Meyerhold in 1913 when he came to Paris at the invitation of Ida Rubinstein to put on d'Annunzio's *La Pisanelle* together with Fokine. I knew little about Meyerhold's productions at the time, but I did know that d'Annunzio was a phrase-monger and Ida Rubinstein a wealthy lady avid for theatrical successes; in 1911 I had seen *Saint Sébastien*, also by d'Annunzio, also written for Ida Rubinstein, and had been irritated by its mixture of decadent aestheticism and a kind of scent-shop voluptuousness. (In Paris Meyerhold made friends with Guillaume Apollinaire who, it seems, realized at once that what mattered was not d'Annunzio, not Ida Rubinstein and not Bakst's stage sets but the inner fervour of the young producer from St Petersburg.)

When I met Meyerhold in the autumn of 1920 he was forty-six; his hair had already turned grey, his features had already sharpened, and his bushy eyebrows and very long hooked nose, resembling a bird's beak, dominated the face.

TEO (the theatrical section of the Narkompros[1]) had its offices in a former private house opposite Alexandrovsky Gardens. Meyerhold darted about the large room, possibly because he felt cold, possibly because also he did not know how to sit in a departmental chief's armchair behind the traditional desk heaped with papers 'for signature'. His utterances were birdlike. He said that he had liked my *Poems about the Eves*; then suddenly he ran up to me and, throwing back his head, which was like a heron's or a condor's, he said: 'Your place is here. October in the arts! You will be in charge of all the children's theatres of the Republic'. I tried to protest: I was no pedagogue, the mofective juveniles of Kiev and the children's playground at Koktebel had been quite enough for me and, what was more, I knew nothing about the art of the stage. Meyerhold interrupted me: 'You're a poet, and children need poetry. Poetry and the Revolution! To hell with the art of the stage! We must have another talk. I've already signed the order putting you on our staff. Be sure you turn up punctually tomorrow morning'.

At that time Meyerhold, like Mayakovsky, was a man possessed by the spirit of iconoclasm. He was not a departmental chief but a fighter, at war with those aesthetics and those 'easy-to-understand' morals of which the hero of *The Seagull* spoke.

I recently appeared on television in Geneva. A young girl barred my way and said that she must make me up. I protested. I was to speak about famine in the economically backward countries; what had that to do with my looks? Besides, it was unseemly for me, an old man, to start painting my cheeks for the first time in my life. The girl replied that rules were rules; everyone had to submit to the process, and she applied a thin layer of a yellowish cream to my face. I think that the light of memory is as powerful as the lights in television studios, and that in speaking of certain people in this book I tend to apply – without wanting to – a layer of paint to soften features that are too sharp. With Meyerhold, however, I am not tempted to do so; I want to present him in every harsh detail, without glossing over anything.

He had a difficult character in which kindness combined with a quick temper, and a complex inner world with fanaticism. Like certain other great men whom I have met, he suffered from pathological

[1] People's Commissariat for Education.

suspiciousness, was jealous without grounds and saw plots and intrigues where there were none.

Our first dispute was stormy but brief. A certain sailor brought me a play for children in which all the characters were fish (Mensheviks were carp) and a 'fishes' Sovnarkom' (Council of People's Commissars) triumphed in the last act. I thought the play a failure and rejected it. Suddenly Meyerhold called me in. The manuscript lay on his desk. Extremely irritated, he asked me why I had turned the play down and, without listening to my arguments, began to shout that I was against revolutionary agitation and against October in the theatre. I flew into a temper in turn and said that this was 'demagogy'. Meyerhold lost control of himself and called for the house manager: 'Arrest Ehrenburg for sabotage!' The house manager refused to carry out the order and advised Meyerhold to get in touch with the Cheka. I walked out in a state of great indignation and decided never to cross the threshold of TEO again. The next morning Meyerhold rang me up: he must have my advice about the puppet theatre. I went, and it was as if yesterday's scene had never taken place.

Then he fell ill. I went several times to see him in hospital; he lay with his head in bandages. He talked to me about his plans and asked what was going on at TEO; had I been to see the new productions? A trace of irony must have slipped into my answers, because Meyerhold accused me several times of lack of faith and even of cynicism. Once, when I remarked on the divergence between many of our plans and the reality, he raised himself up in bed and burst out laughing: 'You, in charge of all the children's theatres of the Republic! No! Dickens himself could not have invented anything better!' The bandages looked like a turban and Meyerhold, thin and big-nosed, like an oriental magician. I burst out laughing, too, and said that the order appointing me to the job was signed by Meyerhold, not Dickens.

I went several times to see *Dawn*. It is a weak play, and the production, too, had many fortuitous elements. Meyerhold was fighting against the 'three walls' that Chekhov's Treplev spoke of, against the footlights, against painted sets. He wanted to bring the stage nearer to the audience. The theatre itself was in thoroughly bad taste: it was the famous 'Aumont' where Muscovites had once ogled half-naked beauties; however, the condition of the auditorium was such that its trappings passed more or less unnoticed. The theatre was unheated; everyone sat in overcoats, fur jackets, sheepskin coats. Thunderous words and delicate clouds of steam escaped from the actors' mouths. Some of the actors sat in the stalls, and would suddenly rush on to the stage, on which there were grey cubes and dangling ropes for no apparent reason. Members of the audience – Red Army men with a brass band, or workers – also mounted the stage from time to time. (Meyerhold wanted to seat several actors in a box; they were to represent S.R.s and Mensheviks, and make suitable interjections. He told me with regret that he had been obliged to abandon the idea: the audience might think that they were real counter-revolutionaries and there would be a fight.) Once I was in the theatre when one of the actors solemnly read out a communiqué which had just been received, announcing the capture of Perekop. It would be difficult to describe what went on in the auditorium.

At an open discussion which followed, the production was attacked. Mayakovsky defended Meyerhold. I hardly know what to say of the performance itself; it cannot be separated from its time; it was closely bound up with Mayakovksy's *agitkas*, with the carnival processions organized by 'Left' artists, with the very climate of those years. Mayakovsky's *Mystery Bouffe*, which I saw in rehearsal, seemed to me to be another of these time-bound spectacles. It was difficult to like them, but one felt like praising, even exalting them. I wrote in 1921: 'Meyerhold's productions are unsuccessful in execution but magnificent in their concept, which is not only to distil the essence of the theatre but also immediately to dissolve it, to destroy the barrier of the footlights, to mingle the actors with the audience'. And Mayakovksy ended his speech at the open debate on *Dawn* with the following words: 'Long live the theatre of Meyerhold, even if this early production is no good'. The young Bagritsky wrote: 'Today Meyerhold has come to replace Molière of the ornate curls. He is looking for new paths, his movements are rough. Tremble, old theatre, in fear: he will subdue you!'

In the summer of 1923 I was living in Berlin. Meyerhold arrived, and we met. He suggested that I should adapt my novel *Trust D.E.* for his theatre, saying that the play should be a mixture of a circus and a propaganda pageant. I did not feel like adapting the novel; I was beginning to lose my enthusiasm both for the circus and for Constructivism, had a passion for Dickens just then and was writing a sentimental novel with a complicated plot, *The Love of Jeanne Ney*. I knew, however, that it was difficult to oppose Meyerhold and said that I would think about it.

Shortly after that an article appeared in a theatrical journal published by Meyerhold's supporters. This article, which took the form of a fantasy tale, described how I had been 'stolen' by Tairov, for whom I had undertaken to turn my novel into a counter-revolutionary play.

(Many times in his life Meyerhold suspected Tairov, that kindest and purest of men, of a desire to destroy him by no matter what means. It was part of that suspiciousness that I have already mentioned. Tairov never had the slightest intention of putting on *Trust D.E.*)

Returning to the Soviet Union I read that Meyerhold was preparing to stage a play called *Trust D.E.* adapted by a certain Podgaretsky 'from novels by Ehrenburg and Kellerman'. I realized that the only argument which might stop Meyerhold would be for me to say that I wanted to adapt the novel myself for the theatre or the cinema. In March 1924 I wrote him a letter beginning 'Dear Vsevolod Emilyevich' and ending 'with heartfelt greetings': 'Our meeting last summer, and in particular our talks about the possibility of my adapting *Trust D.E.*, allow me to believe that your attitude to my work is one of friendship and esteem. I therefore venture, first of all, to ask you – if the newspaper report is correct – to give up the idea of this production. After all, I am not a classic but a living man'.

The reply was terrifying – it contained all the frenzy of which Meyerhold was capable – I should never mention it if I did not love the man with all his extremes. 'Citizen I. Ehrenburg! I fail to understand on what grounds you address a request to me to "give up the idea" of producing Comrade Podgaretsky's play. Is it on the grounds of our talk in Berlin? Surely that talk made it clear enough that even if you were to undertake an adaptation of your novel, you would turn it into a play that could well be staged in any of the cities of the Entente.'

I did not go to see the play; according to friends' reports and articles by critics who supported Meyerhold, Podgaretsky made a poor job of it. The production was interesting. Europe perished amidst a great deal of noise, the panels of the set were hustled off the stage, the actors changed their make-up in a hurry, and a jazz band played deafeningly. To my surprise Mayakovsky stood up for me: at a debate on the production of *Trust D.E.* he said of the adaptation: 'The play *D.E.* is an absolute zero . . . Only a man who stands on a higher level than the authors – in this case, Ehrenburg and Kellerman – can adapt a work of fiction for the stage'. However, the production enjoyed some success, and the Java tobacco factory issued a brand of cigarettes called *D.E.* But as a result of this silly business I did not meet Meyerhold again for seven years.

Whenever I came to Moscow I went to see his productions: *Le Cocu Magnifique, Tarelkin's Death, The Forest.* I bought my ticket and was nervous lest Meyerhold should see me in the theatre. (It would be difficult to see a propaganda pageant in these plays; they could just as well have been staged in the 'cities of the Entente'. Meyerhold never stood still.)

He never followed a smooth, straight path; he laboured uphill, and his path meandered. When his followers were shouting at every crossroads that the theatres must be destroyed, he was already preparing his production of *The Forest.* Many people failed to understand what had happened to the impassioned iconoclast: why had he been tempted by Ostrovsky, the tragedy of art, love? (In the same way the followers of Mayakovsky failed to understand why, having condemned lyrical poetry, he should have written *About This* in 1923. It is interesting to note that *The Forest* was put on shortly after Mayakovsky had written *About This.* Mayakovsky, the poet, was already returning to poetry, while Mayakovsky the LEF man condemned Meyerhold harshly for his return to the theatre: 'I find the production of *The Forest* deeply revolting'.)

Pictures hang in galleries, books are kept in libraries, but theatrical productions that we have not seen remain in our minds as dry reviews. It is easy to establish a link between *About This* and Mayakovsky's early verse, between Picasso's *Guernica* and the paintings of his blue period. But it is difficult for me to judge what, of Meyerhold's pre-revolutionary productions, went into his *Forest* and *Inspector-General.* Doubtless a great deal: a path may meander, but it is still the same path.

The Forest was a magnificent production, and the play moved the audience greatly. Meyerhold discovered many new things in it and presented the tragedy of art in a new way. There was, however, one small detail about the production which outraged (or possibly delighted) Meyerhold's opponents, and that was the green wig worn by one of the characters. The play remained in the repertoire for many years. Once, after a performance in Leningrad, there was a public discussion. Meyerhold was bombarded with written questions; he was pleased, annoyed and jocular by turns. One of the questions was: 'Please explain the meaning of the green wig'. He turned to his actors and asked, puzzled: 'Well, what does it mean, really? Who thought of it?' From that night on, the green wig was seen no more. I do not know whether this display of perplexity was put on or whether he was genuinely surprised, having forgotten a detail which he himself had invented. (Often, in real life, I have heard the same nonplussed question: 'Who on earth thought of it?' sometimes emanating from the authors of various absurdities far more important than the wretched wig.)

Meyerhold was the *bête noire* of people who hated everything new; his name became a generic term. Some critics failed to notice (or did not care to notice) that Meyerhold was going forward: they hurled abuse at him from a wayside halt which he had long since left behind.

He was not afraid to abandon artistic conceptions which only a day earlier had seemed right to him. In 1920, when he put on *Dawn*, he broke away from *Sister Beatrice* and *Balaganchik*. Later he derided the 'biomechanics' he had himself invented.

In the first act of *The Seagull* Treplev says that what matters most are new forms, but in the last act, before he shoots himself, he realizes something different: 'Yes, I come more and more to the conviction that it is not a matter of old and new forms, but what matters is that a man should write without thinking about forms at all, write because what he has to say pours freely from his soul'. In 1938, Meyerhold said to me that the argument was not about old and new forms in art but about art and imitation art.

He never repudiated what he thought essential; he rejected 'isms', methods, aesthetic canons, but not his view of art; he was always rebelling, finding inspiration, catching fire.

What was there to frighten anyone in Chekhov's farces? By that time everyone had forgotten about 'Left art'. Mayakovsky had been recognized as a poet of genius. And yet Meyerhold's productions were violently attacked. He could say the most ordinary things, but there was something about his voice, his eyes, his smile that infuriated those people whom an artist's creative fervour makes uncomfortable.

I saw Meyerhold's *Inspector-General* in Paris in the spring of 1930, at a small theatre in the rue de la Gaîté where an audience drawn from the suburbs was usually regaled with silly vaudevilles or heartrending melodramas. The stage was small and inconvenient; there was no foyer (during the intervals, the audience had to go out into the street); in short, it was a pretty wretched sort of place. *The Inspector-General* impressed me deeply. The enthusiasms of my youth had long since cooled, and my love of Gogol was so great that I was afraid to go and see the play. And then I saw everything that attracted me in Gogol brought to life on the stage: the artist sick at heart and the display of bottomless, cruel vulgarity.

I know that Meyerhold has been accused of distorting Gogol's text, of treating it sacrilegiously. Certainly his *Inspector-General* was not like those productions I had seen in my childhood and youth; the text seemed expanded, but it contained no arbitrary additions: everything was Gogol's. Can anyone believe for an instant that the sole content of Gogol's play is the exposure of provincial officials in the time of Nicholas I? For Gogol's contemporaries, *The Inspector-General* was, of course, primarily a cruel satire on the existing social structure and its morals. But like all works of genius it survives topicality, so that it still moves people a hundred years after Nicholas' mayors and postmasters have vanished from the face of the earth. Meyerhold expanded the framework of *The Inspector-General*. Is that sacrilege? Are not various stage adaptations of Tolstoy's and Dostoyevsky's novels considered praiseworthy although they, on the contrary, narrow the scope of those works?

Andrey Bely did not merely love Gogol, he was obsessed by him; many artistic failures by the author of *The Silver Pigeon* and *Petersburg* should perhaps be ascribed to his inability to free himself from Gogol's domination. And it was precisely Andrey Bely, who, on seeing *The Inspector-General* at Meyerhold's theatre, spoke out in passionate defence of the production.

In Paris, the audience was largely composed of French people: producers, actors, theatre connoisseurs, writers, painters. It was rather like a march-past of celebrities: look, there's Louis Jouvet, there's Picasso, there's Dullin, there's Cocteau, there's Derain, there's Baty. When the performance was over, these people who, one would have thought, had had more than their fill of art and were accustomed to bestow their approval with moderation, rose to their feet in an ovation such as I had never before seen in Paris.

I went backstage. Meyerhold, very excited, was standing in a tiny dressing-room. His hair was whiter than ever, his nose longer. Seven years had passed. I said I had not been able to resist coming to thank him. He embraced me.

After that there was no more estrangement or coolness between us. We never spoke again of our foolish quarrel. We met in Paris or in Moscow and had long talks, and sometimes enjoyed long silences as only the closest friends can do.

When Meyerhold decided to produce *The Inspector-General* he told his actors: 'You are seeing an aquarium in which the water has not been changed for a long time. The water is greenish; the fish swim round in circles and blow bubbles'. He said to me that while working on *The Inspector-General* he often recalled the Penza of his school years.

(In 1948 I was walking along a street in Penza with Alexander Fadeyev. Suddenly he stopped: 'There's Meyerhold's house'. We stood awhile in silence; then Fadeyev, obviously much moved, sighed, made a despairing gesture, and strode off rapidly towards the hotel.)

Meyerhold hated stagnant water, yawns, emptiness; he often used masks just because masks frightened him, not because they suggested some mystical horror of non-being but because they stood for the apathetic vulgarity of everyday life. The final scene of *The Inspector-General*, the long table in *Woe from Wit*, the characters in *The Mandate*, even Chekhov's farces, are all part of the same duel between the artist and vulgarity.

The fact that he became a Communist was not accidental: he was firm in the knowledge that the world must be changed. This knowledge was not based on other men's arguments but on his own experience. Among us, he was a man of an older generation. Mayakovsky was born with the Revolution, but Meyerhold already had a whole complex of experience behind him. Stanislavsky, Komissarzhevskaya, the Petersburg Symbolists, *Balaganchik*, Blok whipped on by snow-storms, *The Love of Three Oranges* and much else. Already in the Rotonde days we had tried to guess what the mysterious Doctor Dapertutto (that was Meyerhold's pen-name) looked like.

Of all the people whom I have the right to call my friends, Meyerhold was the oldest in age. I was only born in the nineteenth century, but he had lived in it, had been a guest in Chekhov's house, had worked with Komissarzhevskaya, known Scriabin and Yermolova. The most extraordinary thing is that he always remained young, forever inventing something new, forever raging like a storm in May.

His whole life was punctuated by his opponents' attacks. In 1911, Menshikov, a contributor to *Novoye Vremya*, outraged by Meyerhold's production of *Boris Godunov*, wrote: 'I believe that Mr Meyerhold has taken these sheriffs from his Jewish soul and not from Pushkin, who gives us neither sheriffs nor knouts'. Certain articles written many years later were, in truth, no cleaner and no fairer than the words I have quoted.

He was quite unlike a martyr. He had a passionate love of life: of children and noisy meetings, of fairground booths and Renoir's paintings, of poetry and the scaffolding of new buildings. He loved his work. I have attended a number of his rehearsals: he not only explained, he acted. I remember the rehearsals of Chekhov's farces. Meyerhold was then over sixty, but he amazed the young actors by his tirelessness, the brilliance of his inventions, his prodigious fund of inner gaiety.

I have said that theatrical performances die and cannot be resuscitated. We know that André Chenier was a splendid poet, but we can only take on trust that Talma, his contemporary, was a splendid actor. And yet creative work does not vanish, though it may become invisible for a time, like a river that flows on underground. I go to the theatre in Paris; all round me people are gasping: 'How novel!' Meanwhile I remember Meyerhold's productions. I remember them, too, as I sit in many Moscow theatres. Vakhtangov wrote: 'Meyerhold gave the theatres of the future their roots, and the future will repay him'. It was not only Vakhtangov who revered Meyerhold, but also Gordon Craig, Jouvet and many other producers of the first rank. Eisenstein once said to me that without Meyerhold he would not have existed.

As early as August 1930 Meyerhold wrote to me: 'The theatre may perish. The enemy does not sleep. There are many people in Moscow for whom Meyerhold's theatre is a thorn in the flesh. Oh, it is too long and boring to talk about it'.

Our last meetings were not gay. I returned from Spain in December 1937. Meyerhold's theatre was already closed down. His wife, Zinaida Nikolayevna Reich, had fallen gravely ill as a result of all they had been through. Meyerhold was sustained by Stanislavsky, who often telephoned him and tried to cheer him up.

During that time the artist Konchalovsky painted a marvellous portrait of Meyerhold. Many of Konchalovsky's portraits are purely decorative, but the artist was deeply fond of Meyerhold and that portrait reveals his inspiration, his unrest and his spiritual beauty.

Meyerhold used to sit at home for many hours, reading and studying books on art. He retained his spirit of venture; he dreamt of a production of *Hamlet*, saying: 'Now, I think, I could bring it off. Before,

I never dared. If all the plays in the world disappeared and only *Hamlet* were left, there would still be a theatre'.

I should like to say that during this difficult time Meyerhold's wife gave him magnificent support. A copy of a letter he wrote to her in October 1938 from Gorenki, a small holiday resort, is before me. 'I arrived in Gorenki on the 13th. I saw the birch trees and caught my breath: look, those leaves are scattered in the air. Scattered, they are immobile, as though frozen. Immobile, they are waiting for something. How they have been ambushed! I counted the last seconds of their life like the pulse of a dying man: would I find them alive if I came back to Gorenki on the next day, in the next hour? When, on the 13th, I was looking at the fairyland world of golden autumn, an inarticulate plea formed in my mind: Zina, Zinochka, look at these wonders and do not leave me, I love you, you, my wife, my sister, my mother, my friend and my beloved, golden like this miracle-working nature. Zina, do not leave me. There is nothing in the world more frightful than loneliness.'

We parted in the spring of 1938: I was going back to Spain. We embraced. It was a grim parting. I never saw him again.

In 1955, the State Prosecutor told me how Meyerhold had been falsely denounced. He read to me a statement Meyerhold had written: 'I am sixty-six. I want my daughter and my friends to know one day that I remained an honest Communist to the end'. As he read these words, the prosecutor rose to his feet. I rose too.

138

20

I SOON returned to my lost paradise: Comrade Adam, having read a note from L. Karakhan, the Deputy People's Commissar, composed in rather haughty terms – namely, 'Ehrenburg stays' – gave us a room. I received a ration and, from February onwards, also a ticket for dinners at the Metropole, where you got thin soup, millet gruel or frozen potatoes. When you left the restaurant you had to hand in your spoon and fork, otherwise they did not let you out. Once a month I exchanged bread for tobacco.

Someone once told me that I had been born in a shirt[1]. The truth of the matter is that I was not only born in a shirt, I actually walked about in nothing more than my shirt; and Moscow in winter is not Brazil.

A long time ago I described in the journal *Projector* how I managed to get clothing for myself at the end of 1920. It is not a very serious story, but it reconstructs certain features of the everyday life of those years; besides, it shows that we were not discouraged by practical difficulties.

I have already mentioned my Paris coat which, with the years, had turned into a sort of threadbare dressing-gown. But I have not yet spoken of the most important thing, namely, my suit: the jacket still held together somehow, but the trousers had disintegrated.

That is when I realized what a pair of trousers means to a man of thirty who has to live in civilized society: to do without trousers is literally impossible. At the office I kept my overcoat on all the time, afraid to allow the skirts of the coat to part by some incautious movement: after all, my office was shared by the poetess Ada Chumachenko and several youthful Froebel girls.

A Red Navy playwright invited me to his house once. He lived in Loskutnaya. I suffered torments during that visit. He gave me wonderful pancakes to eat, but those pancakes were prepared by a young woman. The room was warm, everyone kept begging me to take off my overcoat, but I refused and could not explain why.

[1] Russian equivalent of being born with a silver spoon in your mouth.

Once they would not admit me to the Kamerny Theatre; I produced an invitation, all kinds of certificates and other documents, but the man at the door was inexorable: 'Comrade, you cannot enter wearing outdoor clothing'.

Although I was in charge of all the children's theatres in the Republic and received a ration and a half daily, I suffered from a strong sense of inferiority: I had no trousers.

A hard winter set in. My overcoat gave no more warmth than a lace shawl. I caught cold and coughed and sneezed. Doubtless I was running a temperature, but in those days we paid little attention to such things. By chance I came across one of my old associates from the pre-revolutionary underground organization. He took a look at me and got quite angry: 'Why didn't you tell me before?' He wrote a note to the chairman of the Moscow Soviet and added jocularly: 'The Lord Mayor of Moscow himself will look after your wardrobe.'

Being received by the 'Lord Mayor' was no easy matter. The waiting-room was crowded with petitioners of all kinds. At last I was allowed into a large office; behind a desk sat a most respectable man with a neatly trimmed beard whom I had known in Paris. I realized that he was very busy and was embarrassed. He was extremely amiable, talked about literature and asked about my working plans. How on earth was I to bring the conversation round to trousers? At last, plucking up courage and taking advantage of a pause, I blurted out in despair: 'By the way, I've absolutely got to have a pair of trousers'.

The 'Lord Mayor', embarrassed in his turn, looked at me closely: 'Why, you don't just need trousers, you need a winter coat'. He gave me a note to the managers of one of the departments of the MPO. The text of the note was laconic: 'Comrade Ehrenburg to be clothed'.

The next morning I got up specially early and went off to the MPO (these intitials had nothing to do with air-raid precautions with which they later came to be associated; they stood for *Moskovskoye Potrebitelskoye Obshchestvo*, Moscow Consumers' Co-operative, the department in charge of supplying food and clothing to the population). With the lightheartedness of one accustomed to being fortune's favourite, I asked: 'Where do they issue clothing coupons here?' Someone pointed to an immensely long queue in Myasnitskaya.

It was very cold, and as I stood in the queue I weakly forgot all about the trousers: what I longed for was a warm winter coat. Towards evening I began to approach the magic door. At this point something unforeseen occurred. A young woman wrapped in a warm shawl came up to me and started screaming: 'What cheek! I've been standing here since five o'clock in the morning, and he comes and takes my place!' She hurled herself against me. Her weight was not small. I resisted, but without success: she pushed me out of the queue. I appealed to the people behind: 'Comrades, haven't you seen me standing here all day?' But everyone was hungry, tired and uninterested, and no one supported me. I realized that waiting for justice was futile, walked away a few steps, took a run and, with a flying leap, pushed the impostress out of the queue. Everyone else remained apathetically silent, obviously preferring neutrality. As for the woman, she walked away quite peaceably and started looking for another vulnerable spot in the endless queue.

At last I got inside the manager's office. He read the note and said: 'Look, comrade, we've got very few clothes. You must decide which you want, a winter coat or a suit'. The choice was very hard. Frozen as I felt, I was ready to ask for a winter coat, but suddenly I remembered the humiliations of the past months and shouted: 'Trousers! A suit!' And so they gave me the appropriate coupon.

I went to the depot indicated, but there were no men's suits there; I was offered instead a lady's coat and skirt or a cloak. I naturally refused and was directed to another depot where they showed me a suit evidently made for a midget, which must have survived from Tsarist times for that sole reason. At last, at the depot on the corner of Petrovka and Kuznetsky, I found a suit that fitted me, pulled on the trousers and felt myself a man. Immediately afterwards I drafted ten new projects at the children's section of TEO.

The weather, however, was very frosty and I still went about coughing terribly. The consciousness that I was wearing trousers gave me courage and I began looking for a winter coat.

Being a passionate smoker, I exchanged my bread for tobacco in Sukharevka once a month. In Sukharevka everything imaginable was sold: Chinese vases, lumps of sugar, loose cigarettes, lighter flints, Bokhara carpets, mouldy pre-revolutionary chocolate and Paul Bourget's novels in morocco bindings. In Sukharevka you could also buy a torn sheepskin coat, but it cost not less than fifty thousand. And I had no money. In the pockets of my new suit jacket I kept certificates, projects, poems, an old burnt-out pipe, crumbs of tobacco and sometimes a lump of sugar which I would carry back from the hospitable home of D. P. Sterenberg, the chief of the Department of Visual Arts.

A catalogue of manuscripts which were sold at that time at the 'Writers' Bookshop' has happened to come into my hands recently. The authors include Andrey Bely, B. Lidin, M. Gerasimov, Shershenevich, Marina Tsvetayeva, I. Novikov and many others. I, too, was represented by my *Spanish Songs*, transcribed by Shershenevich, price 3,000 roubles, with a note attached: 'Cost price of 4 lumps of sugar = 2,000 roubles, 1 mug of milk = 1,800 roubles, 50 cigarettes = 6,000 roubles'. Money was so devalued that few people thought about it: we lived on rations and hope.

I nevertheless decided to make some money for an overcoat, and undertook to give a poetry reading at the Café Domino. It was unbearably cold there; customers were given tea with saccharine or a bowl of deathly pale, bluish sour milk. I cannot understand why people went there. The sinister howling of Shershenevich, Poplavskaya and Dir Tumanny rang out in the frosty semi-darkness. The patrons of the Domino consisted of black marketeers, criminal-police agents, inquisitive provincials and melancholy eccentrics.

I took off Akaky Akakiyevich's overcoat, sneezed and began to howl: at that time all poets howled, even when reading something cheerful. One of the black marketeers blew his nose in sympathy. Two others, unable to bear it, walked out. I received three thousand roubles.

I was lucky: a few days later I ran across a highly suspect citizen who offered to get me a sheepskin coat for seven thousand roubles. That was almost nothing. I sold my bread ration for two weeks and lugged the sheepskin coat to the Knyazhi Dvor.

The coat was too small and stank of grease, but to me it seemed an ermine mantle out of a Velasquez painting. I put it on and was about to go off to the Press Club, but at that moment Lyuba returned from art school and ordered me to take the glorious new thing off again at once: the breast of the sheepskin coat was imprinted with an enormous seal. I had been quite right to think the citizen was suspect: he had sold me a stolen coat.

Resignation overcame me: it was better to sneeze and cough than to get mixed up in some ugly business. But Lyuba was not a Constructivist in vain; it was not for nothing that she studied with Rodchenko and talked all day of texture, 'thing-ness' and production aesthetics. She found a way out.

In Moscow in those days there existed so-called 'shops for

un-rationed goods', where you bought frozen apples, Shamo's synthetic tea, saccharine, scrubbing brushes and sieves. I sold two pounds of millet off my ration and bought some leather dye at one of these shops. Lyuba picked up a brush with a practised hand. The sheepskin coat grew more beautiful every moment, beginning to resemble a chauffeur's jacket. Unfortunately, however, the leather soaked up the dye like a sponge. One of the sleeves remained unpainted, and we were out of dye, out of roubles and out of millet.

I could, of course, have walked about in a black sheepskin coat with a yellow sleeve, and no one would have given me a second glance. Everyone was dressed in a most original way. Women with pretensions to smartness wore soldier's faded greatcoats and green hats made of billiard-table cloth. Dresses were made of wine-coloured curtains livened up with Suprematist squares or triangles cut out of old loose-covers. The painter I. M. Rabinovich strolled about the streets in an emerald-coloured sheepskin coat. Yesenin often appeared in a shiny top-hat. But I was afraid that my yellow sleeve would be taken for eccentricity – the declaration of an aesthetic programme – rather than a case of *force majeure*.

Towards the New Year all members of the staff of TEO were given a tin of shoe polish. We regarded this as a misfortune, particularly as the staff of the Department of Music had been given chickens only the day before. But Lyuba found a use for the polish: she spread it over the yellow sleeve.

We saw the New Year in at Rabinovich's. There was a rumour that we might get some supper and even vodka, but no one succeeded in getting anything. We ate gruel and clinked glasses filled with tea, yet we enjoyed ourselves no less than if we had been drinking champagne.

However, the damned shoe polish refused to dry: as soon as there was a fall of snow, it rubbed off. I left my mark on the overcoats of several other people and began to be regarded as something of a menace. I now warned my companions: 'Would you mind walking on my left? On the right you'll get dirty'.

Nevertheless, I was now able to wander at night through the streets of Moscow without freezing to death. Everyone walked in the road: there were no cars, no horses, and the pavements were like skating rinks. In the daytime many people pulled small sledges laden with firewood, paraffin or millet. People got 'registered' or 'de-registered';

this referred to ration cards. (I remember a little verse: ' "What's for dinner, citizen, today?" "Are you registered, citizen, pray?" ')

At night, the dreamers took over. I shall never forget those walks. We advanced slowly between snowdrifts, sometimes walking in Indian file, one behind the other. It is thus that caravans cross deserts. We talked of poetry, of revolution and the new age; we were caravans heading for the future. Perhaps that is why we could so easily bear hunger, cold and much else. The caravans moved through every town in Russia, and Nikolay Tikhonov, then twenty-five, whom I did not yet know, was surely reciting his poem to someone: 'They ought to make nails out of people like these: in all the world no nails would be stronger'.

We walked in Indian file, and the stars shone above our heads: the streets were dark and nothing interfered with the stars shining. On my birthday Yadviga said sadly that she had not been able to get me a present; not a flower, not a boiled sweet was to be had. But, looking at the starry sky, she added, joking: 'I give you Cassiopeia'. We did not suspect that we should live to see the day when the United Nations would discuss possibilities of protecting the planets from unlawful seizure, and when every girl would be able to give her boy a handsome tie made of a chemical substance as a birthday present.

21

I WENT on working in the children's section of TEO. One could, of course, take a sceptical view of our work: it consisted chiefly in drafting projects for children's theatres and obtaining rations for actors. Times were hard; to describe them, let me recall Lenin's words written in February 1921 in connection with the Narkompros's work: 'We are paupers. There is no paper. The workers are hungry and cold, without clothing or shoes. The machines are worn out. The buildings are collapsing'. We did our best to support various ventures. There was the Children's Theatre under the direction of the actress Henrietta Paskar. The sculptor Yefimov and his wife had been busy with a puppet theatre for a long time. The young Natalie Satz appeared, who later did a great deal for children's education in art. Spectacles for children were put on in various workers' clubs. Finally, the famous clown and animal trainer V. L. Durov had the idea of showing four-legged artists to children.

In those days there were more projects than realizations of projects: there was a lot of imagination about but little money. And yet I believe that our work, entirely meaningless as it seemed at first glance, yielded certain results: we helped future playwrights, producers and actors to create extremely interesting children's theatres five or ten years later.

Outwardly there were many amusing features. We worked next door to the circus section, which was run by the actress Rukavishnikova, a poet's wife. Sometimes a horse-drawn sledge would be provided to drive her home. Outside the Manège, the horse would suddenly get on its hind legs as though it were a poodle, or else it began to waltz, frightening the passers-by: it was a circus horse temporarily seconded to sledge-pulling and it was clearly unable to overcome its passion for art. However, our section refused to be outdone by the circus lot: every now and then an emaciated, ascetic-looking camel harnessed to a sledge would stop outside our gate, sent by Durov to take me home.

Various picturesque characters came to call on Rukavishnikova. Jugglers and weight-lifters demanded 'academic' rations. Foreign acrobats protested against too many people being allotted rooms in their

145

flat. A clown would shout at the top of his voice: 'What's it got to do with a Marxist interpretation of events? I refuse to have my jokes taken seriously! That isn't what we made the Revolution for!' My visitors, mostly unsuccessful dramatists, were much duller. An article saying that there was a shortage of plays for children had appeared in one of the newspapers, and presently people from various walks of life began arriving in Moscow from Tambov, Chelyabinsk or Tver, filling my little office with piles of manuscript. The plays were written in green ink on the backs of notaries' deeds, on pages torn out of exercise books, even on wrapping paper. One author would portray the heroic deeds of the juvenile Lassalle, another set out to prove that mermaids were products of bourgeois consciousness, yet another exposed the intrigues of the Entente (for some reason I remember the rhyme: 'That is how it was, you know, When we dealt with Clemenceau'). Some authors would begin to read their works aloud there and then. One man stayed in the section several days, insisting on a room voucher and 'academic' rations.

I went to a club near Taganskaya Square, where a combined company put on a play for children, written by an entirely unknown author and entitled *Pasha's Fate*. The actors on the stage grunted naturalistically, drank tea and talked all the time about the advantages of learning. A middle-aged actress, taking the part of the little girl Pasha, repeated with psychological pauses: 'And so, you see, I grasped the tempo of life and I shut my book'.

Paskar's theatre put on Kipling's *Jungle Book*. The panther stretched voluptuously and generally behaved as if it were not an animal but Wilde's Salome. I thought this decadent and was rather angry. (Today, many concepts have become confused. The *Great Soviet Encyclopedia* includes Cézanne, Gauguin, Rimbaud, Hamsun, Debussy and Ravel – in other words almost all the major writers, authors and composers of the late nineteenth and early twentieth century – among the Decadents. Whereas in fact there really was such a thing as decadent art: it is enough to recall Salome, the novels of Przybyszewski or the paintings of Stuck.) After hearing my criticism, Henrietta Paskar calmly replied that I could put on other plays anywhere I liked, or take up some other occupation altogether. I thought it over and decided that she was right. After that I began to devote whatever time was left from drafting projects to work with Durov, whose animals were neither naturalistic nor decadent.

I had another occupation, too. In Prechistenka, in a building that had caused me much excitement when I was a schoolboy (it had housed the School for the Daughters of the Nobility), was the Military Chemical Academy. The students invited me to teach them versification. Their aim was to be able to write iambics, trochees and even free verse. They counted syllables industriously and searched for rhymes. I doubt whether any of them became poets, but I am sure that for the rest of their lives they remembered their taste for poetry as one remembers one's first love.

There was neither paper nor time for prose at this period. Moreover, prose writing requires a store of inner experience, observation, a critical approach, an ability to grasp events. Prose began to appear several years later. But it was a wonderful time for poetry. In the Soviet Union there is now a regular institution known as 'Poetry Day'. Poets give readings in bookshops and tempt bibliophiles with autographs. At the time I am writing about, however, poetry was read aloud everywhere – on the boulevards, at the railway stations, on icy factory shop floors – and it was not just a day, but a whole epoch of poetry.

I remember a message that came to the Union of Poets: a Red Army unit, about to go South on mopping-up operations against Wrangel's army, was asking for Mayakovsky, Yesenin or some other poet to be sent to their barracks, so that the men might hear some poetry on the eve of departure.

There was a 'Trial of modern poetry', followed by a 'Trial of Imaginism' and various poetical disputations. There was a multitude of literary schools: the Komfuts (Communist Futurists), the Imaginists, the Proletkult group, the Expressionists, the Fuists (Futurists), the Non-objective group, the Presentists, the Accidentists and even some people called *Nitchevoki* (the 'Nothing' group). Of course some of the theoreticians who appeared at the Café Domino or in the Press Club talked a great deal of nonsense; there was often nothing behind the accumulations of strange-sounding words but a craving for fame or a simple showing off. Yet I feel inclined to defend those far-off times. When today we open the book of poets well known far beyond the borders of our country we see how many splendid poems were written during the years of War Communism. Never had people lived so badly, and never, it seems, were they gripped by such creative fervour.

Inside the houses it was dark, cold and uninviting, and at night people besieged the theatres. The characters of Hoffmann, Gozzi, Calderon, Shakespeare thronged the stage. The artists Vesnin, Yakulov and Ekster dazzled audiences with the magnificence of their costumes and décors.

Romanticism was a literary movement during the first half of the nineteenth century. But the romantic element is always present in art: the artist sees what no longer exists or has not yet existed in reality. Meyerhold put on *Lake Liul* at the Revolutionary Theatre; Tairov put on *The Man Who was Thursday*, and lifts soared skywards on the stage, while in Moscow itself no lifts were working. Students at *Vkhutemas* worked on new designs for telephones, but most of the telephones in town had been disconnected. I remember Mayakovsky saying to me, smiling, at one of the rehearsals of *Mystery Bouffe* at Theatre No. 1 of the R.S.F.S.R.: 'Just wait and see: in the next scene you'll get the world of the future, with skyscrapers, electric tractors and enormous sugar loaves'.

Lyuba was studying under A. M. Rodchenko, who made Cubist designs for newspaper kiosks. Forty years later I saw in a number of countries newspaper kiosks, exhibition pavilions and even dwellings that recalled Rodchenko's old designs – though, of course, in a milder, watered-down form. Lisitzky was working on models for the books of the future. It was from a work of Tatlin's that I received the greatest impression of all. A *maquette* of his monument to the Third International was exhibited at the House of Trade Unions. It consisted of two revolving cylinders and a revolving pyramid: glass halls circled by a steel spiral. The Constructivists were fond of talking about logic and the functional purpose of art. According to Tatlin's project, the hall in which the *Sovnarkom* held its meetings was supposed to revolve. This was nonsensical from the functional point of view, and yet it was part of the genuine romanticism of the period. I stood for a long time in front of the large model and eventually went out into the street deeply shaken: it seemed to me that I had glimpsed the twenty-first century. Today I think otherwise: what struck me was the peculiar beauty of the design; art is outside matters of future town-planning and of the advantages of industrialized architecture.

The ways of art are highly complex. Cervantes, wishing to ridicule courtly romances, created a knight who alone survived his epoch and who has come galloping into our own times on his pathetic Rosinante. Balzac believed that he was glorifying the aristocracy, whereas in reality he was burying it.

Naturally, like all the friends I met at that time, I looked eagerly into the future. There were no newspaper kiosks whatsoever, never mind Cubist ones, and we read our newspaper not at the breakfast table but in the streets: they were pasted up on walls. Wrangel's army had been smashed; the Civil War was won. At the *subbotniks*[1] people were trying, with great courage, to vanquish hunger, disorganization and poverty. Various, often contradictory events were taking place in the world. The reaction triumphed, yet a rebellion in Saxony or a British miners' strike would suddenly flare up; India demanded independence. The world revolution appeared to us not as a vague ideal but as a thing of tomorrow. Sometimes, however, I fell prey to doubts: I could not understand why nothing, absolutely nothing, was happening in France – which I knew well – after the terrible war years and the first soldiers' mutinies.

Sometimes it is said of a person that 'he can't sit still', and this relates to space. At this point, however, I am speaking of time: we were impatient to cross over into the next century. All concepts had been turned upside down: one of the most backward countries of Europe found itself far ahead of the others. It lived by those ideas, those literary and artistic concepts which were to shake the West several decades later. Yet life – I mean everyday life – was prehistoric, the everyday life of the cave age.

Everyone wanted to know everything. There are many books describing the storming of fortifications, fortresses and strongholds. But this was a time when the people were storming knowledge. Old women sat over their ABCs. School textbooks became a rarity, like first editions. The *Vuzy* (higher educational establishments) were overcrowded with young enthusiasts. It was impossible to get inside a lecture hall: people elbowed their way into the auditorium of the Polytechnical Museum as they did into the rickety tramcars. Lecturers were bombarded with written questions, and it is amazing what these questions were about: strikes in Westphalia, Pavlov's reflexes, Suprematism, the struggle for oil, eugenics, Mayakovsky's rhymes, the theory of relativity, Ford factories, the abolition of death and thousands of other topics.

Comrade Adam managed to get a little coal and the Knyazhi Dvor began to be heated. Friends often came to see us in the evenings. Boris

---

[1] Voluntary unpaid communal work on Saturdays.

Pasternak, who lived next door, came almost every night. We argued about world events, about the duel between the Futurists and the Imaginists, about the paintings of Rozanova and Altman, about Meyerhold's productions: we wanted to turn a page of history.

I often got muddled and contradicted myself. I was enthusiastic about the cities of the future which would look like Tatlin's projects, but being 'Paul the son of Saul' I wrote: 'I see a dread city, a beehive, glass and steel of faceless honeycombs and, in the echoing streets, carnivals that are like military parades. Shadows of the spirals of future times, the yoke of thought-out equations and the concrete of a new paradise fall on waste patches'.

Among the snowdrifts of the Moscow lanes, clad in a sheepskin coat partially painted with black shoe-polish, I did not for an instant doubt that all these projects would become reality and that a new and extraordinary city would grow up in the place of the crooked little wooden houses familiar to me since childhood. Had I been ten years younger I should have smiled enthusiastically; but, born in 1891, rank-and-file representative of pre-revolutionary Russian intelligentsia that I was, with Korolenko's words that 'man is made for happiness as birds are made for flight' firmly imprinted on my mind since my boyhood years, I was often tormented by speculations about what the life of man in that city of the future would be like.

Emotion and irony, faith and logic struggled within me. Once I met a Belgian visitor at the Third Hostel of the Narkomindel. He talked about the lamentable state of our transport and about the advantages of constitutional guarantees. I retorted sharply: the bourgeois world was doomed, a lean christening was much more attractive than the most opulent funeral. He called me a fanatic. But, speaking frankly, I no longer in the least resembled the sixteen-year-old lad who had sneered at Nadya Lvova because of her admiration for Balmont. Many things troubled me and even aroused my indignation: over-simplifications, intolerance, contempt for the culture of the past, a phrase which I heard many times: 'What's the point of all this jabber, everything's perfectly clear'. But I now knew that history is not made according to one's own volition nor according to the magnificent novels of the nineteenth century. I knew that my destiny was closely bound up with the destiny of the new Russia.

That winter I celebrated my thirtieth birthday. The figure shocked me; I thought disconsolately that I had not done anything yet: all I had produced so far were writing exercises, trial runs, rehearsals. It is a curious fact that the rhythm of life had speeded up, aviation and the cinema had appeared, historical events overtook each other, yet my contemporaries were formed much more slowly than the men of the slow, unhurried nineteenth century. Babel did not properly begin to write until he was thirty, Seyfullina until she was thirty-two, Paustovsky thirty-four. But Gogol wrote *The Inspector-General* at twenty-seven. One of the most astonishing works in our literature, *A Hero of Our Times*, was written by a young man of twenty-six. I do not know; perhaps the speed and feverishness of the events gave us no chance to think deeply, to grasp what was going on, to understand ourselves and others.

It would be foolish to regret those years. Even if we were only the wood with which the fire was fed, that is no cause for resentment: the fire flared up, and it has turned out to be a great deal more lasting than a human life.

There were many things I wanted to describe: pre-war Paris, the trenches of the Somme, the Revolution, the Civil War, the designs, the projects and the snowdrifts; above all, I wanted to anticipate the future. I realized that I could not do this in verse. The idea of the novel was taking on flesh. One day, remembering the stories Diego Rivera had told me, I decided that the hero of my satirical novel would be a Mexican.

Looking up from projects for puppet theatres, I would begin – to my own surprise – to think about the chapters of *Julio Jurenito*.

22

ALTHOUGH V. L. Durov did not approve of the Futurists he was himself an eccentric, and the opening production at his children's theatre had an eccentric title: *Hares of All Lands, Unite!* I remember the occasion very well indeed. At the beginning, a hare held up a large wooden book-cover inscribed with the words DAS KAPITAL. He turned the pages, then summoned some other hares, of whom there were at least twenty. In the next scene there was the model of a palace on the stage; it was guarded by rabbits holding rifles. Hares pushing a toy cannon came running out from the wings: they fired the cannon at the rabbits and, having routed them, hoisted a red flag over the palace.

The curtain was raised and lowered by a bear-cub in a blue smock.

The children's delight was indescribable; pale and thin, they laughed to split their sides. And after the curtain had fallen the hares and rabbits came round to the front, and that intermingling of actors and audience of which the producer of *Dawn* dreamed took place. (On entering the theatre the children were given small pieces of carrot with which they later seduced the actors.)

This part of the show took half an hour, but it required lengthy preparatory work. Durov explained to me from the start that he meant to overthow a number of false ideas about animals. For example, it was traditionally believed that hares were cowards, and also, in Russian folklore, that they were squint-eyed; consequently it had to be shown that hares could fire a cannon.

Durov was then fifty-seven years old. He was Russia's most famous clown. I had seen him in the circus as a boy and had carried away a memory of a funny man in brightly-coloured clothes wearing a multitude of fantastic medals. Long before I was born the brothers Durov had been the favourites of all Russia. Chekhov had laughed at the antics of Vladimir Durov's mongrel Zapyataika. It may well be that the clown I saw as a child was not Vladimir Durov but his brother Anatoly, who at first was the more popular. Originally the brothers appeared together; later they quarrelled. Vladimir began billing himself as 'Durov the Elder', Anatoly as 'The Genuine Durov'. (He died before the Revolution and left instructions in his will that the same words – The Genuine Durov – should be inscribed on his gravestone.)

In any case, by the time I met Vladimir Durov he was Durov the One and Only. Members of the circus section of TEO tried to lure him to join them, but he was absorbed in his animals. I remember the occasion when he first came to see me: would we help him to organize a theatre for children in his house in Bozhedomka? He talked about the works of Pavlov, about conditioned and non-conditioned reflexes; he gave the impression, not of a famous clown, but of a venerable professor.

I was invited to one of the first rehearsals. Durov was trying to cure the hares of their nervousness; this was not easy. Although, according to him, animals were governed by various reflexes, whereas, unless Descartes was mistaken, man thinks and therefore is, there is much in common between the behaviour of men and animals; in particular, it is easier to intimidate the boldest of men than to make a hero out of a coward. Durov used to say that if a worm crawls away from a chicken, the chicken will eat it, but if, on the contrary, the worm crawls towards the chicken, the chicken will retire hastily. (There is, by the way, a Russian proverb – 'Brave before sheep, a sheep himself before a brave man' – which was not invented by hares or chickens.) The rehearsals took place at night. Durov patiently fed the principal performer – a most charming hare – with carrots, and the trainer's hand withdrew timorously all the time. As for the cannon, it frankly ran away from the hares. At the end of two or three weeks the hares realized that they were stronger than anyone. Durov called this method of training 'fear deception'.

Carrots played the dominant part in the producer's work. They were placed between the pages of the book, and in order to get a piece of carrot a hare had to pull the cord which made the cannon go off.

During rehearsals it transpired that rabbits had nothing against headgear, while hares broke formation if made to wear anything on their heads. Durov gave in, and the hares stormed the palace bareheaded.

Someone supplied Durov with carrots; the bear-cub, however, had a hard time. I applied to MPO for permission to issue rations to the bear-cub as a member of the cast. Although the rations were small, the cub grew and its smock was soon too small for it. Durov wanted me to get some cotton material for another smock. In vain did I tell him that this was extremely difficult, that I had spent months getting a pair of trousers for myself and that the bear-cub could perfectly well appear without a smock. In the end we got the cotton.

Durov was terribly upset by the death of a young elephant, called Baby, which he had temporarily housed in the Zoological Gardens. There was no coal. Baby caught cold and died. It weighed about three tons; the meat was shared out among the zoo staff. But Durov kept repeating: 'You never knew Baby . . . Baby had extraordinary gifts'. Five years later he wrote: 'My best, my true, devoted comrade died, my Baby died, a child I had brought up and invested with a part of my soul'.

The second item on the bill was a scene which Durov had first produced at the beginning of the century under the title *The Hague Peace Conference*. Now the name was different. Sworn enemies – a wolf and a goat, a cat and a rat, a fox and a cock, a bear and a pig – sat next to each other round a table.

Durov explained to me in detail how he had prepared this scene. The cage containing the rat was equipped with casters and hung all over with bells; it was lowered on rails from the table to the basket containing the cat. The clatter of the cage and the ringing of the bells frightened the cat, and it gradually began to be afraid of the rat, whereas the rat grew bolder every hour. Durov trained the other performers in the same way. The strong ceased to be confident of their invulnerability and the weak were cured of their fears. On this basis, 'peaceful co-existence' was established.

During the winter of which I am speaking I often saw Durov, tried to help him and became extremely attached to him. Later we met rarely, but he amused, delighted and inspired me on each occasion. He was one of the most fantastic men I have ever met. In the circus ring he wanted to preach and teach, gave scientific explanations, talked about reflexes, and at the same time came out in his dazzling costume driving dogs four-in-hand or riding on a pig. At home in Bozhedomka, where his visitors included eminent scientists, such as Chelpanov and Bekhterev, he would suddenly interrupt a serious discussion with a clown's jest. He was a poet by nature, and he found poetry in the world of four-legged actors.

He often became muddled when talking to people. He was apt to confuse materialism with Tolstoyanism and Marxism with Christianity. He signed his theoretical works 'Durov, Self-Taught Man'. But he was truly at ease with animals. He wanted human beings 'to feel a personality in the animal, conscious, thinking, rejoicing and suffering'.

Fantastic plans took shape in his head.

In one of his books he quotes the text of a letter received in August 1917: 'The Naval General Staff has considered Mr Durov's suggestion that he should train animals, to wit, sea lions and seals, for purposes of naval warfare, and regards the suggestion as highly interesting'. The letter was signed by the Naval Chief of Staff, a Rear-Admiral. One can easily guess the state of mind of the naval command at that time if it seriously hoped to use trained seals against German submarines.

Later, everything settled down again. No one was tempted any longer by the idea of mobilizing seals. In 1923 Durov was sent on an official mission to Germany, where he picked up some sea lions. He thought very well of them and rated them higher than dogs. I remember being taken by him to the pool and introduced: 'This is Ilya Grigoryevich, poet and friend of animals'. The sea lions came out, began to applaud with their fins and drenched me in icy water. Meanwhile Durov was saying: 'You ought to see the convolutions of their brains!'

He was convinced that human beings did not understand animals. Why did the Russians say 'blind as a hen'? A hen could see a hawk long before a man did. Stubborn as a donkey? Not a bit of it: the donkey was mercilessly exploited and only occasionally offered passive resistance. The pig was the cleanest creature and wallowed in the mud only in order to rid itself of parasites; housed in a clean place, it would score points over many human beings.

Why had his proposal to use sea lions against submarines been turned down in the end? Why had no one given consideration to his plan for setting fire to bombers with the help of tame eagles? Say what you will, people were very difficult to deal with.

Many years earlier Durov had fallen ill and made a will giving instructions that if he died, animals should escort him to the cemetery. The church regarded this wish as blasphemous. Alas, people did not understand that animals had souls. Ten or fifteen years later, the word 'soul' had disappeared, to be replaced by 'reflexes'. Yet people still

155

went on smiling sceptically. For example, physiologists claimed that dogs could not distinguish colours. Durov was indignant: 'All my dogs, even complete beginners, puppies, can tell a green ball from a red one'.

Anna Ignatyevna, Durov's wife, was very fond of animals. Yet he once told me, sadly, that only monkeys, dogs, cats and parrots were allowed into the bedroom. Badgers or geese, for instance, were excluded. 'It isn't right . . . it isn't fair.'

Once he came to see Lunacharsky with his usual sort of request: would Lunacharsky sign this paper? Lunacharsky said he must think it over. Then Durov's favourite, the rat Finka, jumped out of his pocket and stood on its hind legs in front of the People's Commissar. Lunacharsky, who was afraid of rats, shouted 'Take it away!' Durov only sighed: 'Sorry, Anatoly Vasilyevich, I can't do that. It's pleading on behalf of its comrades. Solidarity, you know'.

Ten years later he appeared at the Coupole in Paris with another rat and was most surprised when women started screaming hysterically; he tried to explain that this rat was an artiste, but no one listened.

When he went out to dinner he would talk about science and progress, and then suddenly he would pull out of his pocket, together with his handkerchief, a raw fish or a lump of meat: all his pockets were crammed with titbits for animals.

As he looked at people, he thought of animals. Describing how his toy terriers, when pleased, smiled and wagged their behinds, he added: 'The way feelings are expressed is very often the same. Take the wagging of the behind. I have often noticed, particularly at dances, that a young man going up to ask a lady to dance will wag his behind quite unmistakably'.

When he and Anna Ignatyevna came to Paris we took them to a dance-hall in the rue Blomet which was frequented by Negro students, artists and models. Durov watched the dancing couples with great attention and suddenly cried out with delight: 'Mummy, look how they rub their bellies together! It's the same reflex as parrots'.

Anna Ignatyevna said to my wife: 'I was hoping to buy a few dresses in Paris, but Volodya has bought a giraffe. Giraffes are awfully expensive and, besides, it's got to travel in a special truck'.

Durov adored his chimpanzee Mimus, and reported to me in detail on his progress: 'Mimus has learnt to pronounce syllables. He can say several words. He's beginning to write; the only letter he's really sure of is "o", but now I'm teaching him "ж" '.

Then a disaster occurred. Durov was to go on tour to Minsk. He took special care of Mimus and never showed him in the ring, but he took him along to make sure he was looked after. The ape, who had already been ill several times before, caught a cold which developed into pneumonia. Durov told me how it died: 'He slept in my bed at the hotel. It's the most difficult thing to house-train an ape. A kitten will behave properly very soon. But apes are so absent-minded. They know they ought to go out, but they're distracted by something amusing, and so they make a mess. But not Mimus. I saw him get up, take some toilet paper and go towards the chamber pot. He never got there: he died on the way'. And there were tears in Durov's eyes.

I have already said that it was sometimes difficult to understand his view of the world; but he hated war and spoke of this both in the circus ring and at scientific gatherings. In 1924 he wrote: 'Soviet Russia was the first to take a bold initiative in the matter of disarmament and is still openly calling on other nations to follow its example.' (It is sad to think that thirty-six years have gone by, that a war such as history had never known has taken place and that Durov's words read as if they had been copied from today's newspapers.)

Durov's whole life was one of poetry and eccentricity. At a scripture examination in the third form of the Moscow Military Gymnasium, Vladimir Durov, son of a nobleman, walked into the examination hall on his hands. The examiners had not heard of the medieval *jongleurs* and sent the impudent boy packing.

In his old age Durov was surrounded by scholars; Professors Kozhevnikov and Leontovich wrote a preface to one of his books. One might ask: what was there in common between Durov and a clown? And yet he remained a circus man to the end, cursing the ring, yet unable to live without it.

When Durov died in the summer of 1934, the funeral procession moved off from Bozhedomka towards the circus. Thousands of people came to bid farewell to a clown who had amused many generations.

But the dogs listened, sniffed and waited. The sea lions waited. The raven waited, uselessly repeating his name: 'Voronok . . . Voronusha'. Durov did not come. We shall not look upon his like again.

At the beginning of 1921 he and I were driving from TEO to Bozhedomka, pulled along by the emaciated but still cheerful camel. Suddenly Durov said: 'Why do they keep saying "clown, clown"? Let me tell you a secret: clowns are the most serious people'.

23

ONE very cold winter day I ran into Sergey Yesenin in Tverskaya. He suggested that we should go and have some real coffee in a mysterious place which he called 'Kislovka'.

The woman who opened the door to us began twittering rapturously: 'Oh, Sergey Alexandrovich, I thought you were never coming again, it's been such a long time!' Judging by the bric-à-brac on the dressing-table and the old English engravings on the wall she had formerly been a lady of means and now kept an 'underground' eating place for actors, writers and black marketeers. Yesenin whispered something in her ear, and soon a coffee pot, sugar bowl, plate of pastries and even a decanter with liqueur appeared on the table. My own life was rather ascetic and I had not so much as suspected that such establishments existed. Seeing my surprise, Yesenin was as delighted as a child: 'Isn't it just like a Paris café? Well, isn't it?'

Our hostess made a complimentary remark about his tie and he was again delighted. He was wearing a light-coloured coat and black patent-leather shoes. He showed off like a country lad and grinned when passers-by recognized him.

We did not have much to drink – the decanter was tiny – but we did not feel like leaving the warm comfortable room. Yesenin surprised me by turning the conversation to painting: he had recently seen Shchukin's collection, and Picasso had aroused his interest. It turned out that he had read Verlaine and even Rimbaud in translation. Then he began reciting Pushkin: 'Bitterly I complain, and bitter tears I shed, yet cannot wash away the shameful lines.' Suddenly he began attacking Mayakovsky: 'His Tit and Vlas . . . What does he know about them? And even suppose he did, what sort of poetry do you call that?' (He was referring to a propaganda rhyme of Mayakovsky's in which there were two peasants called Tit and Vlas.) His words caused me no surprise: not long before, I had spent a whole evening listening to Mayakovsky and Yesenin abuse each other at the Polytechnical Museum. All the same, I asked him why Mayakovsky infuriated him so much. 'Mayakovsky is a poet *for* something, I am a poet *because of* something. I don't know myself because of what. He'll live till he's eighty and they'll put up a monument to him.' (Yesenin always passionately longed for fame and, in his mind, monuments were not bronze statues but the embodiments of immortality.) 'And I'll die in the gutter, under a fence on which his poems are pasted up. But still I wouldn't change places with him.' I tried to argue. Yesenin was in a generous mood and reluctantly admitted that Mayakovsky was a poet, although an 'uninteresting' one. He began inveighing against the Futurists. Art was an inspiration to life, it could not be dissolved in life. Certainly he, Yesenin, had scrawled obscene verses on the walls of Strastnoy Monastery, but that was due to high spirits, not part of a programme. The people? Shakespeare was surely popular enough for anybody, he did not spurn fairground amusements, yet he created Hamlet. That wasn't anything like Tit or Vlas. Then he began reciting Pushkin again, saying: 'Just to write a quatrain like that! Then one wouldn't be afraid to die. Because I'm certainly going to die soon'.

When we took leave of each other in the street, Yesenin said: 'Poetry isn't like pastries, you don't pay for it in roubles'. I remember these words because they struck me deeply: that day I saw Yesenin for the first time, although we had met earlier and I had long loved his poems.

In Petrograd in the autumn of 1917, a young poetess called Shkapskaya, whom I had met in Paris, invited me to her house. Nikolay Klyuyev, dressed in a peasant shirt, was seated at the table, drinking noisily from a saucer. He struck me at once as an actor performing a well-memorized part for the thousandth time. Topics of conversation were running out when a new guest arrived: a young and handsome lad looking like Lel[1] from the opera; smiling, he introduced himself: 'Sergey Yesenin. Seryozha'. He had limpid, innocent eyes. Shkapskaya asked him to read some of his poetry. I realized that a great poet was before me; I wanted to have a talk with him, but after sitting there smiling for a while he left.

Later we met several times in Moscow and talked of poetry and events. Unlike Klyuyev, he varied the parts in his repertoire, talking now of the indoclave, now of the dynamism of images, now of 'Scythianism'; but he could not (or would not) stop acting. I often

[1] Slav heathen god of love and marriage.

heard him answer someone he was talking to with the tinge of a sneer, opening wide his sky-blue eyes: 'I don't know how it is where you come from, but we in Ryazan province . . .' In May 1918 he said to me that it was necessary to overthow everything, to change the structure of the universe, that the peasants would set fire to things and the world would be burned down. He gave me a book of his with the following inscription: 'To I. Ehrenburg, my dear adversary in our views on Russia and the Storm, in memory of his sincerely affectionate S. Yesenin'.

Now, after our long talk in Kislovka, I saw the real Yesenin. How many Yesenins he acted! Ivanov-Razumnik, after hearing his *Inonia*, gushed: 'Here is genuine revolutionary subjectivism'. Various 'Scythians' regarded him as the spokesman of their ideology, and I remember A. A. Schreider in Berlin arguing that Yesenin's 'Bring forth your calf, O God' would convulse bourgeois Europe. The young poets, on the other hand, saw Yesenin as the creator of a new poetry: 'Imaginism' was served up, not as one of the numerous existing literary trends, but as the tablets of the law.

It would be wrong to think that Yesenin deceived or, if you wish, mystified others: often he played jokes on himself; the feelings which possessed him demanded a form of expression, and he would then give way, turning nostalgia into a programme and inner confusion into a literary school

He was exceptionally lucky. Mayakovsky subordinated his moods to an idea. Yesenin, as he once confessed to me, was able to 'play the fool' at the Domino or Pegasus's Loosebox, yet he wrote, without hesitation, exactly as he wanted to at any particular moment.

Admitting his spiritual defeat at the end, he wrote: 'I accept everything. I take everything as it is. I am prepared to walk on trodden paths. I'll give my whole soul to October and May, but I will not surrender my beloved lyre'.

Mayakovsky had to fight incomprehension, the sneers of some and the coldness of others. Yesenin was well-loved during his lifetime. His poetry had a sincerity, an extraordinary musical quality which enthralled even those who disapproved of him after hearing of his absurd tavern antics. He dreamt of fame and had his fill of it. At the age of twenty-five he addressed his parents in a poem: 'Oh, if only you could understand that your son is the best poet in all Russia!' The famous Isadora Duncan, whose dancing I had admired as a schoolboy, loved him. Her love enchanted him as a mark of universal recognition. He wanted to see the world and was one of the first Soviet citizens to travel right across Europe. He saw America. Women fell in love with him. Old Negroes and Paris urchins winked sympathetically at him. Gorky wept when Yesenin read him his poems. He did whatever he wanted, and even the stern guardians of Soviet morality turned a blind eye to his wild escapades.

Yet it is difficult to imagine an unhappier man. He could not find a place for himself anywhere. Love oppressed him. He suspected his friends of intrigue. He was a hypochondriac and always thought that he would soon die. I know the explanation offered by smug philistines: 'Too much drink'. But one must not confuse the effect with the cause. Why did he drink too much? Why did he overstrain himself at the very start of his life as man and poet? Why is there so much genuine bitterness even in his early poems, written at a time when he neither drank nor brawled? They say that under NEP the vermin crawled out of the cracks, and *Tavern Moscow* was born; but the *Confession of a Hooligan* was written before NEP, during a winter when Moscow was like a phalanstery or a monastery under strict rule. Why did Yesenin hang himself when he was thirty, at the zenith of his fame, before he had even heard the distant footfalls of old age?

I have sometimes read that Yesenin's tragedy was that he was divorced from his times. I don't think it is a matter of the times. Certainly Yesenin lived during a very difficult period, and he often railed at his epoch; but he also often declared his love for it. He reacted to the Revolution in his own way: in 1921 he was still attracted by the element of rebellion and still dreamed of writing a long poem to be called *Gulyay-Polye*. We saw each other shortly before my departure for Paris. He gave me his book *Treryadnitsa* with the following inscription: 'You know the smell of our earth and the pattern of our climate. Tell Paris I am not afraid of it: on the snows of our country we shall once again be able to stir up a blizzard equally terrible for them and for these'. This was in the spring of 1921; one would have thought that by this time everyone had forgotten all about 'Scythianism', but Yesenin still had visions of a defiant band of freebooters galloping on fast horses over the length and breadth of our planet.

Forty years have passed. Yesenin is read and loved in our country and no one gives any thought to the tangled skein of his political ideas. He wrote in 1920: 'I want to be a yellow sail to the country to which we are sailing'. But five years later, a little before his death, he admitted that on that ship he was not a sail but one of the passengers: 'Well, which of us never fell on the broad deck, never spewed and never cursed? They are few, with experienced souls, who remained steadfast on the rough sea. Now years have passed. I am at another age. I feel and think in other ways. And across the festive wine I say: praise and glory to the helmsman!'

He rushed through Europe and America and saw nothing. He wrote in his letters: 'My top hat and my cloak made by a Berlin tailor drove everyone mad ... Such vileness, monotony, such spiritual poverty it makes one spew'. 'Apart from the foxtrot there is almost nothing here, they stuff themselves and drink and do the foxtrot again.' Of course, apart from the foxtrot, the West also saw in those days bloody demonstrations, hunger, Picasso, Romain Rolland, Chaplin and much else. Yet I can understand Yesenin's state of mind. It was not just a matter of his love for the Russian birch tree that has been so much written about. What matters, too, is that he saw from far off a people rushing headlong towards the future.

On his return to Russia he tried to draw conclusions: 'I do not like our scarcely cooled-down nomads' camp. I like civilization. But I very much dislike America. America is that stinking fog where not only art, but also all the best impulses of mankind perish'. He published a naïve and helpless article in a newspaper, yet the name he found for America was extraordinarily accurate: the Iron Mirgorod[1]. It should be recalled that this was in 1923, when LEF was extolling the beauty of New York skyscrapers and when NOT (*Nauchnaya Organizatsia Truda*, Scientific Organization of Labour) was all the fashion – two years before Mayakovsky went to America.

Yesenin was above all a poet. Historical events, love, friendship, all these took second place; poetry came first. He had a rare gift of song. For a zoologist, a nightingale is one of the birds of the thrush family, yet no description of the nightingale's throat can explain why its song has enchanted people in all parts of the world. No one can explain why we are moved by many of Yesenin's poems. There are poets full of lofty thoughts, brilliant observation and passionate feeling who spend whole decades acquiring the art of passing their spiritual wealth on to others. But Yesenin wrote poetry simply because he had

[1] Mirgorod: Gogol's typical provincial backwater.

been born a poet. 'Not everyone knows how to sing, not to everyone is it given to fall like an apple at other men's feet.'

Profound sadness was an innate characteristic of Yesenin's poetic voice. This sadness cannot be blamed on the times, even though it led Yesenin to blame many things on the times: 'It's all very well for them to stand and watch, painting their mouths in tinny kisses: I alone, like a psalm singer, must chant hallelujahs over my native land'. He knew that no one was to blame for his loneliness and his misery. 'Whom should I call? With whom should I share the sad joy of having remained alive? Here, even the windmill – a bird of logs with a single wing – stands with closed eyes. No one here knows me, and those who once remembered me have long forgotten.' Such feelings can arise in no matter what epoch.

Perhaps that is why Yesenin's poems do not age. 'Oh the bush of my head is withered, the captivity of song has sucked me in. I am condemned, in the hard labour of feelings, to turn the grindstone of poetry.' Or: 'And now I speak not to my mother but to an alien, jeering mob: It doesn't matter, I have stumbled on a stone. It will all heal by tomorrow'. When were those lines written? Forty years ago? A hundred years? Yesterday? I do not know. It is of no account.

During the war years I often heard it said by young lieutenants in the front line, straight from the schoolroom – and young people say the same today – 'I love Yesenin'. I can understand that. Young people, unless they are poets or specifically interested in poetry, rarely take a volume of verse down from the bookshelf when they feel happy: they are off to a football match or a dance, go for a walk with a girl, dream aloud or argue heatedly. The need for poetry is felt in hours of sadness, and that is when Yesenin comes to the rescue, Yesenin who died long ago and of whom they know nothing except the most important thing: he wrote marvellous poems.

He never said how poetry should be written; he never identified the poet's craft with industrial production; yet it is absurd to claim that he was a 'simple songster'. Anyway, has there ever been such a thing? The legend of François Villon, the 'ingenuous poet', drunkard and criminal, who wrote poems just as they came to him, was accepted for five centuries. Recently Tristan Tzara made a discovery: the last lines of Villon's ballads are in code; they tell the truth about the poet's tribulations in love and about his crimes. Truly, one needs great skill to write lines in which every fifth or seventh letter is in code and which, nevertheless, seem completely natural, so that no one will suspect the technical difficulties. Yesenin often told me that he worked for a long time on his poems, crossing out and tearing up. Mayakovsky called him: 'Bright-voiced guttersnipe apprentice'. Yesenin said: 'I came as a stern craftsman'. (Yesenin was right: sadness turned him into a 'guttersnipe', he was never 'bright-voiced', and the question whether he was 'apprentice' or 'craftsman' has been answered by time.) He often called himself a 'hooligan', but there was one thing he respected: skill. Bryusov was as alien to him as any poet could be, yet on hearing of his death Yesenin wrote: 'The news is painful and hard to bear, particularly for poets. We all learned from him. We all know the part he has played in the development of Russian verse'.

Yesenin's poetry is gentle and human; there is no cruelty, no mental coldness in it. His poem about a bitch whose puppies have been drowned was written during the war when people were beginning to be inured to callousness. A little before his suicide he wrote a poem called *The Black Man*. The image was evidently suggested by Pushkin: the 'black man' is pursuing Mozart. But Mozart's man in black is death. Yesenin, on the other hand, recognized in him also the pangs of conscience: the man in black is cruel; he insists: 'He was elegant and a poet besides, of tenacious if not great power; he would call some woman of forty-odd a naughty little girl and his darling. Listen, listen! he croaks looking me in the face, bending over me closer and closer, I have never seen any scoundrel suffer so unnecessarily and so stupidly from insomnia.'

In life he was tender and touching but also, in the fury of his inner conflict, insufferable. I have known him gentle, calm and attentive; I have known him, too, in a state bordering on insanity. I do not want to speak of things that are more related to pathology than to a poet's psychological make-up.

In Berlin I saw him several times with Isadora Duncan. She realized what a terribly hard time he was going through, wanted to help and could not. She was almost twice his age and had not only great talent but also humanity, tenderness and tact. But he was a nomad, a gipsy; nothing frightened him so much as the thought of being emotionally settled.

He was always surrounded by fellow-travellers: Imaginists, Kusikov with his guitar and the 'peasant poets' who looked as if they had stepped

165

off the lacquered lids of Palekh boxes. The poets were elbowed out by plain drunks happy to be tolerated at a famous man's table.

Whereas Futurism, despite the yellow shirts and Burlyuk's lorgnette, was an important artistic and social phenomenon, Imaginism always seemed to me a hastily concocted shop-sign for a group of literary men. Yesenin loved a fight and, just as at school the 'Greeks' had fought the 'Persians', he readily joined the Imaginists in order to fight the Futurists. None of this amounts to so much as a page of his biography; it is no more than a few footnotes which will arouse the interest of literary historians only.

It was painful to see Yesenin surrounded by people of profound irrelevance, by that gang which hangs on to the fringes of literature, liking (as it still does) to drink someone else's vodka, bask in someone else's fame and hide behind someone else's authority. But Yesenin was not driven to his death by this black swarm of midges swirling round his head: he attracted it himself. He knew these people's worth, but in his condition he felt easier among people he despised.

I saw him for the last time in 1924 at the house of mutual friends. He was in a bad state and wanted to leave, to make a row, to fight. I reasoned with him and tried to hold him back for several hours, while he repeated desolately: 'Oh, come on, let me go. You know I don't mean you . . . it's everything, don't you see?'

One of Yesenin's last poems contains the following lines: 'How should I not love you, flowers? I'd like to drink with you like brothers. Rustle your branches, stocks and mignonette, my soul's in trouble; my soul's in trouble, rustle your branches, stocks and mignonette'. We all know that stocks are not oaks, that mignonette is not an elm and that they have no branches to rustle. And yet the lines are beautiful, and it is impossible to say why: such is the nature of poetry. And, remembering Yesenin, I always think: there was a poet . . .

24

WHENEVER I think of Alexander Yakovlevich Tairov I am reminded of Pushkin's lines: 'Once there lived a poor knight, taciturn and simple, dark and pale in looks, bold and straight in spirit'. Tairov's life was as simple as a parable. As a youth he fell in love with the theatre; became an actor in a provincial company; came to Petersburg, where he met the leading poets and artists. Meyerhold was putting on Blok's *Balaganchik*. Tairov took the part of the Blue Mask. But Tairov did not yet exist.

In 1914 he organized the Kamerny Theatre which became the goal, the content and the passion of his life. That wonderful actress Alisa Georgievna Koonen was at his side. Tairov was then a little under thirty. He was fighting for what he believed was the most progressive theatre.

He was not indifferent to the great changes which had taken place in Russia. He was always ready to abandon mistaken opinions; he searched; he was indefatigable, working from morning till late at night. The Kamerny had many friends but also many enemies; and, to go back once more to Pushkin's poem, it was as if those enemies repeated for decades: 'He did not say his prayers, they said; he did not observe the fast'.

In 1949 the enemies won: the Kamerny disappeared. Tairov was sixty-four. A year later he died.

During the winter of which I am speaking Tairov put on *Princess Brambilla*, which had a great success. He began working on *Phèdre* and published a book called *A Producer's Notes* in which he defended his position both against the adherents of the naturalistic theatre and against Meyerhold. It was as if he had grown wings. And our melancholy meetings at the end of the forties cannot obscure in my memory the gay and happy Tairov of the first years of the Revolution.

Moscow was delighted with the bright carnival on the stage. Yakulov's décors were dazzling, like fairy-tale settings. The actors skipped about, played the fool, danced, joked. Moscow also understood the sufferings of Adrienne Lecouvreur. Tairov had transformed

Scribe's sentimental melodrama into a tragedy. Alisa Koonen's acting moved the audience deeply. This may seem surprising: it was not easy to excite pity in those days; everyone was used to death. Adrienne's death moved because it was not naturalistic, as in Scribe's play, but had been transformed by art: it was not death in a hospital bed but the end of Eurydice or Ophelia.

Tairov had a profound understanding of two forms of theatre: the harlequinade and tragedy. During the years I am describing, people lived without the in-between stages: there was gaiety and despair, a troglodyte existence and blueprints for the twenty-first century.

Tairov was not only modest in his own life, he also subordinated his dreams in art to the strictest discipline. They say that a sense of moderation clips the wings of romanticism: that is true if one means shrewd calculation or philistine wisdom. But let us remember: even the artists of the most flamboyant period of Romanticism knew full well what a sense of moderation means; without it, art becomes cant, false pathos and hysteria.

Tairov often talked to me about his attitude to the theatre. He abandoned narrow realism; he did not want to show actors naturalistically drinking tea or yawning on the stage. He was fond of quoting a story told by Coquelin, the famous nineteenth-century French actor. An itinerant player at a fair imitated the squealing of a pig. Everyone was delighted and applauded him. Then a Norman peasant wagered that he could do as well as the actor. He hid a live piglet under his coat and started pinching it. The piglet squealed, but the audience booed: they did not think the peasant was a good mimic. Tairov knew what art means and would not recognize a theatre based on imitating life. He often said 'the theatre must become theatrical'; at first this strikes one as absurd, like saying that water must be liquid. Yet all around there were theatres which had renounced the idea of spectacle. Whereas Tairov did not believe in descriptive poetry, literary painting, or a theatre like a room from which the fourth wall has, for some reason, been amputated.

Tairov did not deny either the playwright's or the stage designer's role, but he wanted all the elements on the stage to be subordinated to one thing: the theatre.

At first, as a tribute to Decadent art, he put on *Salome*. He was not the only one who felt enthusiasm for the play. Tairov staged it in 1917, Mardzhanov in 1919. No one later remembered Mardzhanov's sins, but people refused to forgive Tairov his *Salome*. And yet many other people besides Tairov went through a Decadent phase. I heard Lunacharsky recite Balmont's most Decadent poems with fervour in 1909. Bryusov not only wrote Decadent erotic verse in his youth, not only decorated his walls with paintings by Rops, but also admired the poetry of Igor Severyanin, who – although he dubbed himself an 'Ego-Futurist' – was really a Decadent for the use of hairdressers and undiscriminating lady-killers. The decadent 'Someone in Grey' stood on the stage of the Art Theatre and announced like a ventriloquist: 'A man is born'. The same ill-starred *Salome* was put on at the Maly. All this was very quickly forgotten. But there are people, it seems, who are born under an unlucky star. Tairov travelled a long and tortuous road, but when he was lying in his coffin, some producer at the memorial service still recalled his past errors – reading them out from a little piece of paper.

When Tairov was asked to speak or write about his life, he began listing his productions: he was a man of one passion. It is impossible to speak of him without speaking of the Kamerny Theatre. It was a marvellous theatre, but it, too, was born under an unlucky star. Let me begin by saying that it was unfortunately named. (I have met many people whose lives were overcast by the fact that their parents had given them an ugly or pretentious name: a delicate youth called Vlas, an experienced engineer called Cain, a flirtatious girl called Constitutia.) In 1914 the word Kamerny (Chamber) Theatre sounded like 'studio': it implied that the young theatre, full of boldness and daring, was not out for financial success. The name remained, and for thirty years its ill-wishers kicked it about like a ball: 'Kamerny means intimate, small-scale, private, a theatre for connoisseurs, for gourmets'. (Many people failed to understand the name. Tairov told the story of how, in a Siberian town where the company was on tour, he was asked before the performance: 'Are all your actors lags or have you got voluntary chaps as well[1]?')

Tairov was appreciated and defended by many people: Lunacharsky, old actors of the Maly Theatre, M. Koltsov in *Pravda*, ordinary theatregoers. Lunacharsky, who was enthusiastic about the production of *Phèdre*, wrote that the Kamerny was in many ways similar to the old

[1] The word *kamera*, as well as meaning 'chamber', also means prison cell.

theatre of the mid-nineteenth century, to the 'glorious Karatygin'. I have already described how amused I was by the old French actor Mounet-Sully, whose acting was no doubt similar to Karatygin's. When I giggled at Mounet-Sully's Oedipus I was a callow youth who did not know anything about art. Years passed. Then I saw Alisa Koonen in *Phèdre*. I did not laugh. I recognized that fulness of art which makes one feel light and a little afraid. (The first men who leave the earth's gravitational field may feel something of the same sort.)

I have been to performances by the Kamerny in Paris and Berlin, and I have seen the audiences' delight. Tairov had the daring to take Racine's *Phèdre* to Paris, and he triumphed. Antoine and Picasso, Léger and Gémier, Cocteau and Jean-Richard Bloch spoke enthusiastically of the Kamerny productions. Actors of the Kabuki theatre in Japan still remember Tairov. Very few artists, one would have thought, have ever done so much for what the newspapers call 'the development of cultural relations'.

It is impossible to imagine the Kamerny without Alisa Koonen. On the stage, this kindly and warm-hearted woman tore the hearts of the audience; anyone who has once seen her must remember her eyes, hands and voice. She seemed to have come into the theatre out of another age; she knew neither past nor future. It was a time of great men and great deeds, but when the curtain went up in thousands of theatres all one saw were prancing *ingénues*, *jeune premiers*, comic old women and *raisonneurs*. Then suddenly a tragic actress appeared, and she came at a time which no one could call an age of *genre* comedy or domestic drama.

Tairov did not look in the least like an actor; his conversation was simple and controlled; he was always master of himself. I have seen him go quickly into the wings at a time of great personal grief: the man facing the actors was a calm, clean-shaven, imperturbable Tairov.

I must confess that I am not a theatre man. But there are many Kamerny productions I cannot forget, from the early *Princess Brambilla* to *Madame Bovary*, staged in 1940. I am grateful for these to Tairov and Koonen: their art has often helped me. Their friendship helped me, too: I knew the back way into the Kamerny, into the flat where they lived. Every injury one suffered was softened by their sympathy and affection.

In 1949 Tairov was directed to work in someone else's theatre. He was a man of great discipline; he waited for work, but there was none for him.

In a book published long ago, recalling the beginning of his work in the theatre, Tairov wrote: 'When the first posters bearing the name "Kamerny Theatre" appeared at long last in the streets of Moscow, we would beg passers-by to read them aloud to us to be absolutely convinced that it was really true and not a mirage'. During the last weeks of his life the ailing Alexander Tairov used to creep quietly out of his house. His friends, worried about his health, followed him to see where he went. He would go to a wall where theatrical posters were displayed and study them carefully. There was no poster of the Kamerny theatre.

25

ONCE, that winter, having got hold of a few sheets of paper, I tried to make a start on the novel that had long been in my mind. After writing a few lines I tore up the sheet. The times were not favourable to novel-writing. It was not a matter of cold and hunger (although I freely admit that I often dreamt of a lump of meat). Nor was it even a matter of the various meetings at which we spent our days. The events were too near and on too large a scale. A novelist is not a shorthand-typist; he needs to collect his thoughts, to reflect, to stand back a few paces (or a few years) from the situation he wants to describe.

I do not think that a single novel was written in Russia in 1920 or 1921. Those were years of poetry and literary manifestos. I am now thinking of the writers of my generation – Seyfullina, Furmanov, Lavrenev, Paustovsky, Malyshkin, Fedin, Babel, Tynyanov, Pilnyak. They were demobilized, carried out various missions, moved from place to place, edited other people's articles, went to meetings, gave lectures; almost none wrote any significant works until later.

A novel that has been thought and lived through but is not written down can drive one to distraction. It seemed to me that I needed only to sit down in some Paris café, ask the waiter for coffee, a few sandwiches and pen and paper, and the book would be written.

I wanted to write a satirical novel depicting the pre-war years, the war, the Revolution; but the last chapter was shrouded in mist. However hard I tried, I could not imagine what people were doing in the West while the Russians overthrew, burned, made projects, fought on ten fronts, hungered, contracted spotted typhus and dreamt deliriously of the future. I said to myself that the circle must be completed, and that I must take a look at post-war Paris.

(I thought a great deal about the book. But I thought not only about that. Paris had been the city of my youth; I had come to love it and I had left many friends there. Sometimes I missed Paris badly and I do not want to leave that out of my story.)

Once I talked this over with an old friend who had been a fellow-member of the underground Bolshevik organization; I talked about it not as of a realistic wish but rather as of a dream, and I was extremely surprised when I was summoned to the Narkomindel and asked to fill in a form.

Although I was living in the Narkomindel's Third Hostel, I never set foot in the building where I had delivered the sealed bales the previous autumn. I do not know what duties the numerous members of this Commissariat's staff performed (I used to meet some of them in the passages of our hostel). I suppose they attended meetings. After all, there were practically no diplomatic relations with other countries at that period. Having suffered a defeat in their efforts to overthow Soviet power, the governments of the West were now trying to convince others – if not themselves – that Russia did not exist. (The German Republic did not recognize Soviet Russia until 1922, Britain and France not until 1924, the United States not until 1933.)

An elderly but extraordinarily temperamental woman was raging in the waiting-room of the Narkomindel. Having reduced the Narkom secretary to a wreck, she turned her artillery on me for some reason: 'They've got absolutely no right to do this! Ask any lawyer. I have a Swiss passport, and I refuse to be treated like this. I'm not a bourgeoise, I used to work as a governess, I deserve protection. Of course my savings are in gold, I'm not so mad as to hold on to scraps of paper that are worth less and less every day. I'm going to write to Berne. I shan't rest till I get satisfaction'. I got rid of her with considerable difficulty and sat down to fill in my form.

To a question about my purpose in going abroad I answered: 'I wish to write a novel'. The secretary smiled and made me fill in the whole thing over again. He dictated: 'Artistic mission'.

A few more weeks passed and Comrade Adam, the warden of the hostel, said that I was wanted at the Cheka. Noticing my nervousness, he added: 'Main entrance. To see Comrade Menzhinsky'.

V. R. Menzhinsky was ill and lay on a couch which was too short for him. I thought he was going to start asking me whether I had ever had any dealings with Wrangel's army; instead, he said that he had seen me in Paris; was I still writing poetry? I replied that I wanted to write a satirical novel. Since the conversation was about literature, I told him of some of the things that worried me: there was too much pretentious poetry about, but Blok was writing nothing. Menzhinsky smiled and nodded, and occasionally frowned. Suddenly I pulled myself up short: the man was busy, and unwell into the bargain, and here was I carrying on as if I were at the Press Club. Menzhinsky said: 'We don't mind letting you go, but what the French will say is quite another story'.

I was issued a passport for foreign travel stamped with a Latvian visa. My wife received a similar passport.

It was a brilliant spring day. The snowdrifts were settling, collapsing, slipping away. Melted snow dripped from the roofs. Boys called to each other in high, clear voices.

Spring in Moscow is extraordinary. People who live in the blessed South know nothing like it: it is not a change of season but an event of prime importance in everyone's life; and although the Moscow of today had little in common with the Moscow through which I walked in April 1921, our springs are still the same, one is like the other, and none is like anyone or anything else. You have to have lived through that interminable winter, to have switched on the light on waking in December, to have been cold, to have seen the earth eternally swathed in a shroud, to have been blinded by blizzards in March, in order fully to appreciate the thaw, the breaking of the ice, life's boisterous housewarming.

It was precisely on such a riotous, sunny day that, as I walked back to the Knyazhy Dvor with my passport in my pocket, I suddenly stopped and thought: Good heavens, I'm leaving!

It was hard to tear myself away from Moscow life, perhaps because that life itself was so hard. Since Meyerhold had left TEO, the meetings in the children's section – where we continued, by the force of inertia, to work out various projects – had begun to seem meaningless to me. It would be far more sensible to try and write a novel. And yet it was difficult to leave: I realized that real life was here, in Moscow.

That day, or on one of the days that followed – I cannot remember, but anyway it was shortly before our departure – I tried long and earnestly to tell myself that I must 'sum up'.

This idea of 'summing up' was one of the last naïve impulses of my passing youth. I did not know that I should need more than an hour or two to grasp the full significance of those years during which I wandered about the cheerless streets of Moscow, travelled across dismembered, lacerated Russia, educated 'mofective' children, argued about 'Left art', despaired, joked, starved, struggled to provide myself with bread and cheap shag. All of us, in those days, wrote in verse or in prose of the 'historic age'. But living from day to day you do not

174

see the age: you do not see the wood for the trees, and individual trees, too, are obscured by the wood.

Today I want to look back and reflect on that far-off tangle of hopes and doubts.

I have already said that history is not made by man's volition. Neither is it made according to that perfect logic which is the strength of science. As a boy, I had often heard it said in P. G. Smidovich's circle that the way to Socialism would be opened by the proletariat of the most advanced industrialized countries.

In 1946, a worker living in 'Iron Mirgorod', or rather Detroit, said to me: 'Why do you keep talking about American capitalists, mono- polies, exploitation? Do you think we don't know all about that? We do, I assure you. But we have a better life, with capitalists and all, than you have without'. Lack of class consciousness? Of course. But not only that: a different approach to life, a cult of prosperity, a fear of heroism, of sacrifice, of the unknown.

Be that as it may, Russia, with her backward industry, was the first State where the Socialist Revolution was victorious. Out of every three citizens of the young Soviet Republic, two had to put crosses instead of their signatures. In 1918 I happened to visit villages in the Moscow and Tula provinces. In the peasant huts you could see plush armchairs, gramophones, even pianos taken out of the landowner's house or received from city folk in exchange for a sack of potatoes. But the villagers' life was still pre-revolutionary, the kind of life described by Chekhov and Bunin. There was a great deal of cruelty, ignorance, darkness. Libraries were burned. Townspeople were hated as 'spongers'; some people in the villages were positively glad that the cities were starving to death. This may partly explain the confusion which sometimes beset our intellectuals and which is reflected in Gorky's articles.

Young people, freshly arrived in the cities and swept along by the whirlwind of events, were only too ready to accept the simplified ideas of Proletkult extremists, later to become the *Napostovtsy*[1]. I often heard remarks like: 'Why be so complicated? It's all rotten intellectual rubbish. Have you seen the papers? Well, then, everything's perfectly clear. All these whys and wherefores are just bourgeois talk. No point in racking your brains.'

In the autumn of 1920 Lenin addressed the Komsomol in the

---

[1] A group round the journal *Na Postu*: 'At Your Post.'

following terms: 'If a Communist took it into his head to boast about his Communism because of the ready-made conclusions he had acquired, without putting in a great deal of serious and hard work, without understanding the facts which he must examine critically, he would be a very deplorable Communist. Such superficiality would be decidedly fatal'.

I have spoken of the thirst for knowledge which gripped millions of young men and women at that time. The people had opened the ABC. A word should also be said about those who taught literacy, gave lectures on history and geology, rescued books from burning, protected museum buildings and – though perhaps they were even hungrier than anyone else – defended culture: in short, about the Russian intelligentsia. Of course I do not mean that section which went abroad and there tried to smear their own people. I am speaking of the intelligentsia who accepted the October Revolution and was yet full of doubts. Re-reading the early stories of Vsevolod Ivanov, Malyshkin, Pilnyak and N. Ognev, or Tikhonov's early poems it is clear that those doubts arose precisely from the desire to adopt that critical approach to facts of which Lenin spoke.

A poster proclaiming 'Long Live Electrification!' was put up in Strastnaya Square. Beneath this poster Yesenin once recited Pugachev's monologue to me: 'O Asia, Asia! Blue land strewn with salt, sand and lime. The moon travels slowly across the sky, its wheels creaking like a Kirghiz cart's. But who would guess how turbulently and proudly the wool-yellow mountain streams leap there! Is that why there the Mongol hordes shrill all that is savage and evil in man? Long, long have I hidden my yearning to join them, their nomad encampments, to take my stand with the battering waves of their gleaming cheekbones at the approaches to Russia, like the shade of Tamurlane'. But it is not poetry that concerns me at the moment. Gangs of bandits roamed the country. In the villages 'Food Detachments' were shot at. The fields were unsown. The lost children of the Revolution – *besprizornye* – already loitered near the railway stations. The towns were starving; mortality was rising steeply.

All this reads now like ancient history. 'Blue Asia' is busy with industrialization, helped by the Soviet Union. Whereas at the end of the thirties certain politicians in the West still called our State a 'colossus with feet of clay', they were soon to be convinced that the 'colossus's' feet were entirely sound.

176

I was recently told a story that is apparently going the rounds in New York. An American says to his friend: 'Isn't it terrible? They say the Russians have stolen all the secrets of our atomic industry.' The friend replies: 'That's marvellous! Now they'll be five years behind us'.

Last summer, some magnificent rudbeckias, large and brilliant like stars in an ancient mosaic, blossomed in my garden. I had bought the seeds in Paris, at the famous Vilmorin's, and they had a Russian name: Sputnik.

When I look at Moscow I cannot believe that this is the city in which I spent my childhood. As you travel to Vnukovo airport you are astounded each time: it is no longer houses you see growing up but whole streets and districts.

It is, of course, perfectly true that we are better at making jet planes than ordinary saucepans. But we shall learn how to make saucepans as well. The fact is that Western politicians today hardly speak of anything else but the 'colossus's' ballistic feet.

By nature I am one of those people known as 'Doubting Thomases'. During the years I now have in mind — 1920 and 1921 — I had many doubts, but they were quite unlike the chatter of those who believed that Russia was collapsing, that new Varangians must come to establish order, and that the whole thing would end in a moderately Liberal bourgeois regime. There was one thing I did not doubt: the victory of the new social system.

Daily life was horrifying: *psha* (millet gruel) and dried fish, burst sewage pipes, cold, epidemics. But I and all my friends knew that the nation which had beaten the Intervention would also beat the economic dislocation. A few months later I tackled my first novel. Speaking of the extraordinary city of the future, all steel, glass and organization, Julio Jurenito exclaims: 'It shall be so. Here, in poverty-stricken Russia, I speak of it. For it is not those who have a superfluity of stones that build, but those who are not afraid to bind the stones together with their living blood'.

My doubts were not connected with thoughts about the house but with thoughts about the people who would live in it. In a play by Yuri Olesha, the heroine makes two lists: one is of the Revolution's 'blessings', the other of its 'crimes'. Later she realizes her mistake, and the title of the play is *List of Blessings*. I never made such lists either in thought or on paper: life is more complex than elementary logic, many crimes can lead to blessings, and there are blessings which may be fraught with crimes.

(Speaking of the shortcomings of our life, people sometimes add that they are 'remnants of capitalism'. Sometimes this is true and sometimes it is not. A bright light casts dark shadows, and good things may have bad consequences. Let me take the most obvious example: that of bureaucracy. Lenin wrote about it and our newspapers are still talking about it today, forty years later. Can anyone really believe that this paper dropsy, this hypertrophy of those who record, discuss, check, file, is nothing but a 'remnant'? Is not this disease – which, in the last analysis, can and must disappear – part of the development of organization, accounting, production control, all of which are progressive and useful?)

I remember a young country girl who worked as a cleaner at the Military Chemical Academy, singing a ditty which went like this: 'I'll be in trouble, that I know. I'm going to the closet with no pass to show. I'd be happy to get one, but, alas, there's no one about to issue a pass'. At first, when I heard it, I laughed. Then it made me think.

Any worker knows that a machine, however complex, is made by man and serves man. In 1932 I saw the building of the Kuznetsk plant. People coming from the villages regarded the machines with hatred or with holy dread. Some broke their lathes by pulling furiously at the levers if the machine refused to work, just as at home they had lashed their overworked horses. Others addressed a blast furnace (*domennaya pech*) respectfully as 'Domna Ivanovna', a Martin furnace as 'Uncle Martin'.

Naturally enough, I thought above all of the future of art. The chart displayed in Bryusov's office had not only surprised but also frightened me. Literature was shown in terms of squares, circles and rhomboids, the cogs of an enormous machine.

Once I spoke to Lunacharsky about my doubts. He replied that Communism must lead to multiformity, not uniformity, and that an artist's works cannot be cut from a single pattern. He spoke of the *Derzhimordas*[1] who cannot understand the nature of art. A year later, in an article published in the journal *The Press and the Revolution*, he used the same definition. Saying that censorship was necessary in a

---

[1] Name of police chief in Gogol's *Inspector-General*.

period of transition, he went on: 'But the man who says "away with all these prejudices about free speech: State control of literature is inherent in our Communist system: censorship is not a dreadful concomitant of a period of transition but a proper feature of ordered, socialized, Socialist life" – the man who concludes from this that criticism itself must become a kind of informer's report or the forcible fitting of works of art on a primitively revolutionary cobbler's last, this man will merely show that if you scratch him a little, you will find under the Communist a Derzhimorda and that, having in some measure come to power, he has derived nothing from it but the pleasure of swaggering, bullying and, above all, ordering people to "go there" and "keep out of here".'

The journal *Na Postu* was not yet in existence. Exhibitions of artists representing different movements, from Brodsky to Malevich, were still held simultaneously. Meyerhold still rampaged a stone's throw from the Art Theatre. Yet I could not get the chart with its squares and rhomboids out of my mind.

Cautiously, as though it were a piece of fish full of bones, we munched our two ounces of bread. The poet Polonskaya wrote: 'Yet I feel sad that we shall forget the worth of those humble, faithful, voiceless friends, birchwood logs, a handful of salt, a jug of milk and the poor fruits of a bare, stern soil'. In those years all of us were romantics, although we were ashamed of the word.

It was not the epoch that I quarrelled with, but my own self. There was a great deal of confusion in my mind. I was for industrial aesthetics and planned economy; I hated the chaos, the hypocrisy, the gilded trappings of capitalism (which I knew more intimately than out of books). Yet I often asked myself: what would happen to the vast variety of human character in the new, more rational and more just society? Would not the improved machines, which I myself extolled, become a surrogate for art? Would not technology suppress those emotions which, troubled though they sometimes are, humankind holds dear?

Forty years later I published in *Komsomolskaya Pravda* a letter from a Leningrad girl describing a worthy engineer who despised art, remained indifferent to the tragedy of Manolis Glezos, had little feeling for his mother or his friends and believed that love in the atomic age was an anachronism. In the same paper I read a letter from an expert in cybernetics making fun of a girl who could 'cry into her pillow' and of anyone who, in our day and age, still admired Bach's music or the poetry of Blok.

Many of the doubts I entertained in 1921 were naïve and have been proved wrong by life: many, but by no means all.

Above everything I feared indifference, the mechanization of feeling – not of production – the atrophying of art. I knew that the wood would grow, and thought of the fate of a live, warm tree, with its complex roots, its fanciful branches, the rings of its core.

Perhaps such thoughts came to me because, at the age of thirty, I was about to sit for an examination which would entitle me to call myself a writer. I did not know, of course, what difficulties awaited me; but I realized that it was not simply a matter of constructing a novel or turning a phrase. Chekhov says in one of his letters that the writer's job is to stand up for man. That sounds very simple, but it is very difficult.

26

TIME went by quickly in those days, but trains travelled slowly. It took us a long time to get to Riga: plenty of time to think of this and that.

Our diplomatic couriers were travelling in the next compartment. I glanced at their wax-sealed bags and smiled. All we had was a single shabby suitcase containing copies of the journals *Unovis*, *Art of the Commune*, *Artistic Word*, and books by Mayakovsky, Yesenin and Pasternak.

When at last we crawled into Sebezh, one of the couriers said to us: 'Comrades, we're about to cross the Latvian frontier. There'll be a station buffet. Remember your country's prestige and try not to hurl yourselves at the food'. I decided not to get out of the train.

We arrived in Riga at nightfall. Having deposited our suitcase in a small hotel I said to Lyuba: 'Now for a restaurant'. I looked stealthily about me as if going to an illegal meeting: the situation was embarrassing; people might say, here's a Soviet citizen just arrived and all he thinks of is his dinner.

I do not know whether the portions were so large or whether we had become unused to eating, but I could not manage even half my beefsteak. I felt rather sad: here was the piece of meat I had dreamt of for so long, and I could not eat it.

It was not easy to curb our psychological hunger. After a meal I would still stop outside a bakery or a delicatessen, studying various kinds of rolls, sausages and pies. It is thus that collectors gaze at rare objects in the windows of antique shops. I also studied the menus displayed outside the entrances to the numerous restaurants: the names of dishes had the ring of poetry.

I had brought along a passport issued to me by the representative of the Provisional Government in 1917 in order to prove to the French that I had lived in Paris. This document was by now quite ancient and looked like a museum piece. When I held my Soviet passport out to the French consul, he drew back his hand as if I had offered him a hot iron to touch. He read the other, tattered passport and said with disgust: 'You were a political émigré? That's no recommendation'. He asked me what I had been doing in Moscow during the past months and why I wanted to go to Paris. I replied cheerfully that in the last few months I had been helping Durov to train rabbits and that I hoped to write a long book in Paris. The consul said darkly: 'I doubt whether that's where you'll write it'.

I wrote to friends living in Paris and asked them to do what they could about my visa. By this time I had eaten my fill and no longer stopped to examine shop-window sausages. I knew no one in Riga. A cold rain fell steadily. Once a melancholy little man turned up, said that he was starting a publishing house and wanted to publish Soviet authors, and bought my book of poems called *Reflections*. From time to time I went to our embassy, read *Pravda* and argued with the First Secretary, who thought highly of the Imaginists. The French consul kept on saying: 'As I thought, there's nothing for you'.

The visas came when I had given up hope. The consul absolutely refused to put them in our Soviet passports, and issued us with special passes instead. I went to the German embassy for transit visas. The consul was very surprised that I, a Soviet citizen, should have received a French visa. This struck him as highly suspicious and he said he could not grant us a German visa. We had to take a different, very complicated route: by ship to the Free City of Danzig, then to Copenhagen and thence, via London, to Paris.

In Danzig we were allowed on shore. Crowds of speculators selling various kinds of foreign currency milled about in the narrow medieval streets.

The Danes picked us out and invited us to step into a motor-car. I decided that we were on our way to gaol, but we were taken to the public baths; while we washed, our clothes were disinfected. This was understandable: typhus was still raging in Russia. In London, however, the police took me for a madman solely because, to the question: 'How did you manage to escape from Russia?' I replied that we had left with proper passports.

I shall speak in later volumes of life in Western Europe during the years following the First World War: on the way from Moscow to Paris I was too preoccupied to observe much. Although I knew the West well, everything astounded me. There were too many goods. The people seemed drowsy and apathetic.

We were in Copenhagen on May Day. An orderly demonstration,

singing and munching sandwiches, proceeded along the street. The pigeons round the Town Hall were so fat that they seemed unable to fly. Sentries in immensely tall hats stood outside the royal palace. In the working-class quarters people jostled outside the little shops, not, apparently, interested in the overthrow of capitalism but in buying margarine, just then coming into fashion.

In London there was another palace and more sentries in gigantic hats. Some tubthumper in Hyde Park was explaining to bystanders that the rights of man had been violated in Fiume and Vilna and that the British must protect freedom everywhere. I remembered the English soldiers in the streets of Feodosia, and walked on.

At last I was back at the Rotonde. Everything was in its place. A painter greeted me and remarked: 'Haven't seen you about for quite a time. Been away?' Then, without waiting for an answer, he launched into a flood of local gossip.

The proprietor of the Hôtel Nice where I had lived for many years had come back from the front safe and sound. We embraced as friends.

Yes, everything was as before. But I was different. Only at the Rotonde did I become aware of the change that had taken place inside me. Things that had once seemed natural now astonished and sometimes enraged me. Paris was beautiful; I wandered, enchanted, along the quays of the Seine and visited all the places where I had passed my youth. It was easy to get on with the city; people were much more difficult. I did not know how to explain to them what had happened to us in Russia.

I had left Paris in a summer of fierce battles and it was difficult for me to understand why the French seemed to have forgotten the war years. Only the advertisements of travel agencies – 'Cheap Excursions to Verdun: Visit the Famous Battlefields!' – served as a reminder of the recent past.

One of the newspapers ran a competition: which Marshal was the most popular in France? Men were strangely dressed, in short, tight-waisted, pigeon-chested coats; respectable family men looked like homosexuals. I saw the foxtrot for the first time. Couples jerked backwards and forwards like mechanical toys.

All the things I speak of are indicative not so much of the Paris of 1921 as of my own state of mind at that time. I wrote a poem (containing archaisms which still appealed to me despite my enthusiasm

183

for 'Left art'): 'Yes! my country, knowing no moderation, has carted the chattels of many centuries to the bonfire. The dim, cold ashes will not warm the dark caves. Well, Ehrenburg, you are in Paris: transform this ample prosperity into well-groomed odes. But Russia's language is wild and sorrowful, and it will not be a Russian who today extols the triumphant victor rushing in his Ford to smother with truffles the after-taste of death'.

As a matter of fact, there was no shortage of Russians ready and willing to extol their 'generous hosts'. The émigrés had not yet realized what future lay before them in foreign lands. The passions of the Civil War had not yet cooled. In *The Common Cause*, a newspaper edited in Paris by Burtsev, Russia was never referred to otherwise than 'Sovdepia'. I remember an item which appeared in this paper: animals still remaining alive in the Moscow zoo were being fed on the carcases of people who had been shot. Zinaida Hippius accused everyone who had stayed in Russia of having 'sold out to the Bolsheviks': Blok had sold out, Bely had sold out, and even A. F. Koni. Bunin, whom I met at Alexey Tolstoy's, would not even speak to me. The delightful Tolstoy himself, uneasy yet affectionate, grumbled: 'They've filled your head with every kind of nonsense there, Ilya'. As soon as I mentioned that I had left Russia on a Soviet passport, the émigrés turned away from me, some in disgust, others just to be on the safe side.

The former Rotonde crowd welcomed me warmly. I say 'former' because the Rotonde as I had known it was no more; I realized this three days after my arrival. It was not just that the café itself had changed hands. The times had changed. Foreign tourists were displacing the painters and the writers. The disordered, semi-pauperized existence of former years had become a fashionable mode of life for people playing at being Bohemians. The Rotonde was surrounded by other cafés, old and new, where some of the veterans sought shelter and where novices came. At the Dôme I came across some old friends: Fotinsky, Diego Rivera, Marevna, Zadkine. Léger still occasionally dropped in at the Rotonde. Young Americans sat in the Select; I did not know them, and it was not until I met Hemingway many years later that I learnt that he had planned his first novel there.

I talked about Moscow art exhibitions, Meyerhold's productions, recited from memory the poems of Mayakovsky, Yesenin and Pasternak.

Picasso embraced me and immediately declared: 'You know, my place is over there. What is there for me to do in the France of Monsieur Millerand?' Albert Gleizes told me that he had recently exhibited a panel entitled 'Project for decorating one of the Moscow stations'. Léger dreamed of working for the Moscow theatres. Diego Rivera wanted to know how he could get to Russia. The poet André Salmon read me his poem with the Russian title *Prikaz*, in which he glorified the heroism of the Russian people.

It seemed as though bourgeois France could safely set aside its worries: the dangerous years lay behind. The demobilized men had had time to forget about the army mutinies. The wave of strikes was ebbing. But you could still see posters on the walls showing a most terrifying creature, a man holding a knife between his teeth: this was the bogy the ruling circles used to scare the average Frenchman. The propaganda was not very subtle: the Communists were Asiatics, savages, they had nationalized their women and were putting the entire nation through its paces, as on a parade ground. There was another argument, too, more forcible than the 'nationalization of women', namely the Russian loans, the savings of average Frenchmen who had bought what they thought to be good securities at the bank. 'Our money's gone!' the rentiers wailed in anger and despair.

It would be incorrect, too, to say that the French bourgeoisie had enjoyed a breathing space. True, France itself was calm, but only six months earlier the workers in nearby Italy had seized one factory after another. Only two months previously the newspapers had reported a rising in Saxony. Slogans were painted, chalked, scribbled on the walls of Paris: '*Vivent les Soviets!*'

I was in France in the spring of 1946. Then, too, the bourgeoisie was uneasy. It did not like the fact that municipal councils in the working-class suburbs of Paris were naming streets after Stalin. But the cold war was only just beginning, the Soviet Union was still officially regarded as an Allied Power, and representatives of right-wing parties saluted the 'great Marshal' at street-naming ceremonies with mixed feelings of hatred, fear and respect.

There were no streets named after Lenin in France in 1921, but Lenin seemed to be alive in the working-class areas. He was no Marshal but a man who had spent many years in Paris, a man whom some people had met and still remembered. The extraordinary story of the man in a worker's cap who had become the head of a vast, mysterious country, of Russian workers, hungry and ragged, armed with old rifles, repulsing the interventionists' attacks, haunted the suburbs of Paris and disturbed the conquerors' slumbers.

I began to realize that my first superficial impressions had been deceptive. There was a great deal that was new in the West. I bought a book which gave a popular explanation of the theory of relativity. I was enthusiastic about Blaise Cendrars' latest book *La Fin du Monde*, illustrated by Léger, a satire about the end of the capitalist world written in the style of a film scenario.

I saw several films of Charlie Chaplin, who had meanwhile become world famous. At a Picasso exhibition thirty paintings clashed, yet all of them were united by the indomitable desire to express the new age in a plastic form. I realized that there was much I had to read, see, think over.

Diego was delighted to learn that the hero of my novel would be a Mexican. He was just off to Italy, but promised to tell me about the environment of Julio Jurenito's childhood and early youth.

I bought a block of paper and decided to settle down to write the novel. My literary plans, however, were unexpectedly interrupted by the French authorities. Comrade Menzhinsky had been right.

I do not know the precise reason for my expulsion. When I asked why I was being deported, the official at the *préfecture* said: 'France is the freest country in the world. If you're being expelled that means there must be a good reason for it'. One of my friends who tried to get the deportation order rescinded was told: 'But you don't know: he's a Bolshevik propaganda agent'. Undoubtedly, police informers had sat on the café terraces where I had met my friends. The French call these people *mouches*, and they really are a pest like flies in autumn, with the difference that flies have a short life, whereas informers sometimes survive not only ministerial changes but even complete reversals of the regime.

Early one morning a shabby-looking individual with bleary eyes and a weedy moustache turned up at my hotel and showed me a badge: he was an agent of the *préfecture*. Another agent arrested my wife. The hotel proprietor was indignant: 'I am ashamed for France!' This made not the slightest impression on the police agents. I was taken to the *préfecture* and told that we must leave France that very day.

'But where are we to go without visas?' I asked innocently.

'The Belgian frontier is the nearest.'

'We haven't got Belgian visas.'

'And you won't get them either. The Belgians will send you back to the French frontier.'

'And then?'

'Then we shall arrest you for crossing the frontier illegally. You will serve your term of imprisonment, after which you will not be expelled but deported.'

I did not see the difference between the two concepts of 'expulsion' and 'deportation'. The official explained:

'You will travel to the frontier in an ordinary railway carriage at your own expense. You will be accompanied by a member of our staff in civilian clothes. But when you are deported, you need not worry about tickets as you'll be taken to the frontier under escort. At this stage you are free. The member of our staff will only be accompanying you.'

'But when the Belgians have sent us back and I've done my time in prison, where will you deport us to?'

'Why, to Belgium.'

I realized that the idea was to turn us into footballs to be kicked about between the French and the Belgians. This did not appeal to me. Nevertheless, we had to have a meal. We went to a restaurant across the road from the Rotonde, where we met a sculptor we knew. We told him we were being deported. He ran across to the Rotonde, and soon we were surrounded by a dozen friends. Everyone was furious. The police agents sat at the next table and ate with enjoyment: they were perfectly used to being called *sales flics* – they heard this every day – but the food at Baty's was good and the *flics* had special expense accounts for occasions of this kind.

It occurred to me that my expulsion order had been signed by Briand, that skilful orator, that 'parliamentary nightingale'. The thought cheered me up. During the war I had been introduced to Briand as the correspondent of the *Birzhevka* and he had sung me a brief but tender aria. Now Briand was afraid of me. Like Durov's hares, I began to realize that I was quite a fearsome animal.

The train was leaving late that night. At the station, one of the *flics* said that he would buy our tickets for us. 'Third class, of course?' We had travelled third class to Paris, but the *flic's* tone of voice annoyed me and I replied: 'First class, of course'. In the event, this saved us.

There were three of us in the compartment: Lyuba, myself and the *flic*, who left the train at the French frontier. I advised Lyuba to lie down and pretend to be asleep. A Belgian gendarme entered; I pointed at Lyuba, as if to say that it would be a pity to wake her. The Belgian nodded good-humouredly: policemen treat first-class passengers with respect. I showed him a half-rotted piece of paper, my 1917 passport. He looked in vain for a Belgian visa. Finally he folded the paper with care and whispered to me: 'Your passport's out of date, you ought to get it renewed'. I replied, also in a whisper: 'You're quite right, I'll attend to it as soon as we get to Brussels'.

The game of football did not take place. We travelled on, unmolested.

27

In Brussels, opposite the Gare du Sud, we saw two hotels: one was called *Providence*, the other *Hope*. We were not in a despairing mood and so we went to the one called *Hope*. Here, however, we were asked to fill in a form containing a perfidious question about entry permits.

My youth had been spent in that archaic age when civil aviation, radio broadcasting and visas did not exist. Aeroplanes are a splendid invention; a radio set can be useful, and, what is more, one need not turn it on – it is a matter of choice; but visas cannot possibly be included among the inventions designed to make human life more agreeable. I should not like to count up the amount of time, effort and nervous energy I have spent on visas in the course of my life. Furthermore, visas, like bacteria, can be divided into groups and families. There are entrance and exit visas, transit visas with and without permission to break one's journey, visas for one or several frontier crossings with or without indication of frontier station; it is not easy to sort them out, still less easy to obtain them.

We hastily left the hotel lobby. I drew a playful little line instead of giving an answer to the question about entry visas. Our success of the previous night might have led to a very unpleasant situation in broad daylight: we had got into Belgium without entry visas.

I have already mentioned that before the war, in Paris, I had edited a small poetry magazine called *Evenings* together with Nemirov, who came from Rostov. He had a charming wife, cheerful, very slightly cross-eyed and fond of singing; her name was Marusya. Soon afterwards they had separated and, during the war, I had often seen her in the South of France. Before I left for Russia I heard that Marusya had married the Belgian poet Franz Hellens.

As I walked out of the hotel I had one thought only in my mind: how could I find Hellens? There is no such thing as an address-finding office in Western countries: people want to be left alone, and only God and the police know who lives where. There wasn't a Hellens in the telephone directory (I did not know then that Hellens was a pseudonym). I went into a bookshop and was told: 'We sell serious books, not poetry'. I began looking into the windows of other bookshops and found one which displayed a book by Hellens; I burst in joyously, but was disappointed: they only suggested that I should write a letter care of the publishers. I could not explain that by the time my letter reached Hellens, I should no longer be at the *Hope* but in an ordinary gaol.

In the end I was lucky: at the fifth or tenth bookshop I ran into a poetry-lover who turned out to have a kind heart. He told me that I should find Franz Hellens at the Chamber of Deputies; his real name was van Ermengem and he was the parliamentary librarian. I felt at a once as if I had grown wings: a parliament was something quite different from the Rotonde.

Hellens and Marusya received us like old friends. I droned on about the visa. Marusya recalled old times. Hellens said nothing and smiled gently. He was forty; his stern, northern face was lit by a pair of eyes belonging to a child or a dreamer.

Hellens told one of the Ministers that I was a poet, that for some reason I had been expelled from France and now wanted to spend a few months in Belgium in order to write a book. The formalities took two weeks. I wandered about Brussels, so noisy near the Stock Exchange and so quiet in the old quarters, where there are many ash-black houses with gilt decorations, neat old women and unhurried dreamers who smoke their pipes at the end of the working day and gaze with pale eyes at the pale sky.

Hellens and I made friends. He is a wonderfully pure and melancholy man. He is above all a poet, not only because he writes poetry and has always done so, but because his prose, and indeed the whole of his life, are soaked in the very essence of poetry.

During the spring when we met, he was writing a novel entitled *Bass-Bassina-Boulou* – that was his name for a Negro god that stood in his study. In the novel this god, wise and naïve, omnipotent and powerless, comes to Europe from darkest Africa and describes with sad irony what he sees all round him. I have read Gorky's letter about this book: it is dictated by love, not by ordinary politeness. (They met later, in Sorrento in 1925; in another letter, Gorky recalled Hellens' eyes in which, despite their sternness, one guessed at a childlike melancholy and tenderness.) Stefan Zweig liked *Bass-Bassina-Boulou* and wrote a preface to the German edition.

I told Hellens a great deal about Moscow. He became very interested in Yesenin's poetry and began to translate it into French with Marusya's help.

Later, Hellens and I would meet from time to time, in Paris or Brussels. Years passed; a whole lifetime went by. Everything today is different, yet Hellens is still the same: children do not age, dreamers do not betray and, therefore, do not change.

One day Hellens introduced me to the painter Permeke, now well known to all art lovers but in those days still counted among the 'young' artists (he was aged thirty-five, but the war years had been deleted from his life: he had been severely wounded during the defence of Antwerp and had remained alive despite all prognoses). I do not know the reason for it – is it to be found in the strong traditions or in the special nature of the landscape, or rather the light, of Flanders? – but the Belgians are magnificent painters. There is no need to speak of Memling or van Eyck, it is enough to look at the works of Ensor. For some reason, Permeke was classed as an Expressionist, although he never neglected the painterly qualities of art for the sake of literary expressiveness. He liked to paint weatherbeaten, sombre fishermen, peasants of the coastal area, mothers, old women. His long landscapes show a flat earth, with a haystack or a solitary tree – always squat and beaten down by the winds – scarcely rising above the skyline; the greenish or leaden sky plays an enormous part. Unrest and an element of tragedy were inherent in his nature. For a long time I lost sight of Permeke; we met again a quarter of a century later, shortly before his death. I went to see him; he was living near Ostend, huge, ailing and lonely: his wife, with whom he had spent his whole life, had died. A canvas which I cannot get out of my mind hung on the studio wall: Permeke had painted his wife on her deathbed; the colours expressed the artist's mental state.

I was still waiting for the Minister's decision. Merry-go-rounds turned outside the window of the *Hope* till late at night, and street-organs tried to drown each other.

At long last I received a permit to stay in Belgium. It was June; we went away to the coast, to a little place called La Panne near the French frontier. The hotels were empty – there were still a few weeks to go till the holiday period. Here and there, along the coast, one came across ruins: houses destroyed during the war had not yet been rebuilt. The sea was large and angry. At low tide it receded a long way, harbouring its anger; at high tide it hurled itself straight at the hotel.

When the sea ebbed, seaweed, starfish and many pieces of broken wood were left lying on the sand. I picked them up mechanically, remembering how on the beach at Koktebel I had looked for wood to burn in the *mangalka*.

All round there were sand dunes with grey, prickly grass sprouting here and there. These dunes shift from place to place: the wind blows the sand about. When I climbed to the top of a dune I could see France.

I worked from morning until late at night in a little room with a window looking out on the sea. I wrote *Julio Jurenito* in one month, writing as though someone dictated it to me. Sometimes, when my hand got tired, I would take a walk by the sea. A fierce wind knocked over the chairs on the empty café terraces. The sea seemed irreconcilable. This landscape corresponded to my state of mind: I felt not as if I were making marks with a pen on a sheet of paper but as though going into a bayonet charge.

I did not know how to write. The book contains many unnecessary episodes, it is unpolished and there are many clumsy turns of phrase. But I love this novel.

They say that all authors love their first book. That is untrue. I know some authors who cannot bear it if their early works are mentioned in their presence. But why speak of other authors? My own first volume of verse seems absurd and repugnant to me. I have tender memories of the time when I wrote those poems about *marquises*, and even of the printer who printed them, but the poems are rotten and, above all, they are not my own. I love *Julio Jurenito* because, for all its multitude of faults, this book was written by me, was the product of my own experience, is really and truly my book.

I have often, as a writer, aped others. I have already spoken of the imitative nature of my early verse. But later, soon after *Julio Jurenito*, I fell victim to the literary fashion then in vogue. Like some other literary contemporaries, I was seduced by Andrey Bely's rhythmic prose and Remizov's fanciful syntax. What was natural to those writers looked like a parody when I adopted it. I cannot re-read some of my books of that period: all the time I itch to put the adjectives and nouns back in their proper places. The style of *Julio Jurenito* is sometimes clumsy, but it is simple, without verbal acrobatics.

I learned from reviews that my novel was an imitation of *Candide*. I must confess to my shame that I read *Candide* only after seeing those reviews: in my youth I had read a great deal but without method, and to this day there are large gaps in my literary knowledge. Still, I can understand the critics' assumption. Of course, my workmates at the Vaugirard goods station had not read *Candide* any more than I had, but their jokes reflected the same characteristics of French irony that we admire in Voltaire's works. On the other hand, the author of *Candide* may well have influenced the development of the national genius of France.

I love *Jurenito* because I was driven to write it by an inner need: I did not yet regard myself as a writer. The book had a very long gestation period. There may not be enough literature in it (I lacked experience and skill) but there is no literariness whatever.

I have written many books and I do not care for all of them by any means. Some of them I rarely remember and never re-read. For younger readers, I came into being as a writer during the years of the Second World War. Not many people in my country other than old-age pensioners remember *Jurenito*, yet it is dear to me: in it I expressed many things that determined not only my literary development but my whole life. Naturally it contains many false judgments and crude paradoxes; I was trying all the time to look into the future; some things I succeeded in seeing, others I missed entirely. But by and large it is not a book that I would disown.

In *Julio Jurenito* I pilloried racial prejudice and nationalism of all kinds, exposed war, the cruelty, greed and hypocrisy of those who started it and who still do not want to abandon war, the cant of the churchmen who bless their country's guns, of pacifists who discuss 'humane methods of exterminating humanity', of pseudo-socialists who justify the terrible bloodshed. In 1960 I still subscribe to those ideas; and if I hate racial prejudice and fascism, if I find the strength to take part in the struggle for peace, it is because, in half a century, a man wears out many suits of clothes but remains himself for all that.

In *Jurenito* I showed the hypocrisy of the world of money, the false freedom governed by Mr Cool's cheque-book and Monsieur Delet's social hierarchy which has established sixteen classes even for burial. Twelve years before Hitler came to power I drew the portrait of Herr Schmidt who 'can be a Socialist and a nationalist at the same time', who says to the Russians and the French: 'We must organize you', who prescribes: 'colonize Russia and destroy France and Britain as thoroughly as possible . . . The place must be left completely bare . . .

Between killing one weak-minded old man and ten million people for the good of mankind there's only an arithmetical difference. Yet killed they must be . . .' If I had not written this in 1921, I could not have written *The Fall of Paris* in 1940.

Sometimes I made mistakes; at other times I saw pretty clearly. Long before the incinerators of Auschwitz and the pits of Babiy Yar I put the following advertisement in *Julio Jurenito*: 'Solemn Performances of the Destruction of the Tribe of Judah will take place shortly . . . The programme will include, apart from the traditional Pogroms – a public favourite – a series of historical reconstructions in the spirit of the age, e.g. burning of Jews, burying same alive, sprinkling of fields with Jewish blood, as well as modern methods of "evacuation", "removal of suspicious elements", etc., etc.'

I knew that *Julio Jurenito* must arouse the wrath of the upholders of law and order: 'What consul will now stamp my passport with a visa? What mother will allow me to cross the threshold of her home where honest youths and pure girls are growing up?' I was not surprised when the White émigrés received my novel with indignation. But I was under cross-fire: the *Napostovtsy* never referred to *Jurenito* otherwise than as a 'calumny on the Revolution'. The term 'slanderer' was attached to my name in almost every issue of their journal.

In the previous chapter I spoke of my dread of the mechanization of feelings and the regimentation of art. These thoughts are reflected in *Jurenito*. At the time I exaggerated certain dangers and failed to see others. The critics called me a 'cynic' and a 'nihilist', but if there was any charge I deserved it was rather that of suffering from hypertrophied romanticism.

Julio Jurenito was read by readers and abused by critics, abused thoroughly and at length; in discussing my later books, the critics always brought out my first novel as the chief item of evidence against me. Recently I happened to come across an issue of *Novy Mir* published thirty-five years ago containing an article about me, long quotations from *Julio Jurenito* and the following conclusions: 'The Russian bourgeoisie, defeated in open struggle, is persisting in the spiritual fight . . . Ehrenburg is a real servant of his class . . . Ehrenburg is the last-born of bourgeois culture . . . The history of Russian literature would have lost nothing if Ehrenburg had not "chosen" to become a writer'. I am quoting from what was, perhaps, the mildest article.

In Kiev in 1924 I went to see a stage adaptation of *Julio Jurenito*. On the stage there was Ilya Ehrenburg, with the American Mr Cool sitting astride his shoulders and shouting: 'Faster, faster, my bourgeois steed'. My father-in-law Dr Kozintsev was outraged; I found it funny.

Of course there were hours when I, too, was unhappy: shells not fired by the enemy but by my own side were falling on me. However, the shells at that time were fortunately made of paper. Gradually I became accustomed to various accusations; a partial immunity was established which later was often to save me from total despair.

The form of my first novel was also attacked. I believe that it was not the shortcomings of my style but its unusual nature that provoked irritation. Critics have asserted ever since that I am a journalist who writes novels as if they were *feuilletons*; in their opinion, I am a gate-crasher in the precincts of literature. For me, however, the penetration of the newspaper into the novel was bound up with the search for a modern form of narration. There are people who believe that a detailed description of a character's appearance or a landscape gives living flesh to a dry thesis and turns a leading article into a novel or a short story. Whereas, to be honest, this is just gilding the pill. It is like glamourizing a boring meeting with theatrical lighting. I am sure that *My Past and Thoughts* has a better right to be regarded as 'pure art' than *On the Eve*.

Jurenito was published in 1922 by the Helikon Press in Berlin and by the State Publishing House in Moscow. I was pleased that Mayakovsky liked my book and that some Petrograd writers whose opinion I valued spoke of it with approval. (In 1942 Alexey Tolstoy recalled my satirical novels in one of his articles and had a kind word for *Julio Jurenito*.) Later I read in Krupskaya's memoirs of the way in which Lenin responded to my first novel; this gave me great moral support.

Soon afterwards *Jurenito* appeared in German (it was published by a Communist publishing house), in French with a foreword by Pierre MacOrlan and in other languages.

I became a professional writer.

But I am anticipating once again. I had just finished writing the last page of *Julio Jurenito*. On it I had written: 'A fair abundance of grey hairs, frequent palpitations of the heart and general debility are my consolation. I have broken the back of life . . .'

I walked to the sea. The tide was roaring in. It was night, and the faint lights of fishing boats bobbed up and down in the distance. I walked into the wind. I felt apprehensive and gay.

A man and a writer may guess many things, but not everything by any means. You see grey hairs in the mirror when you shave; to see the future is more difficult. I did not know that many storms had still to be weathered, and that the wind does not drop while the heart still beats.

INDEX

Adam, Comrade, 124, 126, 139, 149, 173
Afinogenov, A. N., 50
Agnivstev, 77, 115
Aleichem, Sholem, 74–75
Alexeyeva-Meskhieva, 51
Alexeyevich, Yuli, 63
Altman, 56, 60
Angel, 79
Annesky, Innokenty, 68
Antoine, 170
Antokolsky, 117
Antonov-Ovseyenko, 11
Apollinaire, Guillaume, 128
Aragon, 45
Asatiani, Guram, 117
Aseyev, 52

Babel, Isaak, 50, 72, 151, 172
Bagritsky, 72, 131
Balmont, K. D., 18, 19, 32, 39, 63, 65, 107, 169
Baltrushaitis, J. K., 63
Balzac, 54, 148
Baty, 135
Baudelaire, 60
Bekhterev, 154
Bel-Kon-Lyumbromirskaya, 116
Bel, Andrey, 19, 41, 64–65, 66, 99, 107, 135, 142, 184, 192
Bergelson, 87
Blagoy, D. D., 100
Bloch, J.-R., 170
Blok, 14, 19, 26, 32, 60, 66, 106, 184
    Balaganchik, 167
Bloy, Léon, 101
Blumkin, 123
Braque, 59
Briand, 187
Brik, Lily, 66
Brik, Osip, 49
Bryusov, Valery, 15–20, 25, 32, 86, 165, 169, 178
Bunin, 56, 65, 168, 184
Burlyuk, David, 38, 39, 55, 106
Burtsev, 184

Carra, 58
Cendrars, Blaise, 186
Cervantes, 148
Cézanne, 146
Chagall, 68
Chantal, 62, 69
Chaplin, Charles, 186
Chekhov, 19, 51, 54, 60, 180
Chelpanov, 154
Chenier, André, 137
Chernov, 11
Chicherin, 19
Chulkov, G. I., 64, 66
Chumachenko, Ada, 139
Chukovsky, 97
Coats, A., 29
Cocteau, 135, 170
Coquelin, 168
Craig, Gordon, 137

d'Annunzio, 128
Dante, 105, 107
Debussy, 146
Denikin, 81, 85, 89, 90, 92
Derain, 135
Descartes, 125
Dobrushin, 87
du Gard, R. M., 44–45
Dullin, 135
Duncan, Isadora, 161–2, 165
Durov, Anatoly, 146, 152–3
Dzhalalova, Ludmila, 63, 66
Dzhavakhishvili, M., 117

Efron, Pyotr Yakovlevich, 23
Efron, Seryozha, 23, 26, 27, 94
Ehrenburg, Ilya, *passim*, and esp. father, 70; mother, 30, 70; wife, see Lyuba; daughter Irina, 12; aunt Masha, 72
    And Yet it Moves, 57–58
    Blanche's Chemise, 62, 89
    Fall of Paris, The, 194
    Julio Jurenito, 31–32, 46, 57–58, 89, 103, 151, 177, 192–6
    Love of Jeanne Ney, The, 131

Ehrenburg, Ilya, *(cont.)*
  My Past and Thoughts, 295
  Poems about the Eves, 102
  Reflections, 102, 182
  Rvach, 84
  Trust, D. E., 131–2
Eisenstein, 137
Ekster, A. A., 73, 87, 88, 124, 148
Eluard, Paul, 45, 54
Emilyevich, Alexander, 100
Ermengem, van, see Hellens

Fadeyev, Alexander, 38, 51, 136
Fedin, 172
Fedorchenko, S. L., 85
Fokine, 128
Fotinsky, 184
Fragonard, 59
Frank, Leonhard, 94
Furmanov, 172

Gauguin, 146
Gémier, 170
Genke, Margarita, 85
Gerasimov, Mikhail, 68, 127, 142
Gerassi, Fernando, 111–12
Gerzhenzon, M. O., 64
Ghil, René, 19
Glazunov, A., 29
Gleizes, 59, 185
Goethe, 27, 50
Gogol, 53, 54, 72, 134–6, 161
  Inspector General, The, 134–6
Gouchar, Ivan, 85
Gorky, 14, 33, 162, 190
Grazianskaya, Nina, 116
Gudzenko, Semyon, 74
Gumilev, 86

Hainaut, M., 76, 77, 80, 81, 82, 85
Hamsun, Knut, 146
Hellens, Franz (van Ermengem), 189,
  90–91
  Bass-Bassina-Boulou, 190
Hemingway, 184
Hippius, Zinaida, 184
Holzschmidt, 38–39

Ignatyevna, Anna, 156
Ilf, 72
Inber, Vera, 66
Ivanon-Razumnik, 161
Ivanov, Georgi, 40

Ivanov, Vsevolod, 176
Ivanov, Vyacheslav, 41, 63–64, 99

Jordania, Noah (Kostrov), 115, 119

Kamensky, Anatoly, 55
Kaprelevich, Magdalina, 116
Karakhan, L., 139
Kara-Murza, 63, 66
Katayev, 72
'Katya', see Sorokina
Kautsky, 115
Kayransky, 66, 67
Kellerman, 132
Kerensky, 10, 11
Khazina, Nadya, 89
Khlebnikov, 60
Khodasevich, 13
Khodotov, N. N., 115
Kipling, 146
Kitay-Gorod, 17
Klynyer, N., 160
Kolchak, 92, 103
Koltsov, M., 169
Komissarzhevskaya, 136
Konchalovsky, 68, 137
Koni, A. F., 184
Koonen, Alisa, 167, 168, 170
Kornilov, 10, 13
Korolenko, 14, 70, 150
Kostrov, A., see Jordania
Kotsyubinsky, 75
Kozhevnikov, 157
Kozintsev, Dr., 92, 95, 99
Kozintsev, Grisha, 89, 90
Kozintseva, Lyuba, see Lyuba
Krupskaya, 195
Kudasheva, Maya, 98–99
Kutepov, 92
Kvitko, 87

Larionev, 68
Lavrenev, 172
Lebon, Philippe, 15
Léger, Fernand, 42, 55–56, 59, 88, 170,
  184–5, 186
Lenin, 33, 145, 175–6, 185, 195
Lentulov, 68
Leonidze, G., 117
Leontovich, 157
Levinson, Andrey, 44
Lidin, 13, 63, 66, 142

Lipskerov, 66
Lisitzky, 26, 148
Livshits, Benedikt, 86
Lunacharsky, 39, 156, 169, 178
Lvova, Nadya, 20
Lyuba, 73–74, 96, 99, 100–1, 110–14, 119,
  120–2, 124, 126, 127, 142–3, 148,
  174, 181, 186, 188

MacOrlan, Pierre, 195
Makhno, 79, 121
Makkaveysky, Vladimir, 86
Malevich, 56, 59, 60, 68
Mallarmé, 17
Malyshkin, 172, 176
Mandelstam, Alexander, 122
Mandelstam, Osop, 35, 87, 89, 101, 102,
  103, 104–9, 112–15, 119–23
Manteufel, L. A., 91
Mardzhanov, Konstantin, 88–89, 90, 168
Marevna, 184
Markisch, Peretz, 87, 91
Marusya, 189, 190–91
Mashkov, 68
Mayakovsky, 18, 25, 28, 36–46, 49, 51–52,
  55, 56, 58, 59–60, 63, 66, 68, 106, 131,
  132, 136, 148, 159–60, 161, 165, 195
  About This, 43, 133
  Bedbug, The, 41, 43
  Listen You Swine, 26
  Man, 36, 41
  Mystery Bouffe, 58, 131
  Simple as Mooing, 36
  Slap in the Face for Public Taste, A, 38
May-Mayevsky, 92, 93
Meller, V., 85, 88
Menshikov, 136
Menzhinsky, V. R., 173–4
Merezhkovsky, 68
Merkulov, V., 108
Metzinger, 59
Meyerhold, V. E., 56, 60, 61, 84, 124,
  128–38, 148, 167
Mikhailovich, Mikhail, 75
Mirkin, 23
Mitsishvili, N., 117
Modigliani, 101
Mounet-Sully, 69, 170

Nemirov, 189
Neruda, Pablo, 45
Nezval, 45

Nikulin, L. V., 87
Novikov, Ivan, 66, 142

Ognev, N., 176
Okulov, A. I., 33
Olesha, Yuri, 72, 177
Otsup, 86

Paskar, Henrietta, 146
Pasternak, Boris, 41, 47–54, 117, 149–50
  Doctor Zhivago, 53
  My Sister Life, 48, 52
  Safe Conduct, 52
  Urals for the First Time, The, 48
Pastukhov, Panya, 84
Paustovsky, 72, 151, 172
Pavlova, Karolina, 25
Permeke, 191
Petlyura, 76–79, 81, 85, 90
Petrisky, 88
Petrov, 72
Picasso, 17, 55–56, 58–59, 60, 135, 170,
  185, 186
Pilnyak, 172, 176
Pilsky, Pyotr, 78
Pirosmanishvili, 115
Plautus, 91
Podgaretsky, 132
Poincaré, 20
Polonskaya, 179
Poplavskaya, 142
Popova, 56, 60
Pozazhnoy, 93–94
Pougny, 56, 60
Poussin, 56
Pribylskaya, 85
Przybyszewsky, 146
Pugachev, 45, 65, 176
Pushkin, 19, 27, 56, 167

Rabinovich, 88, 92, 143
Rafalovich, 115
Ravel, 146
Reich, Z. N., 137, 138
Remizov, 192
Repin, 56
Rilke, 53
Rimbaud, 146
Rivera, Diego, 55–56, 184, 185, 186
Rodchenko, 56, 148
Rousseau (of Georgia), 115
Rozanova, 60

Rubinstein, Ida, 128
Rukavishnikova, 145
Rylsky, M. F., 72

Salmon, André, 185
Sashunya, 11
Saulovna, Rakhil, 100
Savich, O. G., 111
Savinkov, 11–12
Schreider, A. A., 161
Segher, Anna, 37
Selvinsky, Ilya, 83
Semenko, 87
Severini, 58
Severyanin, Igor, 19, 169
Seyfullina, Lydia, 40, 151, 172
Shaginyan, Marietta, 83
Shakespeare, 50
Shchukin, 17
Shershenevich, 142
Shifrin, N. A., 88, 89
Shkapskaya, 160
Shklovsky, Victor, 41, 49, 87 *Zoo*, 60
Shkuro, 92–93, 95
Skoropadsky, 76, 78
Smidovich, P. G., 175
Sobachka, Gapa, 85
Sobol, Andrey, 67, 100
Sobol, Mark, 100
Sorokin, Tikhon, 10, 12–13
Sorokina, Katya, 12
Spasskaya, 85
Stanislavsky, 137
Stendhal, 60
Stenich, V. O., 32
Stepun, Fedor, 12
Sterenberg, D. P., 142
Stryuk, 79
Stuck, 146
Svetlov, 72

Tabidze, Tizian, 112–18
Tairov, 132, 148, 167–71
  A Producer's Notebook, 167
Talma, 15
Tatlin, 56, 58, 60, 148
Tchaikovsky, 106
Tikhonov, Nikolay, 117, 144, 176
Tolstoy, Alexey, 13–14, 15, 38, 62, 63,
  65–66, 68, 184, 195
Tolstoy, Leo, 61
Triolet,Elsa, 40, 41

Tsvetayeva, Alya, 22, 26, 27
Tsvetayeva ,Marina, Ivanovna, 22–28, 41,
  51, 99, 142
  Craftsmanship,25
  Parting, 23
  Swan's Encampment, The, 24
Tugenhold, Y. A., 68
Tumanny, Dir, 142
Tuwin, 45
Tvardovsky, 35
Tychina, P. G., 87
Tynyanov, 172
Tyshler, Alex, 88
Tyutchev, 17, 27, 32, 51, 60
Tyutyunik, 79
Tzara, Tristan, 164

Udalstova, 56
Ushakov, N. N., 86

Vakhtangov, 137
Vengrov, Natan, 37, 124
Veresayev, 99–101
Verlaine, 17
Vesnin, 148
Villon, 164
Voloshin, 30, 92, 95, 98, 101–4
Voltaire, 192–3
Vrubel, 18

Watteau, 59
Wells, H. G., 58
Wilde, Oscar, 146
Wrangel, 125–6, 149

Yadviga, 89, 100, 101, 110, 114, 119, 144
Yakovleva, Tatiana, 41
Yakulov, 148, 167
Yashvili, Paolo, 113–18
Yesenin, 117, 143, 159–66, 176, 191
  Black Man, The, 165
  Ionia, 161
Yureneva, Vera, 87
Yutkevich, Seryozha, 89

Zabolotsky, 117
Zadkine, 66, 184
Zaitsev, Boris, 13, 66
Zelyony, 79, 81
Zetlins, the, 63
Ziloti, A., 29
Zoshchenko, 72
Zweig, Stefan, 190

200